Victims and Policy Making

Victims and Policy Making
A comparative perspective

Matthew Hall

LONDON AND NEW YORK

Published 2010 by Willan Publishing

Published 2017 by Routledge

2 Park Square, Milton Park, Abingdon, Oxon, OX14 4RN
711 Third Avenue, New York, NY 10017

Routledge is an imprint of the Taylor & Francis Group, an informa business

© Matthew Hall 2010

The rights of Matthew Hall to be identified as the author of this book have been asserted by him in accordance with the Copyright, Designs and Patents Act of 1988.

All rights reserved; no part of this publication may be reproduced, stored in a retrieval system, or transmitted in any form or by any means, electronic, mechanical, photocopying, recording or otherwise without the prior written permission of the Publishers or a licence permitting copying in the UK issued by the Copyright Licensing Agency Ltd, Saffron House, 6–10 Kirby Street, London EC1N 8TS.

First published 2010

ISBN   978-1-84392-824-9 paperback
       978-1-84392-825-6 hardback

British Library Cataloguing-in-Publication Data

A catalogue record for this book is available from the British Library

Project managed by Deer Park Productions, Tavistock, Devon
Typeset by GCS, Leighton Buzzard, Bedfordshire

For Claire and Edward

Contents

List of abbreviations ix
Acknowledgements xi

1 Victims on the world stage 1
Introduction 1
Victimology and victims of crime: an international
'movement'? 15

2 Defining 'victims' 28
The expanding scope of victimhood 29
Defining victimhood: some broad conclusions 57

3 Victims and international organizations 62
The United Nations 62
The Council of Europe 69
The European Union 72
Other international organizations 81
Discussion 86

**4 Victims in domestic policy making: examining the policy
network** 91
Policy theory, policy networks, and issues of generalization 92
Aspects of the transnational and international policy
network impacting on victim reform 95
Victims of crime: a transnational and international policy
network 132

5 Theorizing victims' rights — **137**
Theorizing victims' rights — 138
The formal rights of victims within national jurisdictions — 143
The 'normalization' of victims' rights — 160

6 Compensation, restitution and restorative justice — **168**
State compensation schemes — 169
Restitution — 182
Restorative justice — 187
Compensating victims? — 202

7 Victims in policy making: a comparative perspective — **206**
Societal changes: the macro perspective — 207
The influence of policy networks — 216
A globalization of victim policies? — 224
Victim support as a principle of international law? — 226
Conclusion — 230

References — *235*
Index — *266*

List of abbreviations

AdVIC	Advocates for Victims of Homicide (Ireland)
CEDAW	Convention on the Elimination of Discrimination against Women
CICA	UK Criminal Injuries Compensation Authority
CIViTAS	Institute for the Study of Civil Society (UK)
CPS	UK Crown Prosecution Service
CRC	Convention on the Rights of the Child
DoJCD	Department of Justice and Constitutional Development (South Africa)
ECtHR	European Court of Human Rights
EG-TFV	Task Force to Combat Violence against Women, including Domestic Violence
HEUNI	European Institute for Crime Prevention and Control
ICC	International Criminal Court
ICCPR	International Covenant on Civil and Political Rights
ICVS	International Crime Victimization Survey
IHRIHL	Basic Principles and Guidelines on the Rights to a Remedy and Reparation for Victims of Gross Violations of International Human Rights Law and Serious Violations of International Humanitarian Law
IOVA	International Organization for Victim Assistance
NAVSS	National Association of Victim Support Schemes (UK)
NICRO	National Institute for Crime Prevention and the Reintegration of Services (South Africa)
NJC	Neighbourhood Justice Centre (Victoria, Australia)
NOVA	National Organization of Victim Assistance (US)

NVCAP	National Victims Constitutional Amendment Passage (US)
NZCVSG	New Zealand Council of Victim Support Groups
OSCE	Organization for Security and Co-operation in Europe
PFI	Private Finance Initiative
POMC	Parents of Murdered Children
PSA	Public Service Agreement
SAMM	Support After Murder and Manslaughter
TIP	Trafficking in Persons Report (US Department of State)
TRC	Truth and Reconciliation Commission (South Africa)
VIS	Victim Impact Statements
VSO	Victim Support Organisation
WAVES	Witness and Victim Experience Survey
YOT	Youth Offending Team (UK)

Acknowledgements

My thanks go to all the policy makers, civil servants, and victim support staff and volunteers who contributed their time and expertise to this project. Particular thanks go to staff at the US Victims of Crime Office, the South African Department of Justice and Constitutional Development, and to Victim Support Europe for the copious amount of information they were willing to share. I am also particularly indebted to all the respondents from the Australian Ministries of Justice, and from Victim Support Australasia and New Zealand, for being so helpful in the arrangement of mutually convenient telephone interviews and discussions.

I would also like to thank colleagues from the University of Sheffield Centre for Criminological Research, and from the University of Sheffield's School of Law, for innumerable discussions, consultations and brainstorming sessions on every aspect of this project.

Finally, I would like to thank my wife Claire and my son Edward, whose support and love is reflected on every page of this volume.

Any errors or omissions remain my own.

Chapter 1

Victims on the world stage

Introduction

> The nature and extent of victimization is not adequately understood across the world. Millions of people throughout the world suffer harm as a result of crime, the abuse of power, terrorism and other stark misfortunes. Their rights and needs as victims of this harm have not been adequately recognized.
> (World Society of Victimology 2006: n.p.)

In this extract from its Strategic Plan, the World Society of Victimology gives voice to a concern being expressed in jurisdictions across the globe for the lack of support, services and rights afforded to many victims of crime and other misfortunes. As a response to such challenges, victims of crime have become a topic of great political interest and policy movement, for both individual jurisdictions and international organizations. Such developments become particularly significant in light of the victim's near indivisibility in criminal justice in past decades[1] whereby, as states assumed responsibility for reacting to crime and pursuing prosecutions, the role of the crime victim in this process became further and further eroded in most jurisdictions (Spalek 2006). The apparent reversal of this trend, witnessed in many countries across all continents in recent years, raises fundamental questions concerning the common influences on policy making between states, the politicization of crime victims and the changing relationship between the state and the individual.

Examples of such developments are diverse and can be drawn from all continents. In North America, the Canadian and US governments were among the first in the world to afford victims an ostensibly significant place on the policy agenda (Rock 1986), with the US Office for Victims of Crime[2] celebrating its 25th anniversary in April 2009. This is not a phenomenon exclusive to the world's richest nations, however. Further south, the Central American states of Guatemala and El Salvador each have well-established programmes to address the needs of victims of domestic violence. Similarly, in South America, the Supreme Court of Argentina has established a dedicated office 'to assist victims of domestic violence, take statements and expedite court cases' (Argentina Ministry of Justice 2009: n.p.).[3] Brazilian literature on criminal victimization is also fast developing (Paes-Machado and Nascimento 2006).

In Europe, where the UK and The Netherlands have traditionally driven much of the academic and policy discussion on crime victims, the 2001 *EU Council Framework Decision on the Standing of Victims in Criminal Proceedings*[4] now requires all EU states to afford victims basic levels of services and support. The European Commission also has a growing role in funding victim assistance initiatives in Member States. Such initiatives are co-ordinated by the newly christened Victim Support Europe, an association of 23 national victim support groups[5] representing around 21 countries. In Australia and New Zealand, restorative justice initiatives have highlighted victim issues, as well as posing fundamental questions concerning the adequacy of the adversarial system in meeting their needs (Dignan 2005). In Asia, the Japanese Basic Act on Crime Victims came into force in 2004 with the goal, as indicated in its preamble, of 'promot[ing] the measures for Crime Victims comprehensively and systematically'. More recently, the Supreme Court of China has called for the creation of a state compensation scheme for victims of violent crime (*People's Daily* 2007). Jurisdictions comprising the region of North Africa and the Middle East have been exchanging best practice in supporting child victims of violence since 2005 (National Council for Childhood and Motherhood 2005) while South Africa has recently introduced its own Victims' Charter to afford rights to victims in the criminal process, with a significant focus on restorative justice options (South African Department of Justice and Constitutional Development 2009).

All this gives a potted and unsystematic indication of the breadth of the victim reform agenda across the globe. The underlying thesis to be presented in this volume is that such developments, while clearly grounded in the particular history and socio-political landscape of each jurisdiction, are nonetheless linked by a broader web of common political and social influences.

In an early examination of such influences, van Dijk (1983) categorizes the reforms witnessed across developed jurisdictions intended to 'do something' for victims into four 'victimogogic ideologies'. The label 'victimogogic' distinguishes such measures from victimology's wider goals of counting and gathering information about crime victims (see below). According to van Dijk, victimogogic measures can be based first on a 'care ideology', emphasizing welfare principles. Second, policies can fall under a 'resocialization or rehabilitation' banner, with offender-based goals. The third victimogogic ideology is the 'retributive or criminal justice' model, stressing 'just desserts'. Finally, the 'radical or anti-criminal justice' ideology involves resolving problems without resorting to the formal criminal justice system. Van Dijk notes two broad dimensions to such victimogogic measures, which remain valid in the recent international policy context. The first is the extent to which victims' concerns are incorporated as factors to consider within the criminal justice process. The second dimension is the extent to which victims' interests are goals in their own right, or whether they are intended to feed back into decision making regarding offenders, system efficiency, or other criminal justice concerns. Van Dijk further notes that many of these measures are 'action orientated', the goal being to intermittently 'do something' for victims, even when such reforms are not evidence based.[6]

Examining why victims have become the subject of an extensive reform agenda in multiple jurisdictions clearly affords insight into the limits of such policies. Nevertheless, van Dijk's construction is restricted to an examination of political ideologies. As such, he does not discuss the wider network of factors, including transnational and international influences or social issues such as race and secularization, that may lead to different policies being put into operation.

In contrast, Robert Elias (1986: 231) argues that victimogogic policies in the USA have from the beginning been used as a tool to facilitate state control: 'victims may function to bolster state legitimacy, to gain political mileage, and to enhance social control'. The argument is that politicians use victims as political ammunition in elections, and as a means of legitimising increasingly punitive measures. Hence, Fattah (1992: xii) characterizes victimogogic measures as 'political and judicial placebos'.

Elias and Fattah therefore look more closely at the driving forces behind such ideologies. This takes our understanding forward, but this concentration on punitiveness may distract attention from a still wider range of influences The further examination of such influences will therefore lead to a more refined understand of *why* political mileage can be gained through the appearance of supporting crime victims in the first place, particularly when confidence in the criminal justice system is lacking (see Garland 2001).

A more direct analysis of the influences behind victims in policy making has previously been undertaken at the national level by Paul Rock (1986) in both Canada and England and Wales (Rock 1990, 2004). In the first study, Rock highlights the complex interaction between various external influences and the social world of policy making in the Ministry of the Solicitor General of Canada which eventually resulted in the formation of victim initiatives. Importantly, many of these influences and pressures had very little to do with victims of crime *per se*:

> In a sense, *reparation* proved to be the Trojan horse which carried victims support schemes to political prominence. Victims support schemes were to be part of the package that were approved by ministers in March 1984 as a 'submission on reparation', and they were to be carried piggy-back thereafter (Rock 1990: 345–46, emphasis added).

In England and Wales, Rock (2004) characterizes domestic 'victim' policies as the products of a broad web of developments. For Rock, there were eight main influencing focal points to this web: the structure of the UK Home Office, the nature of policy making, the growth of the victim as a consumer of criminal justice, the development of human rights, compensation developments, developments in reparation provision, the identification of vulnerable and intimidated, witnesses, and race issues (specifically, the aftermath of the Stephen Lawrence enquiry).[7]

Rock's analyses in both jurisdictions include the role of transnational and international influences in the development of domestic policy. Nevertheless, his main concern is with national policy structures and processes: providing extremely detailed case studies in both jurisdictions. In contrast, the present volume sets out an analysis of common influences across jurisdictions which have contributed to the 'rediscovery' of crime victims (Pointing and Maguire 1988) in multiple criminal justice systems. Genuinely comparative research on this issue is rare. One key exception is that of Brienen and Hoegen's

(2000) analysis of victim reforms in 22 European countries. As in the present research, the authors analysed provisions for victims across European jurisdictions. The work remains a substantial achievement and required reading for any researcher interested in the development of victim initiatives internationally. Importantly, Brienen and Hoegen's research also allows comparisons to be drawn between inquisitorial and adversarial justice systems.[8] Nevertheless, this research was restricted to Europe, was largely descriptive of legislation and programmes and, although covering more countries than the project set out in this volume, was not focused on the *policy-making* process behind such measures specifically. The research is also now ten years old, and was published before the impetus towards giving victims enforceable 'rights' in particular had gathered pace in many jurisdictions. As such, the present volume sets out to complement and, in places, update this earlier study.

In sum, the goal of this volume is to offer a comparative analysis between countries which can help explain the emergence of victims as an international political concern and casts light on the nature of policy making on this issue. In particular, the book will demonstrate how victim policies are part of the wider politicization of law and order seen in most developed nations. As such, victims of crime are often used by policy makers to achieve other, more retributive aims (Elias 1986) as well as financial targets (see Valler and Betteley 2001). It will also be demonstrated that the influences on these policies can be placed in the context of wider social changes, such as those described by Boutellier (2000) and Garland (2001).[9] These include secularization and a dwindling faith in the ability of criminal justice systems to control crime. In particular, it will be demonstrated that victim satisfaction is now used as a proxy measure for the success of criminal justice provisions in many jurisdictions. The research therefore seeks to test the applicability of Boutellier and Garland's thought in jurisdictions beyond the USA and England and Wales, where much of these authors' attention is focused. Common to all these jurisdictions is the tendency for policy makers to accept ever-widening definitions of 'victimhood' (and therefore 'suffering') through which criminal justice may be legitimized. While such developments have brought great benefits to crime victims in all the jurisdictions, it will be argued that these underlying political goals have not always led to the best package of reforms for the victims themselves, particularly for the vast majority who do not conform to ideal images of crime victims.

Introducing the research

The research project presented in this volume compares policies and reforms which relate to victims of crime across nine developed nations, with a view to drawing parallels and identifying common factors influencing their development. The main countries under review here are: Australia, Canada, The Netherlands, New Zealand, South Africa, England and Wales, Scotland,[10] the Republic of Ireland and the USA. The research also seeks to examine the related work of key international bodies such as the United Nations and the European Union.

These countries were selected for a number of reasons. As a group, the large number of jurisdictions was necessary in order to explore the different influences on national, transnational and international policy networks, as explained later. Practically, it was necessary to choose jurisdictions in which government policy on victims was fairly mature. This ensured, first, that there was enough information, reports, and secondary literature available to undertake a meaningful analysis and, second, that relevant civil servants, practitioners and administrators in each country had built up a wealth of experience and knowledge that could be discussed in interviews. As such, most of the nine jurisdictions under review represent a key centre for victim reform on which other jurisdictions have based their own policy agendas. That said, the Republic of Ireland was chosen for inclusion principally because, when this project began in early 2008, the Irish Department of Justice, Equality and Law Reform had only recently set up a dedicated Victims of Crime Office, a development far behind many other European nations. As such, there is very little in the literature on developments concerning victims of crime in the Irish criminal justice system. This afforded the opportunity to examine the development of such policies in one jurisdiction from a relatively early stage.[11]

The chosen jurisdictions have all witnessed recent significant change in the place of victims in their criminal justice systems, coupled with the introduction of wider support mechanisms for victims of crime. One criticism which might be levied at this sample of nations is that, aside from The Netherlands, all these jurisdictions are what Cavadino and Dignan (2007) refer to as 'neo-liberal' states. These are characterized as nations exhibiting right-wing political orientation, a commitment to free-market principles, where imprisonment rates are relatively high and there exist extreme income differentials. As such, The Netherlands was chosen not only because it has been a major centre for victimological research and policy[12] but also because it serves as a comparator 'conservative corporatist' jurisdiction. Cavadino and Dignan describe such countries, in contrast to the neo-liberal states, as being characterized by a focus on rehabilitation in the penal system and in which there is a moderately generous welfare state.

These jurisdictions were also selected to represent as far as possible a divergence of historical and social perspectives from which victim reforms have been approached. Hence, Ireland and South Africa have recent histories of significant political turbulence and violent uprisings. In Canada, this chapter has already noted Rock's (1990) contention that victim policies were originally introduced as part of a wider package on reparation. In Australia, victim support mechanisms arose out of organizations specifically concerned with supporting homicide survivors and women victimized by rape and domestic violence (David *et al*. 1990; Rock 1998, 2007). Both Canadian and Australian jurisdictions have also responded specifically to the victimization of indigenous groups, with developments in the field of restorative justice in particular often being presented and implemented in an indigenous cultural context (Canadian Resource Centre for Victims of Crime 2001; Strang 2001).[13] The USA and England and Wales have a recent tradition of retribution in their criminal justice systems, which raises questions concerning the existence of any zero-sum game between victim and offender rights (Hickman 2004). This sample of countries also allows for comparisons to be drawn between jurisdictions which have been actively involved in victim reform from the earliest days of the victims' movement (USA, Canada, England and Wales, The Netherlands) with a group of countries driven by more recent developments in this movement internationally (South Africa, Australia, New Zealand, Ireland). Scotland is a useful comparator both for its close ties with the English and Welsh system and because its criminal justice system in some ways closely mirrors a more continental model. The Netherlands is interesting for a further reason, in that the victim policy agenda there has been more closely allied with academics in the field than in any other jurisdiction.

It must be emphasized from the outset that comparative research between jurisdictions is always challenging.[14] In particular, the individual researcher may fail to appreciate subtle (or even not so subtle) differences in the social, cultural, historical, and legal context between countries. Selecting nine jurisdictions of roughly the same classification therefore simplifies the process of analysis[15] while still allowing for comparability with a different kind of system (The Netherlands). Of course, this must be weighed against the disadvantage that a volume based predominantly on these countries will have less to say about policy making in a wider range (and type) of jurisdictions. For this reason, while focusing primarily on the countries listed earlier, this book of course also draws on the wider international literature and examples of policy making from across the globe. One objective for this research was to comment on why countries like these and not others appear to be at the forefront of victim policy making.[16] For this reason the choice of countries was again useful, as these are the states to which other jurisdictions are inevitably compared when it comes to supporting victims.

Data for this project were drawn from two key sources. First, a thematic analysis was conducted of policy instruments, documents, and secondary literature concerning victims of crime from and about each jurisdiction. Second, a number of semi-structured, qualitative, interviews were carried out with central policy makers in relevant government departments, and with representatives of victim support organizations in different jurisdictions.[17] Face-to-face meetings were the preferred methodology because such interviews tend to produce the most extensive and rich data, and gave the opportunity for respondents to check information and provide hard copies of documents. They also allowed the researcher to gauge the attitudes and underlying cultures of interview respondents more successfully. Where face-to-face meetings were impossible or impractical, telephone interviews were carried out, specifically with respondents from Australia, New Zealand and the USA. Some supplementary interviews with further respondents from the jurisdictions visited were also conducted in this manner. In total, around 40 interviews were conducted across the nine jurisdictions.

All interviews were digitally recorded (informed consent having been given) and then transcribed. The transcripts were then subject to grounded analysis and coding, utilizing the NVivo software package. The overriding technique employed here has been to identify and code themes emergent from the various data sources in an effort to corroborate or contradict the hypotheses to be discussed in the next section, and to build up an understanding of how victim policies came about in the different jurisdictions. As themes developed, they were used to guide the ongoing progression of data collection and the themes themselves were constantly redefined, making this an iterative process in which data collection should not be separated from outcomes.

Like many qualitative studies, this project therefore owes much to grounded theory (Glaser and Strauss 1967). That said, true grounded theory implies that the data collection continues until 'theoretical saturation' occurs, whereby categories derived from the process which are thought to represent real-world phenomena (in this case regarding the development of victim policies) are no longer developed or refined through the addition of extra data (Strauss and Corbin 1994). In practice, the data were limited by the time and funding available for the research. While this should not undermine the results (the same criticism can be made of most research), it does imply that more data could further enhance the categories (conclusions drawn regarding victim policy making internationally) in Chapter 7.

In the case of official policy documents from different jurisdictions, the above principles were applied as qualitative document analysis, through which underlying themes were again sought out. That said, the reflexive nature of the work may imply a closer similarity with what Altheide (1987) has called 'ethnographic content analysis', whereby once again the initial loosely defined set of themes were open to revaluation and amendment as the data collection process continued.

Clearly this grounded approach can be the subject of criticism. In particular, one might argue that my identification of themes and categories from the dataset was influenced by my hypotheses (set out later) and my existing academic opinions regarding issues like victims' rights, state responsibilities and the effectiveness of different victim support mechanisms. Another criticism of grounded theory rests in the process of splitting up data into component themes, which some argue prompts unnatural distinctions and detracts from the wider context of the issues being scrutinised (Coffey and Atkinson 1996). I would certainly agree with such criticisms, but have responded to them in this project by constantly bearing in mind the relationships between the research questions set out later, and attempting to view the issue of victim policy making as a unified whole. The research presented in this volume therefore endeavours to provide a wide-ranging, international analysis of the issues involved, keeping the wider context of the subject matter at the forefront of the debate.

Theoretical framework, objectives, and hypotheses

The primary goal of this project was to develop a conceptual framework for understanding the development of victim policies internationally. In order to provide structure and to guide the

Victims and Policy Making

research, a draft framework was produced in which a number of hypotheses were set out. These hypotheses and their place in the overall framework were then tested throughout the project. The draft framework is set out later and is followed by a detailed discussion of theoretical perspectives which guided the project.

This project approached victim policy making from the macro level, conceptualizing such developments as the *products* of wider political and societal influences common to many jurisdictions (Level 1 in Figure 1.1). Prominent commentators on this issue include Garland (2001) and Boutellier (2000), who each argue that victims have become a yardstick for judging the effectiveness and legitimacy of criminal justice systems. For Garland, this is because the traditional measure of criminal justice effectiveness, the system's ability to control crime, has become redundant at a time of falling public confidence in these systems. In the face of this growing public concern that little can actually be done about crime, Garland argues that governments deny their failure by turning to ever more punitive policies such as mandatory minimum sentences and 'three-strikes' legislation. Victims, it is argued, are used by governments to justify such measures by reference to their 'need' to be protected and have their voices heard.

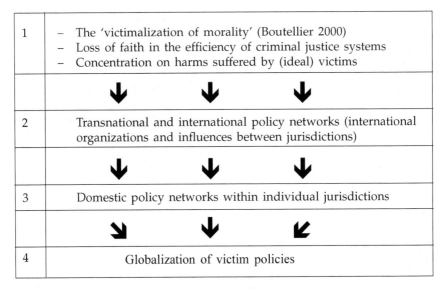

Figure 1.1 Draft conceptual framework of victim policy making internationally

Arguing from a different perspective, Boutellier (2000) notes that, as the process of secularization goes on, common standards of morality decline but common appreciation and sympathy for the suffering of others remains. Boutellier refers to this as the 'victimalization of morality'. Furedi (1998: 82) makes a similar point in terms of social solidarity in the UK context: 'It is difficult to avoid the conclusion that, with British people feeling so fragmented – the ritual of grieving [for victims] provides one of the few experiences that create a sense of belonging'.

This volume will focus particular attention on the way policy makers from all jurisdictions increasingly understand criminal victimization by reference to the suffering or harm experienced by individuals. In both theoretical constructions, victim care becomes the gold standard by which the criminal justice system is legitimized, leading to government implementing appropriate reforms to ensure this standard is met. The difficulty with both discussions, however, is their isolation from the *implementation* of policies. Both constructions take as read the assumption that victims really are being put at the heart of criminal justice in practice as well as in rhetoric. Both authors also draw extensively from the US experience at the expense of a broader international perspective. As such, in testing the place of such ideas in an overall theoretical framework, a further objective of this project was to examine the substance of victim reforms in the countries under review, as well as the rhetoric. The research therefore set out to subject these 'macro' ideas to scrutiny, test their applicability in different jurisdictions and identify any further or alternative prevailing 'macro' influences.

The next stage of the framework (Levels 2 and 3 in Figure 1.1) concerns broader theories from the policy making literature, specifically the development of governance in the formation and implementation of victim policies at the national, transnational and international levels. Bache (2003: 301) defines governance as 'an increasingly complex set of state-society relationships in which networks rather than hierarchies dominate policy-making'. Several authors have drawn links between various aspects of criminal justice policy and the emergence of governance (Crawford 1997; Loader and Sparks 2007). Governance is also a key aspect of Garland's (2001) position given earlier. The concept of 'policy networks' and 'policy communities' (Jordan *et al.* 2005) is also key here, as this project sought to demonstrate how victim policies have derived from multiple, cross-jurisdictional, sources. Peterson and Bomberg (1999: 8) notes that the term 'policy network' 'connotes a cluster of actors, each of which has an interest, or "stake" in a given ... policy sector and the capacity to help determine policy success or failure'. A key argument of this volume is that such policy networks extend across countries, whereby individual jurisdictions are influenced not only by the work of international organizations like the UN and the EU, but by each other. In other words, the influences at work here are *trans*national as well as *inter*national. Hence, Figure 1.1 depicts the influence of transnational and international policy networks feeding into policy networks at the national level. The research therefore set out to identify the stakeholders of victim policies. The project also investigated the assertion that victim policies tend to be highly politicized, driven by a divergent web of inter-related internal pressures (Rock 2004) and often used to achieve political ends (Elias 1983). In this respect, it was again important to compare the policy makers' presentation of victim reform with the substantive reality, and to account for any divergences by reference to processes and pressures going on behind the scenes in each jurisdiction.

The final component of the draft conceptual framework (Level 4 in Figure 1.1) reflects the homogenization of victim policies at the beginning of the 21st century. This is not to suggest that such policies have developed in exactly the same way in each of the nine jurisdictions under review. For example, van Dijk (1997) and Maguire and Shapland (1997) both argue that groups working and campaigning on behalf of victims in the USA have traditionally taken a far more rights-based, political approach compared with their European counterparts, who for many years stressed the need for service provision to victims rather than championing the idea of victims' rights. Australasian victim groups have demonstrated a similar political leaning (Booth and Carrington 2007).[18] As a third category, some jurisdictions (including South Africa) seem to have embarked on victim reform programmes out of necessity. This may be a response to transnational pressures from other states, pressures from international organizations, or a result of the fact that serious impacts of crime in those countries are acute and widely felt among the population (Chankova 1998; Garkawe 2004).

Nevertheless, despite the divergent underlying philosophies just described, not only is the victims' movement in all nine of the jurisdictions under review becoming increasingly professionalised and politicised (van Dijk 1988), but all boast very similar programmes at various stages of development. Typically such programmes include: victims' charters, victim impact statements, the beginnings of victims' rights and fledgling restorative justice schemes. A further objective of this research is to assess the implications of this globalization of victim support.

The above framework was developed to act as a guide for this research, but not to constrict it. Certainly it was recognised from the outset that this model implied a rather simplistic and linear progression of policy development, which is actually characterised by complex interactions and background pressures going on within the policy making institutions of each jurisdiction. Furthermore, Rock (1990) notes in the English context how 'policies for victims sometimes seemed to have little directly to do with the expressed needs of victims themselves and more to do with other politics' (p. 34). As such, a further complication lies in appreciating how other quite diverse areas of policy may feed into and influence reform ostensibly presented by policy makers as being 'about victims'. This project in turn set out to reflect and expose these complexities.

Deriving from the draft conceptual framework described earlier (as qualified by the further complexities alluded to in the last paragraph) the primary research questions and objectives of this project can be set out as follows:

1 To test the overall viability of this conceptual framework as a way of understanding the international move towards victim-based policies, adapting it as proves necessary by the findings.

2 To compare and contrast the 'policy' as presented by policy makers and documents with the substantive reforms rolled out in practice in each jurisdiction, and to explain these differences by reference to the organization of state bureaucracies.

3 To modify or refute the wider macro influences put forward by Garland and Boutellier as the underlying foundation of victim policies internationally.

4 To analyse the implications of the now globalized approach to victim support, both for victims and for the future of policy making in this area (and in general).

These goals were augmented by a number of secondary, more general objectives:

5 To examine the background and driving forces behind victim policies in all nine jurisdictions, drawing out similarities and differences and assessing the extent to which these parallel developments across jurisdictions are driven by common factors.

Victims and Policy Making

6 To assess the extent to which the historical, political and social characteristics of each jurisdiction has impacted upon victim policy making.

7 To critically compare reforms related to victims of crime in each jurisdiction, with particular reference to the differences between the rhetoric and the reality.

8 To investigate the assertions that victim policies are highly politicized, driven by a divergent web of interrelated political pressures (Rock 2004) and used to achieve political ends (Elias 1983).

Book structure

The present volume is organized as follows. The remainder of this chapter chronicles the international development of what has come to be known as 'the victims' movement'. This will cover the various groups that constitute this movement and discuss how the movement became established in all the countries under review. Chapter 2 will examine the definition of 'victimhood' across all the jurisdictions under review, along with the socio-political influences behind such definitions. In particular, the chapter will examine the extent to which policies in different jurisdictions reflect the needs of (relatively rare) 'ideal' victims verses more typical victims of crime. Chapter 3 will review the work of various international bodies including the UN, EU and Council of Europe. Chapter 4 will move on to a thematic examination of policy making in individual jurisdictions. Chapter 5 will discuss the key issue of victims' rights in a comparative context, examining both international instruments and national reforms. Chapter 6 will move on to discuss different methods of compensating victims, including state compensation and court-based compensation. This chapter will also cover the victim's place in various restorative justice schemes: especially in Australia, New Zealand, and South Africa. The final chapter will offer a discussion of all the data put forward in this volume and present comparative conclusions regarding the reasons, rationales, and outcomes of victim policy making across the jurisdictions under review.

A note on terminology

This book will follow the convention utilized in much[19] of the relevant academic and policy literature in employing the term 'victim', as opposed to alternatives such as 'alleged victim' or 'complainant'.

Nevertheless, it is important to appreciate the controversy this engenders for those who argue that labelling complainants as 'victims' prior to the ruling of a court implies the defendant is guilty until proven innocent. As argued by Lord Justice Auld (2001: 500) in his 2001 report on the workings of criminal courts in England and Wales, 'at the pre-trial and trial stages of the process it has yet to be established that the alleged victim is in truth a victim'.

Victimology and victims of crime: an international 'movement'?

Most discussions on the issue of victims of crime and victim policy begin with some historical introduction to the global spread of activist, academic, and policy interest in victims across jurisdictions which are often described collectively as the 'victims' movement'. Such a discussion seems particularly apt for this volume, as it serves to illustrate the international character of these developments from their earliest beginnings. Labelling this as a 'movement' is, however, rather misleading[20] in that it suggests a clarity and consistency of purpose that was often not present, certainly not between jurisdictions and often not within them.[21]

In the literature, reviews of the development of the victims' movement are almost as diverse in scope as the movement itself (see Maguire 1991; Kirchhoff 1994; Jackson 2003). As such, any attempt to summarize this movement should be approached with caution and due regard to Kearon and Godfrey's (2007: 30) warning against the academic tendency to 'force social phenomena into false chronologies'. With such warning labels firmly in place, the following section conceptualizes the development of the victims' movement in three 'waves'. The first of these waves was characterised by a growth of academic interest in victims. The second is the development of victim assistance organizations in the countries under review and elsewhere. The third is the apparent acceptance of victims as the topics of mainstream policy making in the criminal justice systems of these jurisdictions, above and beyond the financing of victim assistance groups and projects. This latter set of developments are demonstrated by the publication of service standards for victims of crime in many jurisdictions and, in most cases, the enactment of primary legislation. Of course, these three stages did not develop in any jurisdiction in a neatly chronological fashion. In reality there has been much overlap and continuing development on all three fronts up until the time of writing, and almost certainly beyond it.

In addition, any review of policy making must be read with reference to the specific point made by Rock (1986, 1990, 1998) in a number of contexts that reforms ostensibly presented as 'victim policies' may derive from quite different political agendas and serve other ends (see Chapters 4 and 5).

The first and second waves

The beginnings of the victims' movement can be traced to the development of the academic study of victimology in the post-war period. This was initially a European development, although Hans von Hentig's *The Criminal and His Victim* (1948), which many consider the founding text of the sub-discipline, was actually produced in the USA following the author's flight from Nazi Germany. Here, von Hentig argued that the traditional distinctions drawn between victims and offenders as entirely separate groups was far from clear-cut, and suggested that individuals could be prone to victimization and (more controversially) even precipitated it through their lifestyle choices. The term 'victimology'[22] is usually attributed to Frederick Wertham (1949) or sometimes to Benjamin Mendelsohn (Kirchhoff 1994). The early victimologists continued these precipitation debates up until the late 50s and early 60s (Mendelsohn 1956; Wolfgang 1958; Amir 1971; Fattah 1992). At this point, Schneider (1991) argues that victimology was set off in two directions: as a discipline concerned with human rights, and also as a sub-discipline of criminology concerned specifically with victims of crime.

A key contribution made by such academic debates was the establishment of victim surveys as the primary method of counting crime and (later) gauging victim satisfaction with various aspects of the criminal justice system. From 1973 onwards, the first surveys were conducted in the USA, followed by The Netherlands in the same year,[23] Canada in 1981, and the UK in 1982 (Rock 2007).[24] A major outcome of such developments has been the establishment of the International Crime Victimization Survey (ICVS), which has now been carried out in a total of 54 countries. In keeping with the concerns expressed by the World Society of Victimology discussed at the start of this chapter, the latest available data from the 2004/05 ICVS reveal that only a small percentage of victims of more serious crimes (burglary or violence) received any help or support from a specialized agency. Less than 10 per cent had received such help in *any* country, although many victims would have appreciated it (van Dijk *et al.* 2008).

Like the victims' movement itself, however, victimology has been far from a unified sub-discipline. The 1970s saw disputes arise between victimologists who focused on the provision of services to victims, and those who were interested in broader, research-driven victimology (van Dijk 1988). Conflict also arose between 'positivist victimology', which employs scientific methods (such as the victimization surveys) to examine criminal victimization specifically, and 'general victimology', which encompasses wider victimizations including natural disasters and war (Cressey 1986; Spalek 2006). Walklate (1994, 2007b) and Young (1997a) have each highlighted the continuing tensions between various groups of victimologists.

Nevertheless, as the view gradually developed that victims of crime were being neglected in many criminal justice systems, the study of *crime* victims took centre stage (Maguire 1991). A major facilitator of this process was the Dutch academic Nils Christie (1977) who argued that the criminal justice system of many countries, having become over professionalized, effectively 'stole' conflicts from their 'rightful owners', meaning victims and offenders:

> The party that is represented by the state, namely the victim, is so thoroughly represented that she or he for most of the proceedings is pushed completely out of the arena, reduced to the triggerer-off of the whole thing. (1977: 5)

Later, in one of the first direct analyses of a working criminal justice system and its interactions with victims of crime, Shapland *et al.* (1985: 177) said of the English and Welsh system:

> The [criminal justice] system is not geared to the perspective of the victim. There appears to be a mismatch between the victim's expectation of the system and the ignorance of and ignoring of his attitudes and experiences by the professionals within the criminal justice system.

Such views have led many commentators to propose alternative justice models, often based (to varying degrees) around principles of restorative justice (Dignan and Cavadino 1996; Braithwaite and Parker 1999; Young 2000; Dignan 2002a, 2002b).[25] For Dignan (2005) this is because the implementation of policies and the reform of practices relating to victims of crime within the criminal justice system have led only to their 'partial enfranchisement' at best within that process. All the countries under review in the present research have experimented with restorative justice, especially in relation to young offenders, and such developments are the subject of extended discussions in Chapter 6.

From its outset, victimology has been a field in which activists and academics tend to overlap. Speaking of Gloria Egbuji, the Nigerian lawyer and campaigner for victims' rights, Jan van Dijk (1998: 2), himself a major figure in the proliferation of victimology across Europe, notes, 'Like many of us, our Nigerian colleague resists to be qualified as either researcher or activist. Most of us are happy to wear both hats'. This blurring of roles (which has been particularly evident in The Netherlands) became more apparent as the second victimological wave took hold and spread from the United States in the late 1960s. Fattah (1992) describes how, at this point, what he calls 'theoretical victimology' gave way to a more political/social model focusing on assisting crime victims, alleviating their plight and affirming their rights within and beyond the criminal justice system. A key aspect of this was a growing appreciation for so-called 'secondary victimization': the notion that many victims of crime are victimized a second time through poor treatment at the hands of the criminal justice system itself (Wemmers 1996). Pointing and Maguire (1988) discuss how the victims' movement in the USA was driven by a host of 'strange bedfellows' concerned with different aspects of victimization in its broader sense. These ranged from feminists[26] and mental health practitioners, to survivors of war and atrocities such as the Nazi concentration camps (Young 1997a) and, particularly relevant for this study, victims of the apartheid regime in South Africa (Garkawe 2004).

These varying camps found a degree of unity in the USA with the formation of the National Organization of Victim Assistance (NOVA) in 1975, the world's first national association of victim assistance projects. That said, Paul Rock (1986: 92) describes the organization in its early days as 'held together only by the deliberate effort of its board to subdue quite manifest ideological and intellectual rifts'. Within the main countries under review in the present volume, NOVA was followed in Europe by the UK with the establishment of the National Association of Victim Support Schemes (NAVSS) in 1979. The UK model was then applied to the Irish Association of Victim Support in 1983, the Dutch National Victim Organization in 1985 and the Scottish Association of Victim Support Schemes, which became independent from NAVSS also in 1985.

Of course, these directly NAVSS-inspired European schemes were not alone. France and Switzerland were among other countries establishing national victim support organizations at about the same time, with a similar model of government funding. In Germany, the nationwide WEISSER RING organization for victims and their families was first established in 1976. The WEISSER RING is itself an interesting case because, unlike most other victim support organizations across jurisdictions, it has from its beginnings been funded not by grants from the German government but by membership fees, donations, and bequests. Van Dijk (1988) notes that this to some extent separates the organization from more grassroots movements found in other countries (including those under review in this research) as in practice the source of this funding tends to be retired police officers and legal personnel. In South Africa, the National Institute for Crime Prevention and the Reintegration of Services (NICRO), which began providing services and support to victims of crime in the late 1980s, has a similar funding structure. NICRO was originally founded in 1910 and was up until this point predominantly concerned with providing probation services in support of offenders and their families. Soon afterwards, all probation officers in South Africa were given specific duties with regards to victims of crime under the Probation Services Act of 1991.

A national umbrella organization of victim assistance and support projects has failed to materialize in either Canada or Australia, although there have been recent moves to establish Victim Support Australasia as the peak body in both Australia and New Zealand (Victim Support Australasia 2009).[27] Despite the success of NOVA in the USA and the WEISSER RING in Germany, one high-ranking civil servant interviewed for this research and involved in the promotion of Victim Support Australasia to the Government of the Australian Capital Territory highlighted the uphill battle of getting anything up and running at the national level in a federal jurisdiction.

Various commentators have attempted to represent the converging interests that made up the early victims' movement in one succinct list of key driving forces. For example, in the US context Young (1997a) lists: the introduction of state compensation schemes; the development of academic victimology; the women's movement; a rise in crime coupled with a loss in faith in the criminal justice system; and the growth of victim activism as all contributing to the birth of the movement. Interestingly, he defines these as 'virtually independent activities' (1977: 194), which refutes the 'movement' label. In Australia, Booth and Carrington (2007) give: the refuge movement, women's support organizations, the women's electoral lobby, aboriginal and community legal services, and sexual assault and advice centres. In England and Wales, Shapland *et al.* (1985) give a predominantly different list of influences: the call for victim aid and assistance, the recognition of victims' poor experiences with the criminal justice system, and state compensation and reparation schemes.

The disparity between the USA, Australian, and English and Welsh lists are indicative of a marked difference of approach taken to victims between these jurisdictions. For example, Maguire and Shapland (1997) argue that groups working and campaigning on behalf of victims in the USA took a far more rights-based, political approach compared with their European counterparts, who for many years stressed the need for service provision for victims rather than championing notions of victims' rights.[28] As noted previously, Australian victim groups have taken a similar politicised stance (Booth and Carrington 2007). This difference in impetus had long-term implications for the way in which victim services and policies were developed and delivered, as can be demonstrated by comparing Europe and the USA.

As has been noted earlier, in the mid-1980s many European jurisdictions followed the English model of Victim Support. This involved governments channelling funding for victim services, which was often *ad hoc* and permanently in danger of being withdrawn (Victim Support England and Wales 2009), though independent charities or other organizations. In time, van Dijk (1988) notes how these organizations took on an increasingly professional, institutionalized role and came to be consulted by national governments on victim issues and policy.[29] Nevertheless, these organizations continued to defended their voluntary, apolitical character and thus rarely found themselves in public opposition to their governments.

By contrast, US victim groups (including NOVA) have a history of being far more vocal in their campaign for judiciable rights for victims of crime. This includes a longstanding call for an amendment to the US constitution to guarantee the recognition of such rights (National Victims Constitutional Amendment Project 2003). As a consequence, an impetus was built up in the USA which saw many states (starting with Wisconsin in 1980) passing a Victims Bill of Rights and amending their own constitutions to guarantee victims the rights they[30] were campaigning for. Such developments spurred on the political debate at the federal level, eventually culminating in the formation of the 1982 Presidential Task Force on Victims of Crime. The Task Force recommended that victims should become the topic of federal legislation, which came soon afterwards in the form of the

1984 Victims of Crime Act. The 1984 Act established (through a 1988 amendment) the federal Office for Victims of Crime, charged with providing leadership and funding for victim support initiatives.

Overall, compared to many European jurisdictions, the US approach of political campaigning and rights-based argument achieved major goals relatively quickly, including the acceptance of victims at the highest level of policy making; the establishment of a fixed and permanent federal agency dedicated to the issue; and a commitment to long-term government funding for victim support organizations. In contrast, Rock (1990, 2004) chronicles the slow and arduous task faced by Victim Support in England and Wales in gaining the government's trust and commitment to financial support. Indeed, requesting more and more funds (and guarding against the possibility that those funds will be withdrawn) has been an ongoing task for the organization ever since (Victim Support England and Wales 2007, 2008, 2009). Of course, like all generalizations there were exceptions to this characterization of the European victims' movement as non political. Heidensohn (1991) for example emphasizes the role played by the European women's movement. Indeed, on this point it is relevant that most European jurisdictions implemented policies and reforms designed to assist victims of rape and domestic violence long before more general policies relating to victims of crime as a whole were in place, as did South Africa (see e.g. Irish Department of Justice, Equality and Law Reform 1999; Scottish Executive 2001).

The third wave: policy acceptance?

As victim support initiatives were taking hold and attracting government finance in North America and Europe towards the end of the 1980s, governments in all the jurisdictions under review began, at least on the face of it, to take seriously the notion that victims needed to become a central plank of criminal justice policy making, beyond the financing of independent support agencies. It has been shown that North America was somewhat ahead in this respect, the USA having already responded at the national level with the Victims of Crime Act in 1984. In Canada, the Ministry of the Solicitor General had introduced the Justice for Victims of Crime initiative in 1982 (Rock 1986). Of course, this latter initiative came about only as a component of a wider package of reform based around reparation (chiefly benefiting *offenders*) which provides an early indication of the differences which can exist between rhetoric and reality with regard to the 'victim centredness' of some of these measures (Rock 1990).

That said, earlier action had been taken in all the countries under review to provide different degrees of state compensation for victims of violent crime. The idea that the state should provide financial reimbursement to victims of crime for their losses was initially propounded by English penal reformer Margery Fry in the 1950s. The first such scheme was introduced in New Zealand in 1963, followed by Britain the following year. The first US scheme was introduced in California in 1965. The first Canadian scheme was launched in Saskatchewan in 1967, with the first Australian scheme opening in New South Wales the same year. Ireland's first scheme began operating in 1974 and The Netherlands followed in 1976. These schemes were for the most part all limited to compensating victims of violent crime, although The Netherlands government had received recommendations from the Dutch Committee on Property Sanctions in 1970 that the planned system for The Netherlands should also offer compensation to victims for any material damages (Wemmers 1996). South Africa still lacks a state compensation programme, although calls for the creation of such a scheme have been growing since the early 1990s (*Noseweek* 2009). Simpson (1996) notes that state compensation in that country is by no means unprecedented, with the pre-1994 government establishing a President's Fund to serve victims of terrorism. It is also important to note that statutory provision for *court*-based compensation, paid for by the offender, has been in place in South Africa since the Criminal Procedure Act 1977. It is however extremely questionable to what extent the majority of victims of crime in apartheid South Africa could avail themselves of this scheme (Schurink *et al.* 1993).[31]

Common to all these jurisdictions then is a sense of 'false start' about the acceptance of victims into official policy. This example helps to illustrate how the growth of the victims' movement was far from an uncomplicated series of simple, chronological breakthroughs. In England and Wales, Rock (1990) draws on the early creation of a state compensation system to explain the relative absence of victims of crime from the policy-making agenda for most of the proceeding two decades. This was after all a costly scheme and, relative to all the other schemes which followed it in Europe, extremely generous in terms of the payments on offer.[32] With such a far-reaching scheme in place, many of those in policy-making circles took the view that that they were already doing a great deal for crime victims, albeit in the absence, at this stage, of any consultation with the victims themselves.

The rekindling of *policy* interest in victims towards the end of the 1980s was heavily influenced not only by the growing prominence of organized victim assistance schemes, but also by the increased attention victims were receiving from international bodies. The United Nations was drawing attention to victims (Joutsen 1989), and various international meetings were hosted on the topic by the Council of Europe and The European Institute for Crime Prevention and Control (HEUNI) throughout the 1970s and 1980s (Mawby and Walklate 1994). A landmark development for all jurisdictions was the introduction of the UN's 1985 Declaration of Basic Principles of Justice for Victims of Crime and Abuse of Power[33] followed, in Europe, by the Council of Europe's Recommendation on the position of the victim in the framework of criminal law and procedure. The 1985 UN Declaration requires victims to be treated with compassion and respect for their dignity. It also requires that crime victims be given access to compensation mechanisms, information about the criminal process, and that the inconvenience caused by this process is kept to a minimum.[34]

Many countries reacted quickly and directly to implement the principles set down in the 1985 UN Declaration. New Zealand responded with the Victims of Offences Act 1987, which placed obligations on criminal justice actors to treat victims with courtesy and afford them access to information and services. The following year, all Canadian Ministers of Justice adopted a uniform policy statement of victims' rights that would be used to guide their legislative and administrative initiatives in the criminal justice area. Other countries, such as France, implemented the principles of the Declaration within new penal codes (Reese 2000). England and Wales did not react with legislation but published the non-statutory (first) Victims' Charter of 1990, which promised similar treatment to victims, albeit with no enforcement structures to guarantee such treatment (UK Home Office 1990).

Not all jurisdictions followed suit at the same pace. For example, in 2002 the Commonwealth Secretariat noted that while Canada, South Africa, the United Kingdom, and some Australian jurisdictions had all initiated 'significant administrative and legal procedures to protect victims' rights and interests' (2002: 5) the vast majority of the 54 nations comprising the commonwealth had failed to take action on implementing the 1985 UN Declaration, some 17 years after its publication. This resulted in the publication of the Secretariat's *Commonwealth Guidelines for the Treatment of Victims of Crime*, which gave new impetus to the Declaration's principles in many commonwealth jurisdictions (Hanly 2003).

The USA is generally considered to have had a head start in

adapting state and federal laws to meet the principles set down in the Declaration (see Goodey 2005). Nevertheless, the 2008 report of Human Rights Watch on the adherence of the USA to international standards on the rights and interests of victims of crime paints a mixed picture, noting in particular that the definition of 'victimhood' used in many US states is restrictive, especially with regard to 'less ideal' victims (Human Rights Watch 2008).[35] Indeed, guidelines accompanying the federal Victims of Crime Act prohibit the federal funding allocated under the Act from being used to offer rehabilitative or support services to incarcerated individuals 'even when the service pertains to the victimization of that individual'.[36]

Broadly speaking, the method of choice for the implementation of the principles set down in the UN Declaration has been the adoption of statutory and non-statutory victims' charters setting out the standards of service victims can expect from criminal justice and other agencies.[37] The enforceability of these charters tends to rest with the internal complaints mechanisms of the criminal justice agency responsible for infringing the relevant standard or pledge contained with the charter. For example, in the South African Charter, victims are informed near the end of the document that they may 'contact the particular government department or service provider if you have any complaints with regard to the service you are receiving' (South African Department of Justice and Constitutional Development 2008a: 4). Similarly, the Irish Victims' Charter divides each page into two sections, with the top section laying out the services that can be expected from each agency, and the bottom section giving the address of the relevant agency's complaints department should the services not be delivered.

Chapter 5 will discuss to what extent provisions backed by such mechanisms can be said to afford genuine rights to victims. Doak (2005) has highlighted the growing international calls for some form of procedural right of participation (for victims) within criminal justice systems. It has been noted above that the movement in the USA and, to some extent, Australia has always been more inclined to campaign in favour of legal rights for victims. This trend has now taken hold in the European victims' movement. In the English and Welsh and Scottish jurisdiction, one of the key precipitators of this change has been the introduction of the Human Rights Act 1998, which enshrined the European Convention on Human Rights into UK law. In wider Europe, the EU Council's 2001 *Framework Decision on the Standing of Victims in Criminal Proceedings* has spurred a revival of 'rights' language (and policy movement) associated with victims because, unlike the various recommendations previously made by the Council of Europe on this matter, a decision from the Council of the European Union is binding on all those to whom it is addressed. The body of case law at the European Court of Justice regarding the 2001 EU *Framework Decision* is growing.[38] Beyond the EU, many international instruments now make mention of victims' rights (directly or indirectly) including: the International Covenant on Civil and Political Rights (ICCPR); the Convention on the Elimination of Discrimination against Women (CEDAW); and the Convention on the Rights of the Child (CRC). In addition, the Rome Statute of 2002 – constituting the International Criminal Court (ICC) to hear cases of war crimes, genocide and crimes against humanity – legislates for the participation of victims at all stages of the ICC process. In addition, the ICC has adopted a judicial code of ethics which includes obligations on its judges to have regard to the interests of victims in their deliberations.[39]

The victims' movement: a reflection

From the early developments in academic victimology, to the establishment of victim support groups and mechanisms, to the *prima facie* acceptance of crime victims as an important concern in national, transnational and international politics (or certainly in rhetoric), the victims' movement has gained much momentum and continues to develop across most jurisdictions. So far it has been shown that developments across the nine main countries under review have been similar, but not parallel with each other. The early politicization of the victim issue in the USA and in the southern hemisphere compared with the more voluntary, service-orientated spirit of European schemes prompted legislation and an early debate on victims' rights in those jurisdictions. This 'rights' question has now developed into the key underlying issue faced by criminal justice policy makers in most jurisdictions. Although the field of zemiology has continued to address victimization through social harms beyond crime and the traditional confines of criminology (Hillyard 2006), victims of *criminal* acts have clearly taken central stage in the national, transnational and international policy spheres, albeit we will see in Chapter 2 that the breadth of individuals falling into this category has been progressively widened. The remainder of this book will seek to explain such developments from a comparative perspective, drawing on the nine main jurisdictions mentioned at the start of this chapter but also drawing on examples from further afield.

Notes

1. Some commentators speak of a prior 'golden age' of victim involvement in criminal justice (see Schafer 1968). Certainly a focus by authorities on victims of crime can be traced back to antiquity. The draft Jamaican victims' charter of 2006 cites the Babylonian Code of Hamnurabi of 1700 BC as prescribing restitution to the victim (the so-called 'wronged man', see Roth (2002)) in property offence cases and the Roman Law of the Twelve Tables of 449 BC as requiring convicted theft offenders to pay a multiple of the value of the goods stolen back to victims, depending on whether they were recovered (Jamaican Ministry of Justice 2006).
2. A federal agency (constituted under a 1988 amendment to the Victims of Crime Act 1984) dedicated to running and funding support initiatives for victims.
3. See also Crawford (1990).
4. Referred to in this volume as 'the 2001 EU Framework Decision'.
5. Originally founded in 1990, and previously known as the European Forum for Victim Services, the organization changed its name in 2008 to convey a more corporate and professional image. All member victim support groups have achieved a degree of official recognition by their national governments, as demonstrated by the case of Victim Support Denmark, which was only invited into Victim Support Europe 'well into the new millennium', after having sufficiently 'matured' as an organization (van Dijk and Groenhuijsen 2007: 372).
6. On which see Chapter 4.
7. See Newburn and Reiner (2007).
8. On this point, the authors conclude that neither system has an inherent advantage in terms of victims' experience of the criminal justice system. They therefore ascribe greater importance to the practical implementation of relevant measures in either system.
9. See below.
10. Scotland having a separate criminal justice system to that of England and Wales.
11. Although this should not be read as suggesting there was an absence of victim support schemes in Ireland up until this point. In fact the Irish Association of Victim Support was established in 1983 by former police Detective Sergeant Derek Nally, who was later to stand as a candidate in Ireland's 1997 presidential election.
12. Presently co-ordinated by the Slachtofferloket Working Group.
13. See Chapter 5.
14. See Nelken (2007a).
15. All but three (the USA, The Netherlands and Ireland) are also Commonwealth jurisdictions and the criminal justice systems of all but The Netherlands have some ancestry in the British criminal justice system.

16 This has been done in anticipation of a future project examining this issue in Asia and South America.
17 All interviewees have been anonymized except where explicit permission was granted to identify individuals by their position within an organization.
18 These issues are returned to later as part of a discussion on the victims' movement.
19 But not all, see Walklate (2007b).
20 Although I do so here out of convenience.
21 See Pointing and Maguire (1988).
22 The term has been described as 'a rather ugly neologism' (Newburn 1988: 1).
23 Although the first European crime victims survey was conducted in Finland (Fiselier 1978).
24 South Africa remains the only state under review in this volume which has not yet completed a national victimization survey, although data from individual city surveys are available from Johannesburg, Pretoria and Cape Town (Louw *et al.* 1988; Louw 1998; Camerer *et al.* 1988).
25 See Chapter 6.
26 The role of second wave feminism for the movement in general has been emphasized by Kearon and Godfrey (2007). It is sometimes presented as the key foundation of the movement in some countries, especially in Canada (Canadian Resource Centre for Victims of Crime 2006).
27 Although a national coordinating body for victim support Groups in New Zealand was established in 1990. This would later become the New Zealand Council of Victim Support Groups (NZCVSG).
28 On which see Chapter 5.
29 Rock (1990) provides an in depth discussion of this process for Victim Support England and Wales.
30 Or, at least, the organizations claiming to represent them.
31 Interviews carried out by Schurink *et al.* (1993) further revealed a lack of knowledge among the population, especially within the rural communities, regarding the Charter and the services on offer to victims of domestic violence and sexual assault in particular.
32 See also Miers (1991) for detailed discussion of this point.
33 Referred to in this volume as 'the 1985 UN Declaration'.
34 See Chapter 3 for a more detailed discussion on these points.
35 See Chapter 2.
36 Victims of Crime Act Victim Assistance Grant Program, 67 Fed. Reg. 56,444, 56,457.
37 See Chapter 5.
38 See Chapters 3 and 5.
39 Both the ICC (2006) and the International Criminal Tribunal for the Former Yugoslavia (Lynch 2006) have actually faced criticisms that defendants are now comparatively poorly serviced by court facilities compared to victims.

Chapter 2

Defining 'victims'

Criminal victimization is a malleable concept. It is a label which can evoke great public sympathy[1] as well as personal catharsis and a sense of closure for all those affected by crime (Miers 1980, 1991). It is the successful attainment of 'victim status' in the eyes of the public and those working within the criminal justice system which in most cases will grant a person access to the range of official and unofficial support mechanisms and financial redress available in many jurisdictions. The recognition of different parties as 'legitimate' victims of crime is therefore a vitally important issue in its own right. As such, this chapter is devoted to a discussion on the meaning and scope of the phrase 'victim of crime' in the jurisdictions under review. Analysis of this issue reveals two underlying themes. First, across all nine jurisdictions one can appreciate an expansion of official notions of victimhood in recent years, to include ever wider categories of individuals affected in some way by criminal (and other) activities. Second, it will be highlighted that victim status is increasingly afforded by reference to the *harms* suffered by a given individual or group. The following discussion will reflect on the implications of such developments, for policy makers and victims themselves, in the nine jurisdictions under review.

The expanding scope of victimhood

Theoretical context

Given the wealth of academic debate surrounding the so-called victims' movement discussed in Chapter 1, it comes as no surprise that victims of crime have been variously categorized and defined by national governments and international organizations. One of the most influential commentators on this issue has been Nils Christie and, in particular, his characterization of the so-called 'ideal victim'. Christie's (1986) argument is that only certain stereotypically victims achieve true 'victim status' in the eyes of the public and within criminal justice systems. Characteristics attributed to this 'ideal victim' include: being weak; carrying out a 'respectable project' at the time of victimization; being free from blame; and being a stranger to a 'big and bad' offender. To be labelled as a *bone fide* victim one must first conform to this ideal and then make one's case known to the justice system. As such, the ideal victim is one that both reports a crime to the police and then co-operates fully with the system by attending court and providing good-quality evidence. Christie's model is arguably incomplete in that he seems to have individual victims in mind rather than groups and does not consider the position of corporate bodies as victims. Nevertheless, the presumption that 'real victims' necessarily become involved with the justice system has resulted in the victim's role often being shrouded in that of the witness in many jurisdictions.[2] Elias (1983, 1986) and Rock (1990) go further to argue that society's narrow conception of victimization is brought about by selective definitions of crime, construed for political purposes. Such ideas may overly simplify the complex interaction of social processes that lead to activities being labelled as deviant,[3] but the point remains very significant in the context of the present volume and its attempt to understand the driving forces behind victim policies across jurisdictions.

Such arguments led to the development of so-called 'radical victimology' and its expanded notions of victimhood beyond simple, criminal classifications. For example, we now know that there is considerable overlap between victims and offenders (Hough 1986; Dignan 2005). Jan Jordan (2009: 3) expresses this reality in the following terms:

Not only can victims become offenders, and vice versa, but in some situations determining who should be viewed as the victim or offender can be problematic. When a burglar is shot leaving a crime scene, for instance, he/she occupies both positions concurrently.

So-called 'indirect' victims are now also widely recognized in academic and policy discussions, including the family, friends and community of the 'primary' victim and the bereaved survivors of homicide (Rock 1998). Of particular importance has been the recognition of 'secondary victimization': the notion that poor treatment at the hands of a criminal justice system can leave people revictimized (Pointing and Maguire 1988: 11). Hence, recently there have been moves to recast victims as *consumers* of the criminal justice process (Zauberman 2000; Tapley 2002).

The harm principle

Underlying the expansion of official notions of victimhood in all the countries under review, and beyond, has been a growing tendency to define victims by reference to the harm they endure. To give an example, Guo-An (2001: 1) reports that in China the term 'victim' in criminal justice means 'a citizen, a legal person or an organization that has directly suffered harm as a result of the criminal act'.[4] In this respect many jurisdictions have followed the definition set down by the 1985 *UN Declaration of Basic Principles of Justice for Victims of Crime and Abuse of Power*:

> 'Victims' means persons who, individually or collectively, have suffered harm, including physical or mental injury, emotional suffering, economic loss or substantial impairment of their fundamental rights, through acts or omissions that are in violation of criminal laws operative within Member States, including those laws proscribing criminal abuse of power. (para. 1)

Harm is therefore defined widely. The 2001 *EU Framework Decision of the Council of the European Union on the Standing of Victims in Criminal Proceedings* follows a similar model:

> 'Victim' shall mean a natural person who has suffered harm, including physical or mental injury, emotional suffering or

economic loss, directly caused by acts or omissions that are in violation of the criminal law of a Member State.' (Art. 1(a))

The South African Victims' Charter utilizes an almost identical definition (South African Department of Justice and Constitutional Development 2008a: 7), as does The Netherlands (Tak 2003). The US Justice for All Act of 2004 defines a victim as 'a person directly and proximately harmed as a result of the commission of a federal offense or an offense in the District of Columbia' (18 USC 3771). Since 1997 it has been clarified that US states receiving federal money to provide victims with services and support under the Victims of Crime Act (42 USC 10601–10603) must extend such amenities to victims of white-collar and financial crimes (US Office for Victims of Crime 1998).

The conceptualization of victims as those who have suffered harm as a result of crime (as opposed to a more technical or prescriptive definition) has two key implications. First, as an underlying principle it gives scope for a wide cross-section of individuals or organizations to be included within the ambit of victimhood, especially given the inclusion of 'emotional suffering' within such definitions. This issue will be discussed in more detail in the section below. Secondly, this understanding of victimhood to some extent allows victims to be self-defined. Such a definition is not, on the face of it, confined to cases where prosecutors in a given state feel there is an arguable case, merely that the victim has been harmed. This is made particularly clear in the English and Welsh Victims Code of Practice, a statutory Code to be followed by all criminal justice agencies:

> This Code requires services to be given to any person who has made an allegation to the police, or had an allegation made on his or her behalf, that they have been directly subjected to criminal conduct under the National Crime Recording Standard. (UK Home Office 2005b: para. 3.1)

It will be noted that this definition does equate the status of victimhood quite closely to a person's co-operation with the criminal justice system, albeit there is no specific link drawn between the reporting of crime and the identification and prosecution of an offender. This means that the victim label in no way turns on a victim's 'success' or 'failure' in giving evidence in court or, indeed, their willingness to give evidence at all. This point has been emphasized in the Quebec Act Respecting Assistance for Victims of Crime 1988 where

> 'Victim of a crime' means a natural person who suffers physical or psychological injury or material loss by reason of a criminal offence committed in Québec, whether or not the perpetrator is identified, apprehended, prosecuted or convicted. (s.1)

In Australia, some states and territories have made reference to the mental element of the relevant crime to clarify the meaning of victimhood. In Victoria, for example, a victim is 'a natural person who has suffered injury as a direct result of a criminal offence, whether or not that injury was reasonably foreseeable by the offender'.[5] Here, injury means actual physical bodily injury, mental illness, pregnancy, grief, distress, trauma or 'other significant adverse effects', loss or damage to property, or any combination of these.

Less developed or extensive official definitions of victimhood were appreciable in Scotland, New Zealand and Ireland. The New Zealand Victims' Rights Act 2002 defines victims as those suffering 'physical injury, or loss of, or damage to, property' (s.4) as a result of crime.[6] Clearly this is a more restrictive understanding of harm than that found in most of the other jurisdictions discussed earlier. In Scotland, the 2001 Scottish Strategy for Victims of Crime issued by the then Scottish Executive defines a crime victim as 'any person who has been the subject of any type of crime' (Scottish Executive 2001: 3). Thus far, the Irish Department of Justice, Equality and Law Reform has not published a specific definition of crime victims, and the Irish Victims' Charter does not carry such a definition.[7] Like all other EU states, Ireland is however bound by the 2001 *EU Framework Decision* and must therefore adopt a compatible understanding of victimization. Of course, to some extent a less prescriptive 'official' definition of vicitmhood can lead to greater flexibility. For example, the International Criminal Court has recently been asked to address the meaning of the term 'victims' in the Rome Statute and to rule whether it is restricted to 'victims who appear before the Court' (Art.43(6)). In reaching its decision, the court took a pragmatic view:

> Therefore, being the obligation upon the Court to protect victims formulated in general terms in article 68(1) of the Rome Statute, such obligation cannot be interpreted as limited to certain categories of individuals. This interpretation is supported by the analysis of the provisions of the founding texts of the Court which refers to the term 'victims' *tout court*'. (para. 27, emphasis in original)

In coming to this decision, the court was also mindful of the wide definition of victimhood given under the 1985 UN Declaration.[8]

In almost all the countries under review then, victims are officially construed as those who have suffered harm, which is generally defined broadly. The focus is therefore on the *outcome* and *impact* of the crime, rather than the legal process. The use of harm in these definitions also recalls the idea put forward by Boutellier (discussed in the last chapter) that the renewed international focus on victims has come about as a result of the appreciation and empathy people retain for the suffering of others. This is reflected not just by the way governments formulate broad brush definitions of who they consider to be victims (at least, rhetorically) but also by developments in the criminal law which expand the scope of victimhood. A case in point is the recent expansion in definitions of rape and sexual assault seen in a number of jurisdictions over recent years. For example, in England and Wales the official legal definition of sexual victimization was expanded in the Sexual Offences Act 2003. This followed long-term arguments from victim groups to the effect that non-consensual oral sex, previously not constituting 'rape' under the law, was as distressing for the victim as 'traditional' rape (see UK Home Office 2000). In accepting these arguments and reforming the law accordingly, the Act may be said to reflect more accurately the harm and suffering of those experiencing such acts, as opposed to restrictive legalistic definitions that exclude many victims. That said, the English statute still restricts 'rape' to non-consensual penetration by the *penis* into the vagina, mouth or anus:[9] meaning those suffering sexual assault perpetrated by a woman cannot usually be recognized by the system as victims of 'rape'.[10]

In contrast, in the United States reforms have progressed further to the adoption of entirely gender-neutral definitions of rape in some states. Epstein and Langenbahn (1994) cite the gender-neutral Illinois Criminal Sexual Assault Statute as the national model for rape laws, albeit many states retain a gender-based definition.[11] Both the Illinois and Michigan criminal codes also refrain from using the term 'rape', and references to this term or its derivatives are inadmissible in court. The US criminal code similarly has a gender neutral definition and also does not use the word rape.[12] The dropping of this extremely emotive terminology is intended to avoid the victim having to label the act as such in order to meet the elements of the crime (Kilpatrick 2004). This last observation raises the important point that for some 'victims' there are *negative* connotations to being labelled as such, which has lead to the term 'survivors' gaining credence, especially in cases of homicide and sexual abuse (Rock 1998).

The harm principle lies at the root of many of the reform agendas across all nine jurisdictions under review and is demonstrated through a number of common developments. For example, reforms intended to improve the experience of victims within the criminal process are generally grounded on the concept of 'secondary victimization' (see below) and the apparent desire to redress the further harm caused to victims by the justice process itself (see Pointing and Maguire 1988). In Chapter 6 I will discuss the expansion of compensation and restorative justice schemes, which aim to redress the harms caused as well as provide symbolic and cathartic benefits to victims. The use of victim impact statements to communicate the effects of a crime directly to a court (see Chapter 4) has for the first time prompted courts in many jurisdictions to formally consider the harm caused to the victim. As such, the harm principle will be returned to a number of times throughout this volume as a means of conceptualizing such reforms.

Indirect victims

As noted in the last section, moves towards addressing the needs of those who have suffered harm as a result of crime have led to the increasing recognition of so-called 'indirect victims'. Shapland and Hall (2007) employ the metaphor of a stone thrown into a pond, and the subsequent rippling out of impacts from those directly involved to their family, friends, local, national and even global communities.[13] Indirect victimization has been a staple of the academic literature in victimology for some time, with particular reference to the families of murder victims.[14] In England and Wales, Rock (1998) has described how policy makers began taking greater account of indirect victims during the late Conservative era following pressure from organizations like Parents of Murdered Children (POMC) and Support After Murder and Manslaughter (SAMM). The Canadian academic Scott Kenney has written extensively about the impacts of homicide on the friends and family of the deceased, arguing that homicide survivors have a greater sense of coping when they engage in activities which enable them to 'compartmentalize their thoughts and deal with them one at a time' (Kenney 2003: 25). In a subsequent paper, Kenney (2004: 244) discusses the long-term implications of such crime for those close to the direct victims:

Subjects [homicide survivors] were very clear that coping is not recovering completely, returning to 'normality', or going back to the way they were before the murder. Instead, subjects referred to the ability to live their lives 'around it' and 'go on'.

As such, it is perhaps with good reason that homicide survivors have been the main focus of both academic and policy attention when it comes to indirect victims of crime in the jurisdictions under review.[15] For example, as is now common in many jurisdictions, the Irish Victims' Charter (Irish Department of Justice, Equality and Law Reform 1999) promises that garda superintendents will 'liaise directly' with families of murder victims through a named member of the investigation team (p. 8). Many criminal justice systems also publish or support special information packs designed for bereaved family members in homicide cases, which include guidance on the criminal justice system and advice on practical issues like who to inform about the death and how to stop unwanted mail (see e.g. Newfoundland and Labrador Department of Justice 2002; Scottish Executive 2004a; Advocates for Victims of Homicide (Ireland) 2010).

For policy makers, this development has been spurred on not only by academic observations like those of Kenney, but also as a response to media campaigning in support of the friends and family of direct victims in high-profile homicide cases. Cases from England and Wales include the racist murder of black schoolboy Stephen Lawrence in 1993, and the subsequent inadequate police investigation and poor treatment of Lawrence's family and community (Reiner 2000). The murder of some 218 people[16] over a 20-year period by Dr Harold Shipman in Greater Manchester similarly raised questions concerning the support being offered to those left behind, including the wider community (Victim Support England and Wales 2002a). More recently, proposals to amend the UK Criminal Injuries Compensation Scheme have been spurred on by the dissatisfaction of victims and relatives of victims who were injured or killed in the London bombings of July 2005 (UK Home Office 2005a). Here, critical comparisons have been drawn with the operation of the US compensation systems after September 11th (BBC 2006; Walklate 2007a). In the latter case, compensation was available for distribution to the spouse, children, or other relatives of people killed in the attack (Maginnis 2002), which is broadly the same as the UK Criminal Injuries Compensation Scheme (UK Criminal Injuries Compensation Authority 2008). However, the English scheme limits compensation in fatal cases to a £12,000 payment, whereas the US scheme paid out considerably more in individual cases and at a considerably faster rate. This is illustrated by the following examples published by Special Master of the US scheme, Kenneth Feinberg:

A married military officer, age 26 with no dependents and a base compensation of $44,000, received a net award of $1,841,128 after offsets of $168,489.

A married broker, age 34 with one dependent and a base compensation of $82,000, received an award of $2,021,046 after $466,000 in collateral offsets.

A married laborer, age 47 with 3 dependents and a base compensation of $58,000, received an award of $1,036,556 after collateral offsets of $298,694. (US Department of Justice 2002: 14)

These compensation figures were high enough to provoke some criticism of the federal government for using the taxpayer's money 'to make millionaires out of the 9/11 victims' (Maginnis 2002: 2). This was despite a near universal empathy for the suffering of these victims, of the kind predicted by Boutellier (2000). An interesting point about the wording of this US scheme is that it phrases the *primary* victim as the beneficiary of the award, even in cases where that person is deceased and actual payment is to indirect victims.

The inclusion of the immediate family of the primary victim is a common theme running throughout relevant policy documents across the nine jurisdictions under review. The families of direct victims are also included in the mission statements of most victim assistance organizations (see e.g. Canadian Resource Centre for Victims of Crime 2010). Hence the New Zealand Victims of Offences Act 1987 maintains that the term victim 'includes the members of the immediate family of the deceased' (s.2), and similarly the South African Victims' Charter holds that '"victim" also includes, where appropriate, the immediate family or dependants of the direct victim' (South African Department of Justice and Constitutional Development 2008b: 1). In the Australian Capital Territory, the Victims of Crime Act 1994 expands this understanding to include 'any person who was financially or psychologically dependent on the primary victim immediately before his or her death' (s.3).

Other jurisdictions have established quite sophisticated systems of classifying victims. For example, in the Australia Northern Territories, the recent Victims of Crime Assistance Act 2008 distinguishes between four different cohorts of victims of violent acts. 'Primary' victims are defined as persons 'against whom the violent act has been committed regardless of whether the person suffers an injury or dies as a direct result of the violent act' (s.9). 'Related' victims are relatives or persons in an intimate personal relationship with the primary victim (s.15). 'Secondary' victims are persons present at the scene of a violent act who suffer injury as a direct result of witnessing the violent act (s.11).[17] This category also includes children or stepchildren of the primary victim or, when the primary victim is a child, parents or guardians if they suffer injury as a direct result of subsequently becoming aware of the violent act (but were not necessarily present). For these purposes, 'injury' includes: physical illness or injury; a recognizable psychological or psychiatric disorder; pregnancy; or some combination thereof. Finally, so-called 'family victims' (s.13) include: the spouse or *de facto* partner of the primary victim of the violent act; a parent, stepparent or guardian; or a child, stepchild, or person entirely or substantially dependent for financial support on the primary victim of the violent act.

In some jurisdictions the recognition of indirect victims has prompted more procedural reforms in addition to the provision of information. Often these are still restricted to compensation provisions (see Chapter 6) but have progressed so far in some jurisdictions as to afford indirect victims the right to speak in court, or even to have their own representation. For example, since 2005 the relatives of deceased victims of violent crime in The Netherlands have been permitted to make a statement in court as to the impact of the crime on them, or have this statement read out by the prosecutor. Slachterofferhulp Nederland (Victim Support Netherlands) provides such victims with assistance in formulating these statements.[18] A similar scheme was piloted in England and Wales from July 2005 onwards. Here, 'victim advocates' were sanctioned for the first time to represent homicide survivors in court. The consultation document published in advance of the English pilots emphasized 'the importance of seeking the view of victims in prosecution decisions' (UK Home Office 2005c: 12). The consultation also envisaged such advocates expressing victims' views to the prosecutor at the pre-trial stage, in order for such views to be taken in to account as part of the decision making exercise. These pilots had three main components: enhanced pre-trial support for indirect victims; a family impact statement to be presented to the court in a manner similar to The Netherlands system; and personal and social legal advice. The last of these components involved the public funding of 15 hours of free legal advice to the families of homicide victims. Such advice was intended to cover personal and social issues directly arising from the death of the (direct) victim, but excluded any pre-existing legal issue or advice regarding the progression of the case through the criminal justice system (UK Crown Prosecution Service 2007).

Despite such developments, substantive recognition of indirect victimization is still notable for its absence in a number of contexts, especially within more binding international instruments which would lead to the tangible commitment of extra resources in individual jurisdictions. For example, in Europe the 2001 *EU Framework Decision* expressly applies only to harm 'directly caused' by the violation of the criminal law of a Member State (Art.1(a)). The exclusion even of homicide survivors from this definition has been a topic of contention at the European level, as articulated in an interview carried out for this research with the Director of Victim Support Europe:

> The Framework Decision has a definition of a victim. We want to extend it to the first line family, who have lost someone. In Holland we are having this discussion as well. I often meet bereaved people who have lost someone from [sic] murder and manslaughter and they should be treated as victims as well. But they are not in the definition as it is now. (interview with the Director of Victim Support Europe 2009)

As a consequence, in England and Wales the statutory *Code of Practice for Victims of Crime*, which is intended to implement the *Framework Decision*, expressly states that it 'does not require services to be provided to third parties or indirect victims' (UK Home Office 2005b: para. 3.2). This is despite the fact that the 1985 UN Declaration includes 'immediate family or dependants of the direct victim and persons who have suffered harm in intervening to assist victims in distress or to prevent victimization' (Annex A(2)). In Scotland, it has been recognised that the Scottish Government's definition of victim of crime 'does not differentiate between some individuals who are directly affected by a criminal activity (e.g. a woman who is sexually assaulted by her partner) and those who are indirectly affected (e.g. children who witnessed the sexual assault of their mother)' (Scottish Executive 2004b: para. 2.7).

Another aspect of the recognition of indirect victimization has been the increasing tendency to cast witnesses as victims of crime, as in the following extract from a Scottish Government report into victim services:

> It is also important to recognise that those who witness crime, for example violent or sexual crime, but who are not themselves the primary victim, should also be considered as victims. (Scottish Government 2007: para. 2.8)

Similarly, 'a person who witnesses the commission of an offence in circumstances in which it is probable that he or she would suffer harm' is recognized as a victim under s.3 of the Australian Capital Territory's Victims of Crime Act 1994. It is important to note here that we are talking about the victimization of witnesses prior to their involvement with the criminal justice system.[19] After coming forward to the system, but before giving evidence in court, several jurisdictions have also passed laws making witness intimidation a specific offence including the UK (Criminal Justice and Public Order Act 1994), Australia (Witness Intimidation Act 2002) and Ireland (Criminal Justice Act 1999). Other countries in the sample have dedicated witness protection programmes (the US, New Zealand, and Canada).

Indirect victims are therefore certainly being considered and, to some extent, catered for by policy makers across the jurisdictions under review: at the level of sympathetic treatment and information provisions, and also at the level of procedural involvement in the justice process.[20] Of course, it should also be noted that recognition of indirect victims, however limited, is not yet a worldwide phenomena. Some developed jurisdictions beyond the main sample under review in this volume have been slow to endorse indirect victimization within the formal criminal justice system at any level. For example, it is clear that, in China, 'victim of crime means the direct victim' (Guo-An 2001: 2). It is equally clear from the above discussion that, even in the countries under review, this category of indirect victims is largely restricted to the family and dependants of direct victims of homicide or violent crime. Such recognition is a significant development, but one which arguably falls far short of recognising the wider array of actors put forward by the academic literature who may be considered 'victims' (see Shapland and Hall 2007; Williams and Hall 2009). For example, none of the policy documents reviewed or the policy makers interviewed for this project made any mention of the concerned relatives of repeat burglary victims, or the lifestyle changes this may provoke (see Mawby 2000). In addition, across all these jurisdictions very few reference have been uncovered to the wider community of the direct victim, be it in a case of violent or property crime.

Given the previous discussion in this chapter, it may be no coincidence that the categories of victim most often singled out for recognition by these jurisdictions are also those whose suffering as a result of such crimes is immediately apparent to most people. Another explanation is that distinctions are being drawn between the kinds of victims suitable for recognition and support by *criminal justice*, and those better suited for redress by *restorative justice* processes. Bottoms (2003) has argued in terms of a separation between the criminal justice and restorative justice systems. This distinction seems to hold weight in this context, given that the majority of the jurisdictions under review in this volume are experimenting with restorative justice schemes, many of which include some element of involvement by the wider community of a primary victim or defendant (Strang 2001; Shapland et al. 2006). This issue will be discussed in greater detail in Chapter 6. The point does however raise interesting questions as to the demarcation of victims into different kinds of justice system.

Secondary victimization

As noted in the last chapter, one of the key developments in the victims' movement has been the recognition that the process of co-operating with an unsympathetic criminal justice system – which ignores the views, perspectives and needs of victims – can itself constitute a secondary victimization. This view was unanimously supported in all the jurisdictions under review and, indeed, acknowledged by all interviewees without exception.

Like victimization itself, secondary victimization has been defined in a variety of ways. A highly detailed discussion of the issue has been produced by the South African Department of Justice and Constitutional Development (2008b: 23), which arrived at the following definition:

> 'Secondary victimization' refers to the attitudes, processes, actions and omissions that may intentionally or unintentionally contribute to the revictimization of a person who has experienced a traumatic incident as a victim through failure to treat the victim with respect and dignity, disbelief of the person's account, unsympathetic treatment, blaming the victim and lack of (or

Defining 'victims'

insufficient) support services to assist the victim at interpersonal, institutional and broad social level).

Most of the reforms and policies covered in this volume could be construed as addressing some aspect of secondary victimization, including the stresses of being denied information about the progress of a case and the feeling that one's views and opinions as to the handling of this case are being ignored.[21] In particular, the 'discovery' of secondary victimization has highlighted the plight of *witnesses* giving evidence in criminal proceedings. It is widely acknowledged that witnesses in court are generally asked to relay information in a very unnatural, unfamiliar way; a courtroom is an unfamiliar environment for most people and can be frightening and intimidating (Hamlyn, Phelps and Sattar 2004; Hamlyn, Phelps, Turtle *et al.* 2004). The evidence is itself elicited from witnesses in a very unnatural manner, with witnesses sometimes being told to present their answers towards a bench or jury while simultaneously receiving the questions from a lawyer standing in another direction (Rock 1993; Hall 2009a). In addition, witnesses are required to present the information at an unnatural speed and volume, and can be persistently interrupted in their flow and asked to slow down or speed up or speak more loudly. In reference to adversarial justice systems, Jackson (2004: 73) summarizes the point in the following terms: 'It is seldom appreciated just what a wide array of cognitive, social and emotional skills the legal system demands of witnesses'.

Brienen and Hoegen (2000) confirm that the same basic difficulties are presented for witnesses in most European jurisdictions, and indeed that most jurisdictions have taken steps to rectify this. The authors also conclude that the differences between adversarial and inquisitorial justice systems do not themselves significantly improve the position of witnesses in the case of the latter. That said, it is important to emphasize that, in the inquisitorial Dutch criminal justice system, victims are often not questioned in court at all, but in pre-trial proceedings. Nevertheless, it is not only the procedure of physically giving evidence that may be difficult for victims and witnesses. In many cases victims will be asked to cope with some very unfamiliar concepts, hearsay being a prime example and one on which witnesses of all kinds receive no information or guidance in any of the published materials reviewed for this project.

The distinction (or lack thereof) drawn between victims and witnesses in the jurisdictions under review is an important one, because it is *witnesses* (as opposed to victims *per se*) who are vital to the operation of any criminal justice system. In other words, by helping witnesses (including victim witnesses) to come to court and give high-quality evidence, the systems also effectively help themselves in terms of efficiency, costs and 'success' rates. As such, commentators such as Elias (1986) have questioned the underlying motives of jurisdictions claiming to put victims at the heart of their criminal justice systems and address secondary victimization by implementing reforms which may assist the prosecution process. Some jurisdictions have responded directly to such charges. For example, the Scottish Strategy for Victims emphasizes that it is concerned with *all* victims, regardless of their contribution to the justice system:

> It is recognized that some victims will also be witnesses; that some will be involved with the criminal justice system, some in civil court actions. The needs of *all* of these victims, irrespective of whether or not they are also witnesses, should be taken into consideration by all the relevant agencies. (Scottish Executive 2001: para. 1.8)

Similarly, the Victims' Charter Act 2006 of Victoria maintains that

> All persons adversely affected by crime, *regardless of whether they report the offence, should be treated with respect* by all investigatory agencies, prosecuting agencies and victims' services agencies and should be offered information to enable them to access appropriate services to help with the recovery process. (s.4(b), emphasis in original)

Nevertheless, there remains a clear sense that much of the reform agenda in all nine jurisdictions is targeted at victims who become involved with the criminal justice system in cases where a defendant is identified and the victim's evidence is needed at trial. As noted by one report into the US system:

> According to the [1985 UN Declaration], a person may be considered a victim irrespective of whether the perpetrator is identified. While this is technically also true in the United States, as discussed below, some victims' rights advocates raise concerns that the systems in place to support victims become effective only after a suspect is identified. (Human Rights Watch 2008: 16)

This type of situation has been most strongly criticized by Victim Support England and Wales in its report *Criminal Neglect: No Justice Beyond Criminal Justice* (2002a: 1):

> In recent years there has been a raft of new developments aimed at tackling secondary victimization of victims, and witnesses – but the issue is that these measures are exclusively contained within the criminal justice system. This is good news for the 3% of crime victims who enter the system – but what about those who do not?

Elsewhere in the report, Victim Support England and Wales identifies areas in which support is required by victims of crime outside the formal criminal justice system. These areas include health provision, financial provision, compensation and help with rehousing. Chapter 6 will discuss the provision of state compensation to victims of crime in all nine jurisdictions in greater detail but, suffice to say, in general most of these systems require the victim to have co-operated with the formal criminal justice system. As for victims' need for support in terms of healthcare and housing, neither issue was raised as a significant area of policy development in any of the official documents analysed for the project, or in interviews carried out across the nine jurisdictions. The needs of crime victims beyond the formal criminal justice system are also highlighted in a report from the Ministry of Justice of New Zealand on the needs of Pacific Peoples when they fall victim to crime. Support from the formal criminal justice system was seen as relatively unimportant by the majority of victims interviewed for this study when compared with health provision and less formal support from friends, family and the wider community (Koloto 2003).

The need to ensure support and services beyond the criminal justice system is included within the 1985 UN Declaration, where states are called upon to 'implement social, health, including mental health, educational, economic and specified crime prevention policies to reduce victimization and encourage assistance to victims in distress' (Art.4(a)). Furthermore, the Declaration requires states 'to promote the observance of codes of conduct and ethical norms, in particular international standards, by public servants, including law enforcement, correctional, medical, social service and military personnel, as well as the staff of economic enterprises' (Art.4(f)). Despite these observations, support to victims beyond the criminal justice system has largely been limited to the central funding of dedicated victim support groups in the nine jurisdictions under review. Of course this might be considered a significant development in its own right, except in so far as the *International Crime Victimization Survey* reveals a lack of knowledge in most jurisdictions about the existence of such services for victims beyond the criminal justice sphere (van Dijk *et al.* 2008). If victims must in practice always be informed about and referred to such organizations through criminal justice agencies, as seems to be the case in most jurisdictions, this once again effectively neglects the needs of victims who never come into contact with the formal system.

Notwithstanding the funding of victim support organizations, most of the policy documents reviewed from the nine jurisdictions under review hint at a 'criminal justice system' bias to the victim reform agenda. For example, in 2003 the Canadian Department of Justice issued ten underlying principles designed to 'guide the treatment of victims, *particularly during the criminal justice process*' (Canadian Department of Justice 2003: n.p., emphasis added). Five of these principles also contain a direct reference to the criminal justice system. In 2009, the Canadian Government restated its commitment to victims in a Federal Victims Strategy comprising of four key goals, three of which invoke victims within the criminal process and the first of which reads: 'Working with partners to enhance victim participation in the criminal justice system' (Canadian Department of Justice 2009: n.p.).

Guarantees made to victims in Canada within the Federal Victims Strategy beyond the scope of the criminal justice system are vague and limited to the provision of information about services: 'Information should be provided to victims about available victim assistance services, other programs and assistance available to them' (Canadian Department of Justice 2003: principle 8). Similarly vague assurances are given in the 2002 Victims' Rights Act of New Zealand: 'A victim or member of a victim's family who has welfare, health, counseling, medical, or legal needs arising from the offence should have access to services that are responsive to those needs' (s.8).

In this last example, the New Zealand legislation does require that any person who deals with a victim should treat that victim with 'courtesy and compassion, and respect the victim's dignity and privacy' (s.7), although the only examples of such persons given within the section are 'a judicial officer, lawyer, member of court staff, police employee, or other official' (s.7). This focus on victims *within* criminal justice is also prevalent at the European level, with the 2001 *EU Framework Decision* being exclusively concerned with the standing of victims in criminal proceedings. The key jurisdiction to stand out in this respect is South Africa, where distrust of the criminal justice system and the widespread failure to report crimes of domestic violence in particular pose very significant challenges for the South African Department of Justice and Constitutional Development. All the jurisdictions under review have attempted to boost reporting rates for domestic violence over the last twenty years but representatives from the South African DoJCD were particularly concerned with community projects designed to raise awareness of and access to external support mechanisms like shelters and advice centres, especially in the rural communities:

> The focus started firstly with victims of gender-based violent crime. It wasn't about any victim, it was more specifically targeting women who were in a bitter relationship. (interview with a representative of the South African Department of Justice and Constitutional Development 2009)

More generally, however, the focus on the secondary victimization of victims *as witnesses* held true across these jurisdictions. The most prevalent demonstration of this has been the introduction of mechanisms and facilities within courtrooms designed to assist witnesses when giving evidence including video-links, screens and/or the facility to pre-record the evidence of witnesses. Such facilities have been introduced on a statutory basis in all the countries under review with the exception of South Africa.[22] The USA and England and Wales have the longest histories of such evidence within the present sample of jurisdictions, although Spencer and Flin (1993) have traced the earliest audio tape recordings of police interviews with abused children to the early 1960s in Denmark and Sweden. The first US state to pass legislation allowing the admission of a videotape with a child was Montana in 1976. It is important to note, however, that at this point much of the literature and policy discussion on this topic concentrated on the practical advantage to the criminal justice system of tape recorded evidence rather than the position of the victims (inevitably children) giving that evidence. Hence, Spencer and Flin (1993) report that when Glanville Williams first advocated the recording of interviews with victims of crime in England in 1963, his argument focused on the benefits to the court of having an accurate record of the proceedings. That said, a report emphasizing the psychological benefits to the *witnesses* of giving recorded video evidence was published in the USA as early as the 1970s (Miller and Fontes 1979).

The USA was followed in the late 70s and early 80s by England and Wales, where the provision of live video-links traces back to the early use of tape-recorded psychiatrist interviews with children in High Court wardship proceedings. Informal use of such facilities appears to have developed throughout this period, although formal legislation on the matter did not arrive until the 1991 Criminal Justice Act (see Hoyano and Keenan 2007), and was only extended beyond child witnesses in the 1999 Youth Justice and Criminal Evidence Act.[23] This legislation drew on Healey's (1995) combined approach to identifying vulnerable witnesses,[24] whereby witnesses could be classed as 'vulnerable' by reason of personal characteristics (disabilities, mental illness or physical disorders) but also for wider circumstantial reasons (being related to or involved with the defendant or being the complainant in a matter of sexual abuse). This model of vulnerability was soon replicated in most Australian states and territories and in New Zealand (Ellison 2001). The Canadian Parliament introduced relevant provisions into the Canadian criminal code in 1988 (para. 700.1). Like the US and English reforms, these were specifically targeted at child victims of abuse. The Netherlands began recording the evidence of child witnesses (usually given outside the formal courtroom in any event) in 1990 (Brienen and Hoegen 2000). The relevant Irish legislation came in the form of the Children Act 1997 (s.21), whereas devolved Scottish legislation came in the Vulnerable Witnesses (Scotland) Act 2004.

Secondary victimization has been addressed further through the enactment of legislation designed to spare some witnesses the onslaught of full cross-examination, by disallowing questions on certain topics unless special consent is obtained. The most notable example is that of questioning about a complainant's past sexual history in support of an assertion that the complainant was either more likely to have consented to the sexual activity forming the subject-matter of the relevant charge, or is otherwise less worthy of belief. Temkin (2002) compares the relevant provisions from Canada, New South Wales and Michigan[25] and identifies notable differences between them. These include the fact that only the New South Wales statute prevents such evidence from being adduced by the prosecution as well as the defence. Temkin also notes that in the original drafting of the provisions in Canada the Canadian criminal code[26] failed to exclude questioning on sexual *reputation* (as opposed to behaviour), as do the English provisions in the Youth Justice and Criminal

Evidence Act 1999 (s.41). Overall, Ellison doubts the utility of many of these schemes, all of which preserve discretionary powers on the part of the judge to allow such evidence in specific situations. This is not objectionable in itself (Henning and Bronitt 1998), however the lack of specific definitions for key concepts within these provisions gives judges wide powers to exercise this discretion. Temkin's (1999) wider work strongly suggests judges are quick to exercise this discretion and allow such questioning. Furthermore, in the Canadian context Gotell (2002) has argued that in order to be spared such questioning a rape complainant must exhibit the characteristics of the ideal victim.[27]

As noted in Chapter 1, the acceptance by policy makers of secondary victimization at the hands of the criminal justice system is an important development in the victims' movement. Furthermore, this development casts light on the continued suffering endured by some of the most vulnerable groups of victims during the criminal procedure itself, including child victims and victims of rape and other sexual assault (Temkin 2002). Nevertheless, this focus on victims *as witnesses* within criminal justice systems does raise questions about the underlying goals of such policies and brings into sharp relief Elias's point that victims can be used to justify punitive reforms, such as barring the defence (but not, in some jurisdictions, the prosecution) from asking questions on certain topics. In combination with the relative absence of reform in all nine jurisdictions specifically focused on victims' needs outside the criminal justice system (outlined earlier), this illustrates how widening the scope of victimhood can bring cost and efficiency benefits to justice systems.

Ideal victims?

The bereaved families of those killed in homicide cases and witnesses victimized through poor treatment at the hands of the criminal justice process both fall broadly within Christie's (1986) categorization of ideal victims. This is illustrated by the following description of the circumstance surrounding the adoption of constitutional amendments to protect victims' rights in California, the so-called Marsy's Law:

> It is named after Marsy, a 21-year-old college senior at U.C. Santa Barbara who was preparing to pursue a career in special education for handicapped children and had her whole life ahead of her. She was murdered on November 30, 1983. Marsy's Law is written on behalf of her mother, father, and brother, who

> were often treated as though they had no rights, and inspired by hundreds of thousands of victims of crime who have experienced the additional pain and frustration of a criminal justice system that too often fails to afford victims even the most basic of rights. (State of California 2008: 128)

The characterization of both Marsy herself and her family as innocent, well-meaning and laudable figures is clear. It is also extremely telling that the law here is presented as having been written 'on behalf of' the victims' family. Witnesses too are ideal in the senses that they have come forward and, in Christie's words, made their case known to the authorities. They are also continuing to co-operate by subjecting themselves to the stresses and inconvenience of giving evidence in court. Homicide survivors, for their part, are generally portrayed as the archetypical wronged party: blameless in the face of extreme suffering brought about at the hands of a monstrous and distant offender.

The principal difficulty with such characterizations of the ideal victims is that not only do the vast majority of victims never become involved with the criminal justice process (van Dijk et al. 2008), but it is increasingly recognized that victims and offenders can often be the same people (Hough 1986; Dignan 2005). As such, to focus policies entirely on the ideal victim not only creates what Carrabine et al. (2009: 159) call a 'hierarchy of victimization', but also effectively excludes the vast majority of victims from the support mechanisms established for their benefit. This has significant implications for a country's accordance with the 1985 UN Declaration, which maintains that its provisions 'shall be applicable to all, without distinction of any kind' (Annex A (3)).

A focus on ideal victims seems to characterize much of the wider victims' movement. The NGO components of the movement are understandably keen to emphasize the blameless position of those they support, and on whose behalf they attempt to elicit public money. For example, a statement from the Canadian[28] Resource Centre for Victims of Crime reads:

> Part of the point of providing victims basic rights is a recognition that they have done nothing wrong, and they are not responsible for what happened although they may bear the burden for the rest of their lives. (Canadian Resource Centre for Victims of Crime 2006: 4)

It is clear that such sentiments have found their way into official policies in the jurisdictions under review. In the USA, for example, Human Rights Watch has been critical of individual states and reforms at the federal level for the restrictive view taken of victims:

> Contrary to the [1985 UN Convention], in certain states incarcerated individuals, persons accused of crimes, and some police officers have been denied victim status or the ability to enjoy all the same rights afforded to other types of victims. (Human Rights Watch 2008: 15)

Elsewhere the report points out that the US Victims of Crime Act prohibits the use of federal funds to provide rehabilitative or support services to incarcerated individuals, even when the service pertains to the victimization of that individual. Furthermore, it is noted that systems set up in the United States to assist victims can break down when the victim and offender have family relationships. This is despite the fact that the provision of services, irrespective of any relationship between victim and offender, is specifically enshrined within the 1985 UN Declaration (Annex A(2)).

In New Zealand, Jan Jordan has spoken of the homogenization of victims in the eyes of policy makers and the public in general, noting that the reform agenda (including the New Zealand Victims of Crime Act 2002) assumes all victims to exude similar ideal characteristics:

> Much of the recent attention given to victims of crime has spoken of them in ways suggesting they are viewed as a conglomerate group, like a huge flock of black and white penguins lacking differentiation – to most human observers anyway. This has translated often into assumptions that all victims will react to crime in a similar way, be impacted on similarly, and have similar needs and expectations. (Jordan 2009: 5)

It has been noted previously that the International Criminal Court has a relatively developed framework of victim support provisions. Yet even here, special distinction is afforded to the stereotypical victim:

> A Chamber in making any direction or order, and other organs of the Court in performing their functions under the Statute or the Rules, shall take into account the needs of all victims and witnesses in accordance with Article 68, in particular, children,

elderly persons, persons with disabilities and victims of sexual or gender violence. (International Criminal Court 2002: Rule 86)

A further revealing case study is that of recent Australian policy on foreign nationals (usually women) who are smuggled into the country as victims of people trafficking. Marmo and La Forgia (2008) have commented that such victims are used by the criminal justice system as a commodity to obtain prosecutions in Australia, before being deported. The Australian Government's Action Plan to Eradicate Trafficking in Persons lays out a framework by which victims of trafficking are granted a so-called 'criminal justice stay visa' for six months and access to the witness protection scheme for as long as the criminal trial continues. At this point, however, only the loosest assurances are given of the *possibility* of continued residence rights. As in the last section, this gives the appearance of a state 'rewarding witnesses, ignoring victims' (Burn and Simmons 2005: 1). More specifically, however, Marmo and La Forgia (2008: 174) comment on how this situation derives from a national tendency to characterize trafficked women as undesirables:

> In Australia, trafficked women are portrayed and maintained as the 'other', as unbelonging matter of the moral and legal community. Trafficked women are dealt with as an external issue – to the point that their conditions and situation are unable to affect domestic policy objectives. Their status as irregular immigrants is used to re-establish a social and moral order, a social identity of the Australian system, which is disturbed by the unwanted presence of trafficked women.

It is worth noting that such an attitude is certainly against the spirit (and possibly the letter) of the 2005 UN Protocol[29] to Prevent, Suppress and Punish Trafficking in Persons Especially Women and Children (which Australia has ratified) which states in Article 14:

> The measures set forth in this Protocol shall be interpreted and applied in a way that is not discriminatory to persons on the ground that they are victims of trafficking in persons. The interpretation and application of those measures shall be consistent with internationally recognized principles of non-discrimination.

The Australian model discussed here is heavily influenced by the model set down in the Council of Europe Convention on Action Against Trafficking in Human Beings of 2005,[30] to which both the UK and The Netherlands are signatories. The Convention requires only that states allow victims of trafficking residence rights for a 30-day 'recovery and reflection period' (Art.13). States must then issue a temporary renewable residence permit to victims in cases where it 'is necessary owing to their personal situation' or 'the competent authority considers that their stay is necessary for the purpose of their co-operation with the competent authorities in investigation or criminal proceedings' (Art.14(1)). The UK Updated Action Plan on Trafficking Human Beings extends the suggested six-month duration of the temporary residence permits in the Convention to one year. However, it does not expand upon the reasons for which such a permit may be granted, and indeed is quite vague on the point, saying only that permits will be granted 'where victims meet certain criteria' (UK Home Office and Scottish Government 2009: 13).

One final point concerning the apparent focus on ideal victims in many of the policy developments across the nine jurisdictions under review is the relative absence of any reference to victims of corporate crime. On this point it can be noted that the majority of the definitions of victimization employed in these jurisdictions refer only to 'natural persons'[31] (this being the phrase used by the 2001 *EU Framework Decision* in its conception of victimhood). The absence of corporate victims from these policy agendas is perhaps not surprising given the fact that, with a few exceptions (Walklate 1989; Levi and Pithouse 1992; Spalek 1999, 2001), corporate crime victims have also been neglected by researchers in this area. Toombs (2005: 272) suggests that, in our society at present, '"conventional criminals" tend to be represented as a burden upon society in a way that corporations will not be'. If victims of corporate crime are to be taken more seriously, a cultural change in which the crimes themselves are seen as such – and are regarded as serious – will be required. On the other side of this equation, Croall (2007) has recently highlighted that the victims of such crimes often find themselves labelled and placed within the 'unworthy' camp. Once again, therefore, the absence of corporate victims from the policy agendas may reflect a preoccupation with the ideal victim (see Williams and Hall 2009).

This focus on ideal victims internationally has significant implications. Not only does it ignore the reality exposed by crime surveys that the vast majority of victims fall outside this category, but the assertion that such ideal victims co-operate with the criminal justice system gives an impression that states are assisting victims for their own ends by boosting efficiency and confidence in the criminal justice system.

Victims of non-criminal acts

Another widespread international development in the conceptualization of victimhood has been the expansion of attention beyond victims of crime *per se* to include those who suffer as a result of non-criminal behaviour. England and Wales has been at the forefront of this trend with the introduction of 'anti-social behaviour orders' (ASBOS). ASBOS were introduced in England and Wales in the 1998 Crime and Disorder Act, later supplemented by the Anti-social Behaviour Act of 2003. Anti-social behaviour is defined within the 1998 Act as behaviour 'likely to cause harassment, alarm or distress to one or more persons not of the same household [as the perpetrator]' (s.1(1)(a)). An anti-social behaviour order can be made against a person acting in this way 'if necessary to protect persons in the local government area in which the harassment, alarm or distress was caused or was likely to be caused from further anti-social acts by him' (s.1(1)(b)). For present purposes, the significance of this lies in the statutory recognition of a much wider category of victims. The UK Home Office website describes such measures as 'protecting specific victims, neighbours, or even whole communities from behaviour that has frightened or intimidated them, or damaged their quality of life' (UK Home Office 2010: n.p.). This amounts to an acknowledgement that victimization can ripple out from a confined set of individuals, as discussed by Shapland and Hall (2007). Furthermore, the inclusion of damage to quality of life indicates a wide conception of suffering.

ASBOS have been a controversial development, as their effect is to 'prohibit the defendant from doing anything described in the order'.[32] In practice the orders have been used to prevent such persons going to certain places at certain times (or at all) as well as obliging them to refrain from anti-social behaviour for the duration of the order (Campbell 2002). These are civil orders but, significantly, breach of an ASBO is a criminal offence.[33] This use of the criminal law to effectively punish non criminal acts has concerned many commentators (see Rodger 2008). Once again, therefore, we see how a measure ostensibly presented as supporting a traditionally overlooked cohort of victims and their suffering can be construed as means of net widening and retribution. In this respect it is significant that, in England and Wales, ASBOs arrived in the context of media-driven moral panics concerning binge drinking and youth gangs, which heightened public concern about the adequacies of the criminal justice system (Jacobson *et al.* 2008). Following on from the previous section, it is also notable that much of the publicity surrounding the use of ASBOS seems to revolve around the ideal victim whose life is ruined by the deviant behaviour of youth gangs or 'neighbours from hell' (McMahon 2005). In reality, however, Nixon *et al.* (2006) demonstrate that, as with victims of *criminal* acts, the victims and perpetrators of *anti-social behaviour* frequently overlap.

A very similar ABSO framework has been exported to Scotland and the Republic of Ireland. In the latter case, a court issuing such an order must have regard 'to the effect or likely effect of that behaviour on other persons'.[34] As in the UK, the measures caused controversy, the Irish Youth Justice Alliance (2005) writing that

> ASBOS encourage net widening, involve the labelling and criminalization of young people and fail to employ positive approaches and supports to divert young people away from behaviour that could lead to criminal activity. In addition, the employment of the media and the general public to encourage the community to police the order is likely to further demonize and exclude children as young as 10 and set communities against families and their children. They are contrary to international standards on human rights and children's rights.

On the last point, the view of the House of Lords[35] in the UK has been that ASBOS do not breach Article 6 Rights to a fair trial under the European Convention on Human Rights for the reason that, while the orders are civil, the standard of proof required is indistinguishable from the criminal standard (See Collins and Cattermole 2003). Nevertheless, the above quotation reinforces the wider point that the expansion of categories of victimization can raise significant questions concerning the scope of the criminal law and its adherence to human rights. Such questions are now being asked in Australia, where the UK ASBO model is being considered in a number of jurisdictions. As well as the general rights debate, concerns in Australia have been voiced regarding the impact of ASBOS on the freedom to use public space (Winford 2006) and the 'creeping control' over tenants' behaviour in housing estates (Slatter 2007). Notwithstanding this, Australian state and territorial governments are continuing to address victimization from anti-social behaviour by other means, particularly through measures attempting to curtail alcohol abuse (Fleming 2008). Similar measures have also been implemented across the USA (US Department of Health and Human Services 2000) and Canada (Collin 2006).

The extension of official interest beyond *crime* victims has in some cases gone further than anti-social behaviour, to include breaches of human rights in general. This has been particularly apparent in South Africa where, in fulfilment of the 1987 African Charter on Human and People's Rights, the African Union adopted in 2001 a set of Principles and Guidelines on the Rights to a Fair Trial and Legal Assistance in Africa. The Principles give certain guarantees of respectful treatment and information to victims of crime, similar to those found under the South African Victims' Charter. However, here 'victims' includes those who have suffered 'loss or substantial impairment of their fundamental rights' (para.S(n)). This mirrors the wording used in Article 1 of the 1985 UN Declaration, which is extended explicitly beyond criminal acts in Article 18:

> 'Victims' means persons who, individually or collectively, have suffered harm, including physical or mental injury, emotional suffering, economic loss or substantial impairment of their fundamental rights, through acts or omissions that do not yet constitute violations of national criminal laws but of internationally recognized norms relating to human rights.

As noted by the South African Department of Justice and Constitutional Development:

> Interestingly, the definition includes violations of human rights contained in international instruments that are not covered in national legislation. This is significant because victims who have been violated can seek redress, even if national legislation does not recognize the violation. (2007: 2)

Of the nine countries under review South Africa has, for clear historical and social reasons, had the greatest difficulty in maintaining standards of human rights. As such, the fact that this issue is highlighted in this context is not surprising. More broadly, however, this demonstrates how different issues within jurisdictions are being increasingly viewed through the 'lens' of victimhood (see Zehr 1991).

Official verses unofficial definitions

So far, this chapter has discussed 'official' definitions of victimhood. That is, definitions specifically laid out or otherwise implied by national governments and international bodies. This focus has been chosen because the broad aim of this volume is to examine victims as the subject of official policy making in the nine jurisdictions under review. However, to some extent, this discussion only exposes the tip of the iceberg. In reality the practical *application* of such official definitions by individuals within the different justice agencies of these jurisdictions will have a significant impact on how such policies work in practice. Indeed, guidelines published by the Commonwealth have gone so far as to explicitly acknowledge that criminal justice actors must exercise a degree of discretion in their identification of 'victims':

> Where practicable, law enforcement officials must inform the victims of crime of the date, place and time of any bail proceedings. [In terms of the general definition of 'victim' there may be a large number of victims of any crime, thus placing an unacceptable administrative burden on law enforcement officials. The qualification 'where practicable' allows the relevant official to exercise his/her discretion in deciding which victims to inform. These will usually be the direct victim(s) of the crime. Alternatively, there should be a system whereby a 'representative victim' of the group victimized could be identified to accept information and act on behalf of the group]. (Commonwealth Secretariat 2002: para. 3)

Researchers working on behalf of the Scottish Government have reflected on this reality in the following terms:

> Although there is a nationally agreed definition of a 'victim', it is clear that this is not in consistent use. It is clear that definitions evolve over time, for example to include the concept of vulnerable witnesses, but one consequence of this is that different agencies, at different points in the adoption process, would use different definitions. (Reid Howie Associates 2005)

In the United States, the reality that individuals, rather than government departments or even criminal justice agencies, effectively dictate who is considered a 'victim' has been recently acknowledged:

> Prosecutors get to, for the most part, decide who the victim is ... Certain crime victims' family members, and I can name cases, have been excluded from the courtroom and from the inside circle of prosecutors' offices because the prosecutor would pick and choose who would get to be [considered as victims'] family members based on whether or not they supported the harshest penalties possible. (an advocate quoted by Human Rights Watch 2008: 15)

This extract draws obvious links between the expansion in definitions of victimhood and punitiveness within a criminal justice system. Notwithstanding this, however, the real challenge posed by the prevalence of such attitudes among criminal justice practitioners is that the more ideal victim is once again likely to receive better treatment. Commentating on the situation in Victoria, for example, Elding *et al.* (1999: 6) emphasize the problems faced by less ideal victims in rural communities:

> Attitudes of police, service providers and the general community are sometimes much more intense in small communities. Judgements around those 'ideal' victims deserving of assistance and others seen as less deserving can be a challenge and are very prevalent, particularly when resources are already limited.

In England and Wales I have previously discussed how lawyers and other criminal justice workers can often subscribe to stereotypical, ideal notions of victimhood, and that this has an impact upon the services they receive from the criminal justice system. This is demonstrated by the views of one English barrister interviewed for that project on what he hoped to see in a victim personal statement:

> What you want from a victim impact statement[36] is '79 year old Doris has been burgled', I want to know and I want to be able to tell the judge that her wedding ring that was taken – from her late husband – is something that she will never get over. (a barrister working in the north of England, quoted in Hall 2009c: 182)

Clearly, the old woman described here is a textbook ideal victim. Of course, that lawyers should think in these terms is not necessarily inevitable. Evidence from Scandinavia indicates that social workers supporting female victims of sexual abuse outside the criminal justice system do not think in terms of ideal verses non-ideal victims. In fact, the study by Ljungwald and Svensson (2007) suggests these social workers do not primarily label such women as victims of crime or think of themselves as a service for victims of crime, but rather as people who can connect such women with helping resources. While there are considerable differences separating the roles, concerns and training of social workers compared with legal practitioners, this does offer an indication that ideal and non-ideal victims can be thought of in other ways by the professionals charged with supporting and providing them with services.

Defining victimhood: some broad conclusions

In its recent call for the establishment of a European centre of excellence within victimology, Victim Support Europe (2009: 8) voices the criticism that 'not even a common definition of a 'victim' has been fully affirmed'). The forgoing chapter confirms this observation both within Europe and outside it. Nevertheless, it is clear that the reform agendas in most of the countries under review share common themes. For example, all these countries have expanded their official concept of victims to include indirect victims and secondary victims. Furthermore, in every jurisdiction we can note some deference to the harm and suffering experienced on the part of the victim, which equates closely with Boutellier's thought that such deference is a key feature of the postmodern world. More recently, Hayward (2004) has drawn parallels between developments in the concept of victimhood and a perceived expansion of 'youth', whereby individuals in their late 20s now go through a period of extended adolescence or 'kidulthood' before succumbing to the responsibilities and pressures of adult life. This is not to suggest that more victims are now being recognized because they are being treated like children, but rather that kidulthood is another demonstration of a wider social tendency to identify and empathize with perceived suffering and a person's inability to cope, which has extended across jurisdictions.

As noted at the beginning of this chapter, using 'harm' as a common denominator in the identification and labelling of crime victims should result in a wide definition, or self-definition, of victimhood based on an individual's subjective experience of suffering. In reality, however, it has been shown in the above discussion that the reform agendas across these nine jurisdictions generally tend to emphasize certain kinds of (ideal, cooperative) victims and certain kinds of suffering (experienced as a result of giving evidence within the criminal justice system itself). In effect, therefore, the definitions of victimhood in use in most of these jurisdictions are much narrower than they first appear. For example, while most systems recognize indirect victimization, most restrict such recognition to family and dependants of the direct victims of homicide or violent crime. In most cases, indirect victims are also excluded from the more enforceable national and international codes and service standards.[37] A wider category of victim does appear in most experimental restorative justice schemes (including the direct victim's neighbours and communities) but this restriction begs the question as to whether different kinds of victims are to be afforded access to different kinds of justice.[38] It is also obvious that victims *as witnesses* feature heavily in these reform agendas despite the fact that most victims will never report their victimization to the authorities. This is demonstrated not just through the increased protection of witnesses both within justice systems (through the introduction of special facilities to help them give evidence) and outside them (through the enactment of witness intimidation laws and protection schemes) but also by the fact that most victims only come to learn about any support mechanisms available to them *through* criminal justice agencies (van Dijk *et al.* 2008).

Of course one might argue that the type of victim being emphasized here is understandable and in keeping with Boutellier's (2000) thesis, given that the suffering of ideal victims – such as homicide survivors or rape complainants willingly subjecting themselves to giving evidence in court – is obvious and readily draws sympathy from the majority of the population. In practice, however, it has been demonstrated that the expansion of victimhood has implications beyond Boutellier's thought. For example, Garland's (2001) view that victims and the treatment of victims is now the yardstick by which a criminal justice system is legitimized helps explain why governments in all the jurisdictions under review appear to be seeking out new kinds of victims to support. In a sense, criminal justice systems now need victims as much as they need convictions and, as such, new types of victim and new types of harm are identified to fill the void left by dropping public confidence in those systems. New victims are also created by statutory changes such as the introduction of crimes of witness intimidation and the expansion of the (legal) concept of rape. The increased attention paid to non-criminal anti-social behaviour is another prime example, where the ASBO scheme in England and Wales sets out to support not only the direct victims of said acts, but also the witnesses of those actions, in effect creating two victims instead of one. From the defence perceptive this has worrying implications; generally speaking, to expand the concept of victimhood is also to widen the category of 'deviant' acts attracting the attention of the criminal justice system. This raises the important concern that expanding the notion of victimhood can serve the ends of retribution and is therefore more properly thought of as part of the growth in populist punitiveness seen in all these jurisdictions.

It is clear that a wider array of victims are now being recognized across the nine jurisdictions than at any time in the recent past. However, as the above discussion demonstrates, some victims appear to be more equal than others in this exercise. On the issue of prioritizing different kinds of victims Spalek (2006: 13) makes the following observation:

> Whilst the terms 'primary', 'secondary' and 'tertiary' suggest that there is some sort of hierarchy in the level of suffering experienced, it cannot be assumed that secondary and tertiary victims necessarily suffer less trauma than primary victims, since secondary and tertiary victims can also face significant physical, psychological and emotional pain.

To this, we can add that ideal victims who assist the justice system do not necessarily suffer more than non-ideal victims who do not. If this observation is correct, the *de facto* prioritization of different forms of victimhood in these nine jurisdictions implies that the degree of harm or suffering experienced by such victims is only part of a much broader picture: a picture clouded by concerns regarding system efficiency and the need to appease populist punitive sentiments. Of course, this is all notwithstanding the probably greater challenge of ensuring practitioners and front line criminal justice workers accept wider and non-ideal images of victimhood, for the suggestion that only the innocent and the helpful suffer is clearly at odds with the reality.

Notes

1 As discussed by Boutellier (2000), see Chapter 1.
2 A development to be discussed in more detail later.
3 Taking us into the territory of what Mawby and Walklate (1994) term 'critical victimology'.

4 The inclusion of corporate victims here is itself an interesting addition not found in many other jurisdictions.
5 Victims' Charter Act 2006, s.3.
6 Although this is expanded to include 'any form of emotional harm' (s.4) specifically for the purposes of providing services to victims at court (s.7) and further afield (s.8).
7 At the time of writing the newly constituted Irish Victims of Crime Office was still in the process of updating this document.
8 See p. 30.
9 The law had previously been extended to cover anal penetration in the Criminal Justice and Public Order Act 1994.
10 The New Zealand Crimes Act 1961 (as amended) has a similar provision, although in both jurisdictions a person who at birth was female can commit rape with a surgically created penis analogous to the naturally occurring organ. New Zealand is presently in the process of reforming its rape laws, specifically in relation to the meaning of consent, which has been defined in statute in England and Wales, Australia and Canada.
11 As do other jurisdictions, including England and Wales and South Africa. In the latter jurisdiction only females can be *victims* of rape.
12 18 USC 2241–2233.
13 UN Guidelines (United Nations 1999) have gone so far as to recommend jurisdictions set aside funding '[t]o provide special support and assistance to victim assistance professionals themselves, who are constantly exposed to victims' distress and may consequently suffer trauma and chronic stress, in addition to the fact that they may also become victims'.
14 'Homicide survivors'.
15 In the USA, unborn children killed or injured as a result of criminal activity can be recognized by the law as victims of crime (18 USC 1841). Similar rules have been proposed in Canada under the Unborn Victims of Crime Bill (C-484), introduced in 2007 and presently at committee stage.
16 The officially attributed number of what may be considerably more victims (Smith 2005).
17 Note that the terminology used here varies from source to source. For the purposes of this volume such victims are termed 'indirect', whereas 'secondary victimization' is reserved exclusively for victimization at the hands of the justice system. Witnesses are also sometimes referred to as 'tertiary victims' (Spalek 2006).
18 The 2005 extension of this scheme to relatives of murder victims and the direct victims of 'serious crimes' was accompanied by an extra 2 million Euros in central funding awarded to Slachterofferhulp Nederland by the Dutch Government.
19 The position of victims giving evidence at trial is dealt with in the next section.
20 On which, see Chapter 5.

Defining 'victims'

21 See Chapters 4 and 5.
22 Which does have relevant equipment in use on a non-statutory basis in some courts (Meek 1999).
23 Now amended by the Coroners and Justice Act 2009.
24 It will be noted in Chapter 4 how the identification of specifically vulnerable groups of victims is an important driving force behind these policies in general across many jurisdictions.
25 Which has informed a large proportion of other US states.
26 The original provisions were enacted in 1982 and were reformed in 1992 in the face of such criticisms. The 1992 version was later confirmed as constitutional by the Canadian Supreme Court in *R v Darrach* [2000] 2 S.C.R. 443, 2000 SCC 4.
27 See the following section.
28 The traditional mistrust of 'non-ideal' sexual assault complainants in Canada was criticized by the Canadian Supreme Court in *R v Seabover; R v Gayme* [1991] 2 S.C.R. 577.
29 To the United Nations Convention against Transnational Organized Crime of 2000.
30 Which itself derives from the Protocol to Prevent, Suppress and Punish Trafficking in Persons, Especially Women and Children, supplementing the United Nations Convention Against Transnational Organized Crime. See Chapters 3 and 4.
31 China being one of the very few exceptions to this rule.
32 Crime and Disorder Act 1998, s.1(4).
33 s.1(10) of the 1998 legislation.
34 Criminal Justice Act 2006. S.115(1)(c).
35 Now the Supreme Court.
36 Despite the English and Welsh scheme being renamed 'victim personal statement' in 2001, the term 'victim impact statement' appeared to have stuck with many lawyers and court workers.
37 See Chapter 5.
38 See Chapter 6.

Chapter 3

Victims and international organizations

The goal of this chapter is to review and critically assess the responses of organizations beyond the nation state to the challenges posed by the victims' movement and the renewed global interest in supporting victims of crime. In the previous chapter it was established that national understandings about the nature and extent of victimhood in the nine jurisdictions under review have been influenced by international bodies. In Chapter 4 it will be demonstrated that such influence goes well beyond matters of definition, to inform specific measures and reforms introduced in the countries under review. This chapter sets the scene for these arguments, and in so doing supports this volume's wider proposition that national victim reforms are heavily influenced by international governance and to some extent are becoming globalized. To this end, the work of international and regional organizations like the UN and EU are considered as well as the relevant work of international courts such as the European Court of Justice and the International Criminal Court.[1] The chapter will also examine the work of international victim support agencies, including Victim Support Europe and Victim Support Australasia.

The United Nations

The 1985 Declaration

Since its inception in 1985, the UN Declaration of Basic Principles of Justice for Victims of Crime and Abuse of Power has remained the most wide-ranging and influential document on the issue of crime victims to appear at the international level. The Declaration was the culmination of various international meetings hosted on the subject by the UN, the Council of Europe and The European Institute for Crime Prevention and Control throughout the 1970s and early 1980s (Joutsen and Shapland 1989; Mawby and Walklate 1994). This was not the first attempt by a major international body to address the victim issue. For example it will be noted later that the Council of Europe had by this time already produced the 1983 Convention on the Compensation of Victims of Violent Crime. Nevertheless, prior to the 1985 Declaration, much of the focus seems to have been on victims' role as part of crime prevention strategies,[2] as opposed to their place, roles, and expectations within criminal justice systems *per se* (Joutsen and Shapland 1989). As such, there is a general consensus on the significance of the 1985 UN measure, described as the 'Magna Carta for victims' by Irvin Waller[3] and set out by Jan van Dijk in the following terms:

This Declaration, although not legally binding by itself, is seen as a landmark achievement of the international movement to advance the interests of crime victims. It can also be used as a benchmark against which progress in domestic policies can be measured. (1989: 12)

The Declaration was originally tabled at the 1985 UN Crime Congress in Milan, after which it was adopted by the General Assembly in November that year. The principles set down in the Declaration have since become staples of the policy discussions going on in most jurisdictions. The Declaration speaks of victims being afforded access to justice (Art.4), fair treatment (Art.5), and of compassion and respect for the dignity of victims (Art.4). The instrument also makes reference to victims being informed about their role and about the scope, timing, and progress of proceedings, as well as the disposal of their case (Art.6(a)). The Declaration further maintains that victims should be guaranteed assistance from the criminal justice system (including information that such assistance is available) (Art.6(c)) as well as formal and/or informal procedures providing them with redress, restitution and compensation for wrongs suffered (Art.8). The document also has provisions protecting victims from unnecessary delay or inconvenience within the criminal justice system (Art.6(d)) and ensuring their concerns are considered (Art.6(b)).[4] As noted in the previous chapter, the document also applies to victims of abuses

Victims and Policy Making

of power and breaches of human rights which do not constitute actual crimes in individual jurisdictions.

The 1985 Declaration has had a profound impact on academic and policy thinking with regard to victims of crime although, as a non-binding statement of principles, it omits any details regarding the implementation of its aims at the national level. Furthermore, it has been noted by the Secretariat of the Commonwealth of Nations that the document also employs 'very general language' with much room for individual interpretation (Commonwealth Secretariat 2002: 6). As such, since its inception the UN has organized numerous meetings and discussions on the Declaration as well as publishing guides for practitioners and policy makers on its implementation in 1989 (Joutsen and Shapland 1989) and 1999 (United Nations 1999). Both documents place heavy emphasis on the impact of crime on victims and, being addressed to practitioners, there is a clear attempt to educate and influence traditional occupational cultures amongst lawyers in particular.[5] The police, as the front end of most criminal justice systems, are also targeted and presented with a goal 'to integrate the philosophy and implementation of victim assistance into routine police policy and practices' (United Nations 1999: 24). The guidelines contain the seeds of many of the national developments to be discussed in the next chapter including a recommendation to produce written standards of service for individuals working with victims, an overview of victim impact statements and a discussion of the benefits of restorative justice to victims of crime.

Much of the UN's guidance on the implementation of the 1985 Declaration focuses on issues concerning victims outside the justice process. This is in sharp contrast to the specific emphasis (explicit or otherwise) on victims *within* the formal criminal justice system demonstrated in many of the subsequent national definitions discussed in the last chapter. Indeed, criminal justice personnel to some extent play second fiddle in the guideline document to a range of other professions and organizations including schools, universities, health-care professionals, media professionals, mental health workers, clergy, spiritual and informal leaders, landlords, housing entities and employers. The guidelines also advocate the wider goal of promoting public awareness of victim issues.

The Declaration and its associated guidelines are openly idealistic documents, as acknowledged by the following extract:

> Not everything outlined in the *Handbook* [guidelines] will necessarily be appropriate or even possible in different

situations. The *Handbook* is not meant to be prescriptive but to serve as a set of examples for jurisdictions to examine and test. The writers are aware of the difficulties faced throughout the world in identifying resources for victim services. Several of the programmes recommended in the *Handbook* require significant investments of time, personnel and financial resources; in addition, some recommendations may require legislative changes. In many jurisdictions, therefore, the recommendations may appear unrealistic. (United Nations 1999: 132)

As such, and as van Dijk (1989) argues, the true utility of the Declaration lies predominantly as a basis of comparison against which national policies across jurisdictions can be measured and compared. As a list of ideals formulated at the international level – without reference to issues like cost, efficiency, or public confidence – it can be argued that the principles being promoted in the Declaration are likely to be less clouded by the competing political and practical factors which influence policy networks in a domestic setting (see Goddard 1997; Egeberg 1999). This argument can be overstated, after all the Declaration itself was the product of considerable debate and development at the international level before it reached its final form, but the view remains that the Declaration constitutes a relatively 'pure' attempt to address the needs of victims. As such, comparisons between the ideals set forth in the Declaration and the implementation of those ideals in the nine jurisdictions under review[6] can provide us with clues as to the other influences at work in each country.

Given the length of time that has passed since the publication of the 1985 Declaration, it has been argued by some commentators that the response of many national governments to its principles has been disappointing. As Groenhuijsen (2006: n.p.) notes: '[T]wenty years after its adoption ... the principles contained in this Declaration have been poorly implemented in national legislation and policies'.

Declarations adopted by the General Assembly of the United Nations are non-binding on UN members,[7] although Hannum (1997: 145) argues that 'adoption by the UN General Assembly and other bodies of formally nonbinding declarations, statements of principles and ordinary resolutions can have an impact on the creation of international law').[8] As a set of ideals, it may in any event be unrealistic to assume that the Declaration could ever achieve universal acceptance (politically or practically) or implementation. This does not remove the document's significant influence across many jurisdictions, as Williams and Goodman (2007: 251) note: 'it has undoubtedly been influential internationally (and it takes a much wider view of victimization than most victim support organization providing direct services)'. Furthermore, Waller (2001: 1) has pointed to the 'exemplary progress' made in some jurisdictions towards the implementation of the Declaration. This follows the 2001 establishment of a joint Liaison Committee between the UN and the World Society of Victimology to promote the wider implementation of its principles.

Other UN measures

The 1985 Declaration monopolizes much of the discussion in the literature on the UN's work relating to victims of crime although there have been several other, more recent, developments. Four years after the Declaration, members of the UN agreed the Convention on the Rights of the Child. With its emphasis on the 'welfare principle' (Leblanc 1995) this document has significant implications for the support of children giving evidence as witnesses in court and, unlike the 1986 Declaration, is binding on those countries that ratify it.[9] In addition, the 1993 *Declaration on the Elimination of Violence Against Women* urges states to ensure women who are subject to violence 'should be provided with access to the mechanisms of justice and, as provided for by national legislation, to just and effective remedies for the harm that they have suffered' (Art.4(11)(d)). The 1993 Declaration also contains further provisions against secondary victimization to 'ensure that the re-victimization of women does not occur because of laws insensitive to gender considerations, enforcement practices or other interventions' (Art.4(11)(f)). Victims also figure prominently in the Vienna Declaration, adopted by the UN General Assembly in April 2000. This document calls for world governments to develop strategies for addressing the risk factors related to crime and victimization, establish funds for victims and develop restorative justice options.

In the year 2000, the 1985 Declaration and subsequent documents were joined by two significant measures: the United Nations Convention against Transnational Organized Crime, and its supplementary Protocol to Prevent, Suppress and Punish Trafficking in Persons, Especially Women and Children. Both documents have been ratified by all nine countries under review in this volume meaning that, unlike the 1985 or 1993 declarations, states are bound to incorporate their provisions into domestic laws. Article 25 of the Convention provides that 'each State Party shall take appropriate measures within its means to provide assistance and protection to victims of offences covered by this Convention in particular in cases of threat of retaliation or intimidation'. Here 'intimidation' generally seems to refer to threats and abuse suffered by victims as potential witnesses outside the court, which might prevent them from giving evidence. In a recent publication, entitled *Good Practices for the Protection of Witnesses in Criminal Proceedings Involving Organized Crime*, the United Nations Office on Drugs and Crime (2008) makes it clear that a state's obligations under the Convention extends to what it calls 'procedural protection' during the trial itself. As such, the *Good Practice* document provides examples of measures and processes in operation in a number of jurisdictions intended to 'prevent the revictimization of victim-witnesses by limiting their exposure to the public and the media during the trial' (p. 31). These include measures such as video-links, screens, and pre-recorded evidence. The *Good Practice* document specifically distinguishes these kinds of measures from the formal witness protection schemes operating in a number of countries to relocate and hide witnesses in order to avoid their intimidation. The argument is made that the admission criteria for such schemes are often 'overly rigid' and therefore exclude a large proportion of 'victim-witnesses' (p. 21). The Convention also requires that crime victims be afforded access to appropriate compensation and restitution, and have their views considered during the justice process.

With regard to the protocol on people trafficking, Article 2 lists one of three purposes of this measure as 'to protect and assist the victims of such trafficking'. In so doing the protocol requires victims of trafficking to be afforded information on relevant court and administrative proceedings and access to compensation mechanisms. In addition, the protocol urges states to 'consider implementing measures' (Art.6(3)) to provide for the physical, psychological and social recovery of victims, appropriate housing, employment and educational and training opportunities. The protocol similarly requests governments to 'consider adopting legislative or other appropriate measures that permit victims of trafficking in persons to remain in its territory, temporarily or permanently, in appropriate cases' (Art.7(1)). This gives states discretion over the guarantees they make to victims regarding residence rights which, as we saw in the case of Australia in the last chapter, has led to the implementation of some restrictive systems.

Another more recent resolution to be passed by the UN General Assembly is the Basic Principles and Guidelines on the Rights to a Remedy and Reparation for Victims of Gross Violations of International Human Rights Law and Serious Violations of International Humanitarian Law (IHRIHL) of 2005. This document relates to victims of gross violations of international human rights law and serious violations of international humanitarian law, rather than breaches of domestic law in individual jurisdictions. The Basic Principles make specific reference to secondary victimization and maintain that 'a victim who has suffered violence or trauma should benefit from special consideration and care to avoid his or her re-traumatization in the course of legal and administrative procedures designed to provide justice and reparation' (para. 10). The document continues to expand upon familiar themes including minimizing inconvenience to victims and their representatives; ensuring victims are protected from intimidation or retaliation; and protection for victims' families and for witnesses before, during, and after judicial, administrative or other proceedings. The Basic Principles also place heavy emphasis on restitution and reparation to victims (para. 15), which will be the subject of Chapter 6.

Also in 2005, the UN Economic and Social Council passed a resolution detailing *Guidelines on Justice in Matters involving Child Victims and Witnesses of Crime*. This document was based on previous (2003) guidelines from the International Bureau for Children's Rights, and were the product of a Canadian-led (and funded) initiative which saw an intergovernmental group of experts convened by the UN Secretary General meeting in Vienna. A particularly interesting feature of the 2005 document is its insistence that each child victim and/or witness must be 'treated as an individual with his or her individual needs, wishes and feelings' (para. 11). This precludes broad brush labelling of children as 'vulnerable' or 'intimidated' and instead envisions that services and support offered to such children both within and outside criminal justice systems should be tailored to the individual. The *Guidelines* also emphasize the need for training among criminal justice practitioners and personnel who work with children 'with a view to improving and sustaining specialized methods, approaches and attitudes in order to protect and deal effectively and sensitively with child victims and witnesses' (para. 23) and to develop 'child-sensitive procedures' (para. 25).

Both the 2005 *Guidelines* documents, like the 1985 Declaration, are non-binding and therefore have only persuasive force in the nine countries under review in this volume and beyond.[10] This does not make them redundant however, for as Ramcharan (2008: 146) writes of the IHRIHL: 'The principles may be far from being applied in practice, but they are vital to attaining justice in the future'.

Overall, the UN has continuously kept victims of crime on its criminal justice and crime prevention policy agendas for the last 20 years. While the instruments at its disposal are often non-binding (or 'persuasive') authorities, arguments to the effect that implementation has been slow perhaps miss a wider point. The UN's goal in this area has been to promote ideals and best practice. To these ends, the UN has built up a framework of language in which victim issues can be discussed at the policy level, as opposed to the level of activism. It has already been demonstrated how this strategy has impacted upon national and international understandings of victimhood. In the next chapter, it will be demonstrated how these ideals have impacted upon specific policy developments in the countries under review. As such, the real achievement of the UN lies not so much in its pushing through of significant, legally binding, reforms in individual jurisdictions, but rather in its various instruments providing the context and the political precedent[11] to allow (and compel) individual governments to move ahead with such measures.

The Council of Europe

At the regional level, the Council of Europe has been active on the issue of crime victims since the 1983 European Convention on the Compensation of Victims of Violent Crime. Ratified by the majority of Council of Europe members, including the United Kingdom (1990) and The Netherlands (1988) (but not Ireland)[12], this Convention sets out minimum standards for state compensation systems for victims of violent crime while at the same time emphasizing that the primary source of such compensation should be the offender (Art.9). The same year, the Committee of Minsters issued a Recommendation (R (83) 7) calling for Member States to develop policies to provide assistance to victims, and to take account of the public's view in forming such policies. The Recommendation pre-empted several ideas put forward in the United Nations Declaration on Basic Principles of Justice for Victims of Crime and Abuse of Power two years later, including the need to provide a special reception or waiting rooms for victims in police stations and court buildings, and the need to provide victims with appropriate psychological, moral, or material assistance.

Since 1983, the Council of Europe has developed a series of conventions and Recommendations on matters pertaining to victimization and victims within criminal justice. One of the earliest such measures was Council of Europe's 1985 *Recommendation on the Position of the Victim in the Framework of Criminal Law and Procedure*,[16] which largely mirrored the provisions set down in the UN declaration of the same year, being mainly concerned with service rights. The EU has focused particular attention on child victims, victims of human trafficking (see Lee 2007) and victims of terrorism (Pemberton 2010). In the latter case, Article 13 of the Council of Europe's 2005 *Convention on the Prevention of Terrorism* (Council of Europe 2005a) makes the following stipulation:

> Each Party shall adopt such measures as may be necessary to protect and support the victims of terrorism that has been committed within its own territory. These measures may include, through the appropriate national schemes and subject to domestic legislation, *inter alia*, financial assistance and compensation for victims of terrorism and their close family members.

The 2005 *Convention on Action Against Trafficking in Human Beings* (Council of Europe 2005b) similarly contains provisions designed to guarantee victims access to services which will aid their 'physical, psychological and social recovery' (Art.12). This includes access to education for children and, for adult victims lawfully residing within a 'destination country', access to the labour market and vocational training. The Convention also guarantees victims a 30-day recovery and reflection period before any extradition proceedings can be initiated, Following this period, the Convention keeps open the possibility of gaining a temporary residence permit either because it is necessary in the victim's personal situation or the victim's stay is necessary for the purpose of co-operating with the authorities in investigating or prosecuting criminal activities. Under Article 20, victims and other witnesses are also afforded protection from intimidation and coercion both outside and within the court room.

The most recent Council of Europe Convention to impact upon victims of crime is the 2007 *Convention on the Protection of Children Against Sexual Exploitation and Sexual Abuse*. This instrument offers a similar protection and recovery mechanism as that afforded above to victims of trafficking. The 2007 Convention also focuses specific attention on the conduct of interviews with child victims and on their appearance in court. Article 35 maintains that such interviews should be conducted without justified delay, in premises designed for the purpose and by trained professionals. In addition:

Each Party shall take the necessary legislative or other measures to ensure that all interviews with the victim or, where appropriate, those with a child witness, may be videotaped and that these videotaped interviews may be accepted as evidence during the court proceedings, according to the rules provided by its internal law. (Art.35(2))

In court, Article 36 maintains that training should be available on children's rights, sexual exploitation, and the sexual abuse of children for all persons involved in criminal proceedings, particularly judges, prosecutors, and lawyers. Furthermore, when giving evidence, national laws should allow a judge to order that evidence be given in private (excluding the public) and for the victim to be heard in the courtroom without being physically present through the use of appropriate communication technologies. In practice, it will be noted in the next chapter that most jurisdictions have gone beyond these minimum requirements in the provision of video-link and other equipment to assist children and other vulnerable witnesses to give evidence.

The above conventions have tackled specific issues relating to victims of crime. More wide-ranging responses to the victims' movement have come in the form of non-binding recommendations issued by both the Committee of Ministers and the Parliamentary Assembly of the Council of Europe. The first, and most influential, relevant provision was the Committee's 1985 *Recommendation on the Position of the Victim in the Framework of Criminal Law and Procedure*. This was a significant early development which, like the UN Declaration of the same year, called for a range of support and protection measures to be implemented for victims across Europe (see Brienen and Hoegen 2000). This was followed two years later by *Recommendation R (87) 21* on Assistance to Victims and Prevention of Victimization, which contained more stringent provisions concerning the setting-up and monitoring of victim assistance organizations and the development of victim-orientated crime-prevention strategies (see Pease 1997).

Recommendations since then have covered areas such as the intimidation of witnesses in court (R (97) 13); mediation in penal matters (R (99) 19); domestic violence against women (1582 (2002));[13] and sexual assaults linked to 'date-rape drugs' (1777 (2007)). The most recent such Recommendation, R (06) 8, focuses attention back on the support mechanisms afforded to crime victims and was written to update *Recommendation R (87) 21* (Reeves 2003). Here, as well as the familiar safeguards against secondary victimization within the criminal justice system seen in previous Council of Europe and UN documents, the Recommendation also touches upon the promotion of equal access to insurance in all Member States. It also includes 'the provision of special measures for the support or protection of victims by organizations providing, for example, health services, social security, housing, education and employment' (para. 4.6). At a conference of the European Ministers of Justice held later that year, participants issued a resolution to abide by and encourage the developments in *Recommendation R (06) 8* and previous instruments and, in particular, called for more action to tackle the issue of domestic violence. The resolution also called for the implementation of restorative justice initiatives in Member States.[14] On the former point, the Council of Europe has a Task Force to Combat Violence against Women, including Domestic Violence (EG-TFV) which produces reports on relevant legislation in all Member States (Hagemann-White *et al.* 2006).[15]

Aside from the analysis by Brienen and Hoegen's (2000), the work of the Council of Europe regarding victims of crime has been relatively neglected by the literature compared with that of the United Nations and the European Union. Like the UN documents, however, the Council of Europe instruments provide an important framework for domestic policies. They also reinforce particular themes and areas of policy interest including human trafficking, terrorism, and childhood victimization.

The European Union

Given that all the Member States of the European Union are also members of the Council of Europe, it comes as little surprise that the EU has developed its own array of measures concerning victims of crime, several of which draw upon the Council of Europe measures noted above. Recent interest in victims of crime at the EU level can be traced to a special meeting held in October 1999 in Tampere on the creation of an area of freedom, security and justice in the European Union. The outcome of that meeting, the so-called 'Tampere Conclusions', included the following undertaking:

> Minimum standards should be drawn up on the protection of the victims of crime, in particular on crime victims' access to justice and on their rights to compensation for damages, including legal costs. In addition, national programmes should

be set up to finance measures, public and non-governmental, for assistance to and protection of victims. (Art.5)

The Conclusions came with a 5-year implementation timetable, leading to a flurry of EU activity on this issue during that time period. The most significant such development came in 2001 when, pursuant to the above aims, Portugal proposed the implementation of an EU Council Framework Decision on the Standing of Victims in Criminal Proceedings.[17] This document, adopted by the Council in March 2001, arguably spurred the recent revival of 'rights' language (and policy movement) associated with victims in Europe.[18] Unlike the various recommendations made by the Council of Europe[19] or UN declarations (see above), a framework decision from the Council of the European Union is binding on all those to whom it is addressed and therefore highly significant politically in the domestic context. The *Framework Decision* makes similar guarantees to victims as most of the UN and Council of Europe documents, including respect and recognition by criminal justice actors, the right to protection from intimidation and the provision of mediation schemes. While these latter schemes are not cast as an alternative to the formal criminal justice system, the *Framework Decision* does maintain that 'each Member State shall ensure that any agreement between the victim and the offender reached in the course of such mediation in criminal cases can be taken into account' (Art.10(2)). The *Framework Decision* also refers to victims having a 'real and appropriate role in its criminal legal system' (Art.2(1)), the implications of which will be discussed more fully in Chapter 5.

As a binding document, EU Member States had until March 2002 to introduce the necessary laws giving effect to most of the provisions, and until March 2006 to implement Article 5 (Communication safeguards), Article 6 (Specific assistance to victims) and Article 10 (Penal mediation in the course of criminal proceedings). At the time Victim Support England and Wales, which was heavily involved in the drafting of the 2001 EU *Framework Decision*, pointed out that while the UK and Ireland had two of the best records on victims in Europe, change was needed in *all* Member States before any could be said to have fully implemented the Framework Decision (see Victim Support England and Wales 2002c).

Van Dijk and Groenhuijsen (2007) have analysed the impact of the 2001 EU *Framework Decision* by drawing on data from Brienen and Hoegen's (2000) study of the implementation of Council of Europe Recommendation R (85) 11 described in the last section. Given that the two documents have similar themes and provisions, it is argued that data concerning one measure can be used to answer questions about the other. The authors admit that this methodology is to some extent crude, but it does provide unique insights into the effects of the *Framework Decision* in domestic settings. Van Dijk and Groenhuijsen's main conclusion is that countries which demonstrate the greatest compliance (on a legal evaluation) with the *Framework Decision* and Council of Europe Recommendation are broadly also those where victims report greatest satisfaction with the criminal justice system.

The EU Commission itself has had considerable difficulties in collecting full information about the implementation of the *Framework Decision*. Under Article 18, states were required to submit reports and materials to the Commission by the deadlines referred to in the penultimate paragraph in order to demonstrate implementation of each component; deadlines which many states missed. The Commission has produced reports pursuant to Article 18 in 2004 and early 2009. In the latter case, the frustration of the author is clearly evident:

> The implementation of this Framework Decision is not satisfactory. The national legislation sent to the Commission contains numerous omissions. Moreover, it largely reflects existing practice prior to adoption of the Framework Decision. The aim of harmonising legislation in this field has not been achieved owing to the wide disparity in national laws. Many provisions have been implemented by way of non-binding guidelines, charters and recommendations. The Commission cannot assess whether these are adhered to in practice. (Commission of the European Communities 2009: 9)[20]

The author of the Commission report was interviewed for this research. On being asked to account for the poor implementation of the *Framework Decision* in Member States she noted that part of the explanation lies with the lack of remedies available to the Commission on criminal matters. Essentially, the only option available to the Commission in the case of a state failing to implement the *Framework Decision* is a naming-and-shaming exercise, as in the reports quoted earlier. In addition, the respondent emphasized the confusing and difficult implementation strategy built into the *Framework Decision* itself:

> The Framework Decision has this extremely unwieldy implementation scheme that I've never seen in any other Framework Decisions and I don't want to see ever again, which is a three stage implementation. (interview with a representative of the European Commission 2009)

The respondent went on to discuss numerous unforeseen internal difficulties at the Commission around this time. In particular the task of monitoring the complex three-stage implementation scheme came at a time when the EU was expanding to 25 members and translation services were significantly backlogged. Furthermore, the respondent acknowledged that the text of the 2001 EU *Framework Decision* was vague and often hard to interpret. This had partly resulted from the fact that in matters of criminal law (third-pillar activities) the European Council adopts a policy of unanimity, whereby all states must agree to any measure. This is because it lacks any clear mandate to harmonize legislation in Member States. The resulting negotiations and adaptations had led to the document containing what this respondent described as 'logical inconsistencies'. The particular example was given of Article 5, which concerns 'communication safeguards':

> Each Member State shall, in respect of victims having the status of witnesses or parties to the proceedings, take the necessary measures to minimise as far as possible communication difficulties as regards their understanding of, or involvement in, the relevant steps of the criminal proceedings in question, to an extent comparable with the measures of this type which it takes in respect of defendants.

This Article had been understood and implemented in vastly different ways across jurisdictions. In some cases it had been thought to concern only the provision of an interpreter for those who could not speak the native language of the court, while in other countries it was being taken as a requirement that victims and witnesses understand the implications of different aspects of the criminal process.[21] To some extent this ambiguity was a result of framework decisions being a relatively new development at the time. As such, the Commission had less experience in drafting such instruments and did not insist upon especially rigorous standards of legal translations into different EU languages.

In response to such difficulties, the Commission has recently adopted a policy of 'producing less legislation but following up better on what we've got' (interview with a representative of the European Commission 2009). This has involved the creation of an 'implementation Czar' (interview with a representative of the European Commission 2009) to visit Member States to meet with those drafting legislation and offer advice and ideas. Respondents interviewed at the European Commission were also adamant that implementation required a combined approach from the Commission, local policy makers, and victim assistance organizations:

> We see very patchy [implementation of the Framework Decision] ... implementation has to be a partnership between the Commission, the [domestic] Ministry[s] of Justice and the people working in the field. I would like to see victim support organizations involved much more in implementation strategies' (interview with a representative of the European Commission 2009).

Given the problems with the implementation of the 2001 EU *Framework Decision*, recent moves have concentrated on its updating and development. A meeting of experts in victims and victim policy was held in Brussels in November 2008 to discuss this. The report from the meeting puts forward a number of ideas for reform, most of which are focused around clarifying the confusing and vague terminologies which frequently arise within the current document. Special mention was also made of the present Article 13 in the *Framework Decision on Victim Support Organizations* (VSOs). VSOs, it is argued, require definition, along with their roles and responsibilities (European Commission 2008). At interview, the author of the 2009 implementation report noted that the different levels of NGOs working in different jurisdictions with different categories of crime victim made it difficult for the victims' movement to present a unified voice and, more practically, to successfully lobby the Commission for funding and reform. It was also noted that some states (including Romania and Malta) still do not fund victim support organizations at all and it was suggested that this should be made an obligation in any new framework decision.

The Commission has also been obliged to respond to a number of legal rulings concerning the 2001 *Framework Decision* from the European Court of Justice. In the case of *Maria Pupino*[22] it was confirmed that a national court must interpret domestic legislation 'to attain the result' pursued by the 2001 EU *Framework Decision* (and all framework decisions) even before national laws had been adopted to formally implement this instrument (see Fletcher *et al.* 2008). The full legal and constitutional effects of this ruling are wide and need not concern us here (see Herlin-Karnell 2008). For victims specifically, the key implication is that national courts must authorize the use of special measures to assist children who claim to be victims of maltreatment to help them give evidence in criminal proceedings, even where the letter of national legislation does not allow this. In coming to this judgment, the European Court of Justice based much of its position on judgments of the European Court of Human Rights (see Arts and Popovski 2006). The problem exposed in the 2001 EU *Framework Decision* was thus that some jurisdictions (in this case Italy) were confused about the meaning of 'vulnerable and intimidated' victims, and for this reason it has been suggested that a definition of this concept is needed in any future framework definition (European Commission 2008). On the point of definitions, it will also be recalled from the last chapter that the Director of Victim Support Europe was very much in favour of including a wider definition of victimhood in a revised framework decision, which would include bereaved family members.

The *Katz* decision of September 2008[23] has exposed another hole in the provisions of the 2001 EU *Framework Decision*. In this case a Hungarian court had prevented a victim from giving evidence in a fraud case because he himself was the prosecutor in a private prosecution (the state having declined to prosecute itself). The European Court of Justice ruled that Articles 2 and 3 of the 2001 EU *Framework Decision* were to be interpreted so as not to oblige national courts to permit victims to be heard as witnesses in criminal proceedings instituted by a substitute private prosecution. However, in the absence of such a possibility, the court ruled that it must still be possible for the victim to give testimony which could be taken into account as evidence. In effect, the Hungarian law preventing the victim giving evidence did not contravene the *Framework Decision*, because the *Framework Decision* was interpreted as affording 'a large measure of discretion with regard to the specific means by which they [national governments] implement [its] objectives' (para.96). However, it was further ruled that the court still had to allow the victim to give evidence in some way short of attending court. The contradiction in this is highlighted in the report of November 2008 (European Commission 2009) with a call for clarification within a new framework decision.

The next chapter will examine more specifically how the 2001 EU *Framework Decision* has impacted upon the policies of Member States within the EU. Already, however, it is clear that the implementation and monitoring of these provisions has been problematic. This again hints at the difficulties and competing influences faced at the national level when more widespread international developments are being implemented. The development and redevelopment of the 2001 EU *Framework Decision* also exemplifies the complex process of forming and enacting such provisions at both the national and international level.

A further development in 2001 was a Green Paper issued by the European Commission on Compensation to Crime Victims. This was adopted in 2004 as an EU Directive binding on Member States. The Directive sets up a scheme whereby, when a person becomes a victim of a 'violent intentional crime' (Art.1) in a Member State other than that where he or she is habitually resident, he or she can submit an application to the body responsible for victim compensation in their home state. Under the Directive, the application is then forwarded on to the appropriate decision-making body in the state where the crime occurred. The goal is to ensure victims can receive compensation in cross-border cases and, in so doing, supports the free movement of individuals. The majority of this Directive was to be implemented in Member States by 1 January 2006. Unlike the 2001 EU *Framework Decision*, the Commission's report of April 2009 on the implementation of this measure is fairly positive and points to a 'substantial degree of compliance' achieved in most jurisdictions, albeit the actual number of cases of cross-border compensation claims has been disappointingly low (European Union 2009: 3). In conclusion, the Report argues that the application of the Directive could be improved on the basis of its current provisions and, as such, there is no need to amend the Directive in the same way as the 2001 EU *Framework Decision*.

During this period the EU, like the Council of Europe, also focused attention on victims of people trafficking and, in particular, the rights of third-country nationals to remain within an EU country, having been brought into the EU as a result of trafficking. A Directive on this issue was proposed in 2002 and came into force in April 2004. As well as the overriding context of the Tampere Conclusions, the UK made human trafficking a priority during its coinciding tenures as president of both the G8 and the Council of the European Union in 2005, driving forward the adoption of an EU Action Plan on this issue in December 2005 (Ferrero-Waldner 2006). The 2004 Directive requires states to permit all victims of human trafficking a recovery and reflection period before initiating any extradition proceedings against them, during which they are to have access to services, support mechanisms and granted standards of living capable of ensuring their subsistence, as well as access to emergency medical treatment. States must also 'attend to the special needs of the most vulnerable, including, where appropriate and if provided by national law, psychological assistance'. (Art.7(1)). Following the reflection period, states must allow such victims a six-month residence permit provided they are willing to co-operate with any criminal investigation. It will be recalled from Chapter 2 that this is very similar to systems adopted in Australia and by the Council of Europe. It is however notable that the Council of Europe version does not mandate a minimum six-months duration for the renewable residence permit and also stresses that it is reason enough to be granted one if it is 'necessary owing to their [victims] personal situation',[24] regardless of the formal position of any criminal proceedings.

Two further recent developments are significant here, both comprising of updates to existing framework decisions adopted by the Council of the European Union in March 2009. The first seeks to repeal and replace an existing 2004 *Framework Decision on Combating Child Pornography and the Sexual Abuse and Sexual Exploitation of Children*. The 2004 document already has provisions relating to the protection of and assistance to the victims of these crimes (Art.9). However, the reformed *Framework Decision* will introduce new provisions 'to ensure that abused children have easy access to legal remedies and do not suffer for participating in criminal proceedings e.g. by limiting the number of interviews, providing for legal aid or for a special representative' (European Union 2009a: 2). Second, the Commission is seeking to update the 2002 *Framework Decision on Trafficking in Human Beings*. The new proposed *Framework Decision on Preventing and Combating Trafficking in Human Beings, and Protecting Victims* contains much expanded provisions relating to the victims of these crimes, especially those considered 'vulnerable'. In particular, child victims of trafficking are to be automatically considered 'vulnerable victims' pursuant to Article 2(2), Article 8(4) and Article 14(1) of the 2001 EU *Framework Decision*, and any adult victim may be so considered subject to individual assessment. The revised (trafficking) *Framework Decision* also requires states to 'take the necessary measures to establish at national and local level appropriate mechanisms aimed at early identification and support to victims, in co-operation with relevant support organizations' (Art.10(3)) as well as assisting and supporting them in their escape from the influence of the perpetrators, and in their subsequent recovery.

The EU and crime victims: a consistent priority?

The above overview demonstrates how, since 1999, the EU has developed a framework of measures designed to meet the goals of supporting and protecting victims set out in the Tampere Conclusion. Interestingly, however, the reader may observe that much of the work discussed here had been completed by 2004. The resurge of interests in refining and amending these measures came only recently in early 2009. In the gap between 2004 and 2009, the policy scene at the EU was relatively clear of victims. This is largely because, when the five-year implementation timeframe of the Tampere Conclusions ran out, it was replaced by the proceeds of the Hague Convention of 2004 in which no mention was made of victims at all. A representative of the European Commission interviewed for this study explained this omission in simple terms: 'I'll tell you why the gap. The political priorities changed' (interview with a representative of the European Commission 2009). The respondent went on to attribute the lack of political will in the EU to address victims of crime at this time with a failure by the European Forum for Victim Services to lobby effectively as a result of what she called 'internal power struggles'. In addition, the Forum had recently failed to provide robust research outcomes following EU grants, a fact admitted by the Director of the newly christened Victim Support Europe when he was interviewed for this study: 'Until now we messed up a couple of European funded projects dramatically. We had a very very bad name. We messed up projects, we didn't deliver' (interview with the Director of Victim Support Europe 2009). Indeed, it was only when the Forum was rechristened Victim Support Europe under the present Director that policy makers at the European Commission regained confidence in the organization, and indeed in the whole victim issue. It was clear that this turnaround was largely down to the personal efforts of the new Director:

> He seemed to be doing all the right things, he'd realized that there was a big pot of EU money available if he could only access it and there were people to lobby and things to do at the European level. He came to see me with a business plan for Victim Support Europe, which was remarkable. (interview with a representative of the European Commission 2009)

The new Director, for his part, emphasized the importance from his perspective of putting Victim Support Europe on a professional footing:

When I started here in the office I said. Listen, we have to do a couple of things. Change this culture in this organization. Start a plan of professionalizing, and professionalizing doesn't mean you're only working with professionals [as opposed to volunteers] you're working with professional standards. We have to see to it that we become more known and respected. (interview with the Director of Victim Support Europe 2009)

The result of this was that victims once again became a major issue towards the end of 2008, and a priority for the Swedish presidency of the Council of the European Union in the second half of 2009. As such, following the expiry of the Hague Convention, victims of crime were once again put on the EU policy agenda in the new Stockholm Programme on justice and home affairs: 'The European Council invites the Commission to put forward proposals in line with what is set out in the Council conclusions on a strategy to ensure fulfilment of the rights of and improve support for persons who fall victim to crime' (Council of the European Union 2009: para. 2.3.4). The episode is interesting not just for historical purposes but also for what it reveals about the policy-making process at the European level. Representatives from the Commission were unanimous in the view that, to a significant extent, victim polices had become a major issue for them as a result of lobbying and successful funding bids by organizations like Victim Support Europe. The need for such organizations to speak with 'one voice' in order to affect policy was a much emphasized theme.

Other international organizations

So far this chapter has focused on the work of large international organizations and regional law-making bodies. While the impact of measures from such organization is to some extent obvious, smaller organizations and NGOs working above the state level have also contributed to the development of victim policies internationally.

International victim assistance organizations

The NGOs referred to at the end of the last paragraph include victim assistance groups with a transitional ambit. For example, it has just been discussed how the reconstitution of the European Forum for Victim Services as Victim Support Europe in October 2007 had a significant impact on policy movement at the EU level. Victim Support Europe's manifesto (launched in February 2008) made a number of significant pledges, including a promise to lobby Member States for the full implementation of Council of Europe Recommendation R (06) 8, discussed earlier, and EU Directive 2004/80/EC relating to Compensation to Crime Victims. The manifesto also calls for the establishment of national victim support organizations in every Member State of the EU and, to this end, Victim Support Europe has pledged to attract funding to develop quality standards and best practice for all national victim support organizations.

Victim Support Australasia has made similar attempts to lobby governments with a succession of position papers on recommended levels of victim service within the Australasian jurisdictions, and on restorative justice.[25] These papers are explicitly grounded on the 1985 UN Declaration and are essentially a call for states to continue working to implement these standards. Victim Support Australasia has not been as successful as its European equivalent in gaining the ear of policy makers at national or regional levels. When contacted for this project the Chair and founder of VSA emphasized the difficulty in straddling the NGO/government divide, particularly in the Australian context.

In the USA, the National Organization for Victim Assistance spawned a 'sister organization' in 2005 in the form of the International Organization for Victim Assistance (IOVA). IOVA has since been particularly concerned with victimization in Latin America, Asia, and Africa. The organization has a stated aim to promote national and international public policy change on victim issues and violence prevention, although it is unclear to what extent it has had an impact in the first 4 years of operation. As noted by Rock (1990) in the context of Victim Support England and Wales, there is a sense that a victim support organization must attain a level of 'respectability', as evidenced by a proven track record, before it is accepted into the 'inner circle' of actors who are able to influence victim policies. This will be discussed in more detail in the following chapter.

The Commonwealth of Nations

As noted in Chapter 1, the Commonwealth of Nations[26] has reacted as an institution to the growing calls for change in the way its constituent criminal justice systems approach victims of crime. Prompted once again by the 1985 UN Declaration, Commonwealth Law Ministers issued their own Statement of Basic Principles of

Justice for Victims of Crime in 2002. Like all such statements based on the 1985 Declaration, the Commonwealth draftsman picked out particular themes to emphasize. In this case such themes include ensuring the prompt return of any property used as evidence in criminal proceedings to victims and the consideration of alternative methods of retaining and introducing evidence, such as the use of photographs. The 2002 Statement also advocates allowing victims and witnesses to be on call for court proceedings, where practicable, rather than requiring them to wait around in court.

Later the same year, the 2002 Commonwealth Statement was followed by the more detailed *Guidelines for the Treatment of Victims of Crime in Commonwealth Countries* (Commonwealth Secretariat 2002). The *Guidelines* are an explicit attempt to fill in some of the detail lacking in the 1985 UN Declaration, with specific reference to the generally adversarial rules of criminal procedure and criminal rules of evidence based on common law found in most Commonwealth states. Given that all but three of the countries under review in this volume (the USA, The Netherlands and Ireland) are members of the Commonwealth this obviously has direct relevance. However, perhaps one of the most interesting features of this document is that it is designed to cater for and reflect the 'human and economic constraints' (Commonwealth Secretariat 2002: 8) of many Commonwealth member countries. Consequently, the Commonwealth guidelines are fairly unique in that they are ostensibly designed to apply in both developed and undeveloped nations. For example, recognizing the provenance of sexually transmitted diseases in many African Commonwealth jurisdictions, the Guidelines make the following stipulation:

> In cases of sexual offences or other crimes involving life-threatening diseases, particularly HIV/AIDS or hepatitis B, law enforcement officials must immediately assist victims of crime to obtain medical testing and preventative medical measures and inform them of any appropriate counselling facilities. (para. 9)

The *Commonwealth Guidelines* also recognize that 'in many Commonwealth jurisdictions, policing powers are not exclusively exercised by members of the police force. The definition here is broad enough to cover all officials engaged in crime detection and investigation' (para. 2.1). This raises the interesting point that more generalized support beyond the confines of the formal criminal justice system, which victims of crime themselves say they need, may be more forthcoming in countries where policing has not become so professionalized or concentrated in one body.

Another significant feature of the *Commonwealth Guidelines* is the general duty placed on parliamentarians to 'consider the impact of any proposed legislation on victims of crime' (para. 1.9). This apparently wide duty is similar to the requirement in some countries to consider the human rights impact of new laws.[27] Again, the Commonwealth moves are commensurate with the wider development of international organizations becoming concerned with victims of crime and making recommendations to Member States. Like other such organizations, the Commonwealth has also been particularly interested in human trafficking (Commonwealth Secretariat 2008) and domestic violence (Commonwealth Secretariat 2009).

The International Criminal Court

It was noted in Chapter 2 that the International Criminal Court (ICC) has adopted a wide definition of victimhood. The ICC is interesting because it is an example of a discreet judicial system developed from the outset with a firm appreciation for the arguments of the victims' movement. As Holder (2007: 11) notes:

> Of course, the International Criminal Court is young and untested. It is nonetheless significant that this and the other initiatives I have mentioned show that court leadership and indeed court delivery of assistance to crime victims is not intrinsically incompatible with court independence and impartiality.

As such, in March 2005 the ICC adopted a *Code of Judicial Ethics*, which included the following requirement:

> Judges shall exercise vigilance in controlling the manner of questioning of witnesses or victims in accordance with the Rules and give special attention to the right of participants to the proceedings to equal protection and benefit of the law. (ICC 2005: Art.8(2))

The rules mentioned here are the ICC's *Rules of Procedure and Evidence* (2002). These contain many safeguards to what are called the rights of victims, including the right to participate in proceedings as a party with legal representation. For example, under these rules the prosecution and defence can agree that an item of evidence will be treated as 'proven' without needing to present it formally in court 'unless the Chamber is of the opinion that a more complete presentation of the alleged facts is required in the interests of justice, in particular the interests of the victims' (ICC 2002: Rule 69).

Indeed, the ICC rules often bring together an 'interests of justice' test with an 'interests of victims' test. This means that victims' views must be canvassed under many of the rules, and their privacy protected. Perhaps most significantly, the rules provide the following general principle for the ICC to work under:

> A Chamber in making any direction or order, and other organs of the Court in performing their functions under the Statute or the Rules, shall take into account the needs of all victims and witnesses in accordance with Article 68, in particular, children, elderly persons, persons with disabilities and victims of sexual or gender violence. (ICC 2002: Rule 86)

While there is clearly a special focus here on ideal victims, the general principle applies to all victims.

Bottigliero (2004) argues that the victims' movement has tended to focus on what she calls 'ordinary' crimes like assault and theft, which can be dealt with in the domestic context, while ignoring the victims of atrocities like war, genocide and crimes against humanity. She argues that the infrastructure set up by the International Criminal Court begins the process of addressing the needs of such victims, particularly their need for restitution. As such, the significance of the ICC in this context lies first in the demonstration of a judicial system which to some extent was built around victims from the outset and, second, in once again opening the debate as to who qualifies as a victim of crime. There is a real contrast here with the criticisms voiced by Rydeberg (2004) of the International Criminal Tribunals for the former Yugoslavia, which was established in 1993 to deal with war crimes taking place in the region in the early 1990s. While the Tribunal has a dedicated Victims and Witnesses Section, Rydeberg notes that victim participation is essentially limited to giving evidence as witnesses. Victims in their own right are afforded only minimal participation in the system and cannot request compensation as part of the main process. The author maintains that the reason for this lies in the focus of the Tribunal being on the restoration and maintenance of peace rather than on individual victims *per se*. Certainly the only mention made of victims in UN Security Council Resolution 827 of

1993, which created the Tribunal, is a guarantee that the work of the International Tribunal shall be carried out without prejudice to the right of the victims to seek, through appropriate means, compensation for damages incurred as a result of violations of international humanitarian law (Art.7). This provision does not place any positive obligations on the Tribunal itself. As such, a comparison between the Tribunal and the ICC demonstrates how far victim issues have come on the policy agenda beyond individual states in the years between 1993 and 2005.

Discussion

Given constraints of space, it is inevitable that relevant work from a number of further international organizations regarding victims of crime has been overlooked in the above discussion. For example, the International Organization for Migration has been particularly active in the support of victims of human trafficking (International Organization for Migration 2008). The African Union (2001) has also addressed the issue of victim care, as has the Organization for Security and Co-operation in Europe (2002). To provide a comprehensive list of such organizations is impossible. What the above discussion does achieve, however, is to demonstrate the breadth of interest in victims of crime developing among international political and economic organizations over the last 20 years, while also shedding light on some of the complexities surrounding this development. It is clear that the measures described in this chapter are interdependent and have influenced each other, with the consequence that they tend to emphasize and repeat consistent themes. These include: the provision of information; protection from intimidation; access to compensation and restitution schemes; and minimizing secondary victimization.

It has been shown here that international organizations also tend to emphasize specific victims including victims of human trafficking, terrorism, domestic violence, and child victims (as well as the overlaps between these groups). Although on one level this could be seen as a restrictive list it is important to note that these are all traditionally neglected and 'invisible' cohorts of victims. To some extent, therefore, it is the *international* policy scene which has brought such victims to the forefront of public attention and, as such, gone some way to rectifying the deficit of attention being paid to the 'unordinary' victims identified by Bottigliero (2004). What these documents contain less of are references to what Ashworth (2000) calls procedural rights, or rights of actual participation in the criminal justice process.[28] This issue will be explored in greater detail in Chapter 5.

It has been demonstrated that the international backdrop of instruments, guidelines and conventions has provided a context in which national governments can work to develop victim initiatives. Nevertheless, it has also noted that these international developments have for the most part been *principled* rather than practically orientated. This reality has two main implications.

First, most of the measures discussed earlier are essentially non-binding codes of best practice. Such instruments can and do have the power of persuasive authority in individual states, but they do not create obligations, at least in the short term. Hence it has been noted that some EU countries still provide no financial support for victim assistance organizations. In the longer term, there is an extended debate among international lawyers regarding the extent to which such non-binding instruments may start to constitute what has come to be known as 'soft law', which in time can give rise to binding customary law (Boyle 2006). This argument will be discussed in some detail in Chapter 7.

The second main implication is that the non-prescriptive nature of these instruments can make them rather vague documents, lacking in clarity and subject to divergent interpretation. Of course, with the 2001 EU *Framework Decision* and the *Katz* ruling, it has been shown that this can also be true of more binding instruments. The difficulty here is that, unlike national legislation, almost all international documents (whatever their degree of enforcement) are the products of extensive negotiations by the very parties who will be bound by them (that is, representatives of individual states). As noted by one interviewee at the European Commission in 2009:

> I can tell you why European legislation is so vague…in the criminal law area. In our area there's no parliament involvement…because of unanimity you have to compromise. I remember the days of 15 [Member States of the EU], it was difficult to get agreement at 15. You can see that 25, and now 27, is more difficult. There's always one that has a problem… they'll, say, have a problem with Article 14. You know that in order to bring them round on Article 14 you're going to have to give them something they want somewhere else. That's why there's some logical inconsistencies within the [2001 EU] Framework Decision.

Of course the fact that international regulations or laws can be rendered ineffective by the level of compromise needed to arrive at a written agreement is an old one (see Brownlie 2008). The wider question, however, is whether victim care and provision specifically is an area of policy which is more or less suited to regulation by international instruments, or whether the impetus for such reform must come from individual states and/or other organizations. For example, the case of Victim Support Europe and the EU demonstrates how the latter required the proactive and effective involvement of the former in order to reinstate the stalled reform agenda on victims of crime in Europe. At the very least, we are forced to conclude that reform relating to victims of crime has become the subject of what Smith (2004) has called 'multi level governance' with national, transnational and international levels.

On one level, we can understand the international influence on victim policy in individual jurisdictions purely in terms of the increasing number of international instruments and documents related to the issue of victims and witnesses. It has been shown how these have broadened narrower conceptions of victimization. As such, it is evident that *specific* international pressures of the kind described in this chapter – from the EU, Council of Europe and UN among others – are another factor complicating the larger framework of interconnected politics set out in Chapter 1. On another level, we might view this as a broad international growth in our understandings of victimhood and victims' needs, reflecting even wider macro developments of the kind described by Garland (2001) and Boutellier (2000).[29]

The next chapter will examine the extent to which the principles set down in international instruments have been applied to the reform agenda in the nine countries under review. In so doing, this discussion will shed further light on the development of international policy-network in this area and the globalization of victim measures.

Notes

1 Discussion of the case law from the European Court of Human Rights will be left for Chapter 5, which focuses on conceptions of victims' rights.
2 See Chapter 4.
3 In an interview conducted in 2003 for the Victim Oral History Project. Waller has been a major proponent of the victims' movement and a key figure in the creation of the 1985 UN Declaration. The Victim Oral

History Project itself is an initiative of the US Office for Victims of Crime and has amassed interviews with key international figures from the early victims' movement. Transcripts of this and other interviews are available at http://vroh.uakron.edu/index.php and, in particular, provide much background information regarding the UN's adoption of the 1985 Declaration.

4 On which see Chapter 5.
5 Although, if this were the aim, there are no data available to demonstrate the extent to which practitioners in individual jurisdictions have ever seen these guidelines.
6 See Chapter 4.
7 In 2006 the International Victimology Institute at Tilburg University in The Netherlands produced a draft Convention on Justice and Support for Victims of Crime and Abuse of Power which presented the principles set down in the Declaration in an enforceable way, complete with provisions related to implementation (Art.12) and monitoring (Art.13) of relevant reforms in individual states.
8 Detailed discussion of this point will be set out in Chapter 7.
9 See Chapter 4. It is notable that the USA delayed ratifying this Convention until 1995.
10 Although see Chapter 7 for a discussion on how such documents might lead to the creation of international law.
11 See Chapter 4.
12 Although Ireland had already introduced a state compensation system for victims of violent crime in 1974.
13 See also *Recommendation R (85) 4* on Violence in the Family.
14 MJU-27 (2006) Resol. 1.
15 See http://www.coe.int/t/dg2/equality/domesticviolencecampaign/Speeches/DeputySG_en.asp.
16 Recommendation R (85) 11. See Briennen and Hoegen (2000).
17 The 2001 EU *Framework Decision* is one of two initiatives relating to victims put forward by individual Member States, as opposed to the European Commission itself. The second was an attempt by Belgium during its presidency of the Council of the European Union and the European Council in the second half of 2001 to spearhead an initiative on restorative justice, which ultimately failed to gain momentum.
18 On which see Chapter 5.
19 Although van Dijk and Groenhuijsen (2007) note that the 2001 EU *Framework Decision* is very similar to the 1985 Council of Europe Recommendation.
20 Two other reports are presently being compiled on the implementation of the 2001 EU *Framework Decision*, outlines of which were presented in November 2008 at a meeting in Brussels. One is being produced by Victim Support Portugal and the other by the Centre for the Study of Democracy in Bulgaria.

21 The report does not specify the respective countries in making this point.
22 Case C-105/03 *Maria Pupino*.
23 Case C-404/07 *Győrgy Katz* v *István Roland Sós*.
24 Convention on Action against Trafficking in Human Beings 2005 (Art.14(1)(a)).
25 See http://www.victimsupport.org.au/policies.php.
26 Formerly the British Commonwealth.
27 For example under the Human Rights Act 1998 in England and Wales, s.19.
28 See pp. 138–143.
29 See Chapter 1.

Chapter 4

Victims in domestic policy making: examining the policy network

The last chapter examined the context of international developments, above the level of the state, in which individual jurisdictions have found themselves addressing the issue of victimization and the place of victims within their criminal justice systems. As set out in Chapter 1, the overriding goal of this volume is to demonstrate how, at the national level, such policy developments are the products of a complex web of political, legal and social influences, of which transnational and international regulation is just one element. As such, the specific purpose of this chapter is to examine the extent to which common themes and drivers behind victim reform can be identified within the sample of nine heterogeneous states under review. Clearly this is a complex task, and care must be taken on the part of both writer and reader to avoid making unfair or sweeping generalizations. Nevertheless, methodologically this is a problem inherent to all transnational or international comparisons. Such disadvantages must be viewed in light of the real benefits accrued from comparative research, particularly where it bridges conventional classifications (e.g. between common law and civil law countries), thus allowing 'difference' (in policies, in justifications, and in practices) to act as a lens for the understanding of policy development.

The secondary goal of this chapter is to present observations and conclusions which have general relevance to the study of modern (national, transnational and international) policy making in the 21st century beyond the specific issue of victims of crime and criminal justice. To this end, links will be drawn with the more general literature on policy making to illustrate how the characteristics of reform in this field may be far from unique, but reflect broader political trends, especially in relation to 'governance' (Crawford 1997; Jordan *et al.* 2005). As such, the chapter begins by setting out some theory regarding policy networks and governance before moving on to examine specific themes drawn from the dataset regarding victims of crime. These themes include the influence of victim support organizations and other NGOs; the development of crime prevention techniques; the 'discovery' of several groups of particularly vulnerable victims; drives to improve efficiency in criminal justice; and a new consumer focus exhibited by many criminal justice systems.

Policy theory, policy networks, and issues of generalization

Recent years have witnessed a growth of academic investigation into the mechanisms by which governments and other organizations form policies both at the national and international levels. Indeed Smith (2004) notes how the integrated domestic, transnational and international elements of modern policy making are often impossible to separate. In light of the preceding chapter, we can see how this observation has particular relevance to victims of crime. The overriding message presented by this literature is that modern policy making across most developed countries has become a multi-facetted, iterative process utilizing an evidence-based approach and drawing contributions from an increasingly wide range of actors. The emerging shorthand for this complex development is that 'governance' is taking over from 'government' in the formulation of many polices. Governance is understood by Crawford (1997: 6) as:

> A pattern of shifting relations which involve: the fusion of, and changing relations between, the state, the market, and civil society; a move from 'social' to 'community'; greater individual and group responsibility for the management of local risk and security; and the emergence of new forms of management of public services and structures for policy formation and implementation.

As noted in Chapter 1, Bache (2003: 301) defines governance more concisely as 'an increasingly complex set of state-society relationships in which networks rather than hierarchies dominate policy making'. One implication of this is that governance tends to be characterized by reduced compulsion on the part of central government agencies, with more deference to local actors and interest groups. This is so-called 'interactive policy making' (Mayer *et al.* 2005) whereby stakeholders such as local communities (Pearce and Mawson 2003; Irvin and Stansbury 2004), the elderly (Priestley 2002) and children (Tisdall and Davis 2004) are given a 'voice' in policy making. In theory, the implication of this development is that all those who will be affected by a policy decision will have some involvement in its formation (Cabinet Office 1999; Williams 1999b). This grouping of contributing stakeholders forms what have been variously termed 'policy networks' (van Waarden 2006), 'policy communities' (Jordan *et al.* 2005), 'policy environments' (Coleman and Perl 1999), or 'issue networks' (Atkinson and Coleman 1992). Whatever term is employed,[1] the basic premise is that of 'a cluster of actors, each of which has an interest, or 'stake' in a given...policy sector and the capacity to help determine policy success or failure' (Peterson 1992: 8). Such ideas have a long pedigree, with Lindblom (1968) arguing that successful policy making requires policy problems to be identified on which there is consensus among all relevant stakeholders. In more recent years, the impact of globalization[2] has prompted renewed interest in this perspective and the question of how policy networks stretch between countries and continents. As Coleman and Perl (1999: 702–3; emphasis added) surmise:

> We can expect the formation of *transnational* policy communities, composed of actors from both the national and international levels, that serve to link national policy communities both to one another and to international institutions.

Of course, before wholly subscribing to such ideas as the basis for an analysis of victim policy movement in multiple jurisdictions we must pause to consider the extent to which these observations are true across all the countries under review. On this point, Atkinson and Coleman (1992: 157) give a stern warning against over-generalizations:

> Study after study has shown us that, within the same political system, things work differently in agriculture, transportation, monetary policy, and so on. We have been forced to accept that, in advanced capitalist economies, the policy process differs considerably across policy domains. Nor do sectors provide a way out: studies of the same policy sector across different states yield diverse findings as well.

Indeed, it is clear that the spread of interactive governance across multiple jurisdictions and policy areas is far from even or universal. For example, Thomas (2005) argues that, contrary to the more prevailing theme of inclusivity demonstrated in the Australian political scene in recent years, the federal government in that jurisdiction has repeatedly failed to consult teachers (as key stakeholders) on education policy. Notwithstanding such exceptions, Atkinson and Coleman (1992: 157) go on to point out that the concept of policy networks 'appear[s] to possess the required elasticity' (p. 157) to serve as a robust analytical tool when drawing comparisons between jurisdictions and policy areas. Consequently, and notwithstanding the above reservations, a considerable literature has grown up around the development of governance and policy networks in the UK (Jordan *et al.* 2005), the USA (Lauman and Knoke 1987; Heinz *et al.* 1990) and Canada (Bernstein and Cashore 2000). The relevant literature is also regularly drawn upon to inform discussion of policies in the Republic of Ireland (Murphy 2005), New Zealand (McLeay 1998) and The Netherlands (Kickert *et al.* 1997). The same is true of South Africa, albeit here attention has tended to focus on the implications of opening up the Republic to the forces of globalization post-1994. As Roux (2002: 430) notes: 'In this day and age, no country can view itself as an island. All countries, great and small, developed or developing, experience the effects of globalisation. Needless to say, this also applies to South Africa and in broader terms, the African continent'. Such views have prompted discussion of how the *transnational* policy communities described by Coleman and Perl (1999) have influenced domestic policies and developments within the republic. For example, it has been argued that South Africa's (2001) adoption of private prisons was heavily influenced by the lobbying of an international corrections-commercial (Lilly and Knepper 1993) coupled with the wholesale export of Britain's 'Private Finance Initiative' (PFI) model of privatization around the world (Prison Reform Trust 1997). In this case the impact of these transnational influences was resoundingly negative: instigating a budget crisis after it emerged that South Africa's first two PFI-based prisons were set to consume 5 per cent of the entire corrections budget for the next 25 years (Goyer 2001). Ijeoma (2008: 105) has gone on to draw links between the increasing pressures of globalization and the need for South African governments to engage with domestic 'public policy communities' in all areas:

> It became apparent for all agencies of change and development in South Africa to be strategically and practically repositioned

towards addressing the unfolding globalization trends. To this end, one principle of an effective new economic order demanded that South African government should bring strategies to harness all resources in coherent and purposeful efforts that can be sustained at local, provincial and the national spheres of government. This can only be effective if and when all policy making stakeholders and pressure groups are made part of the policy making process.

In sum, while it is certainly true that robust generalizations are difficult to make in comparative work, not least on the subject of policy making, it is equally clear that policy networks exist and have been the subject of academic scrutiny in all the jurisdictions under review. This includes South Africa where, given the previous impediment of non-democratic government, one might expect such moves to be less developed. The analysis of national, transnational and international policy networks therefore provides a useful starting point for understanding the development of victims of crime as a policy area in the nine countries under review.

Aspects of the transnational and international policy network impacting on victim reform

Victim support organizations

In keeping with the notions of governance and inclusive policy making discussed earlier, victim support groups and other non-governmental organizations (NGOs) involved in victim care seem likely candidates for inclusion as key participants and stakeholders in any policy network surrounding victim reform within or between the jurisdictions under review. Indeed, the importance of victim support organizations in policy development has already been noted in the previous chapter, where the examples were given of Victim Support Australasia and Victim Support Europe, the latter having rekindled the European Commission's interest in victims thanks largely to the work of a new and forward-looking Director.

Evidence of a close interaction between domestic victim support organizations and government departments was present in most of the jurisdictions under review. For example, Victim Support New Zealand (2008: 2) regularly updates a briefing note to the incoming Minister of Justice in which its intentions to exert influence over policy are clearly spelled out:

This briefing provides information about Victim Support. It outlines priorities, as identified by Victim Support, for ensuring that New Zealand's response to victims lives up to its national and international obligations. As an independent and demonstrably successful advocate on victims' issues and a 24/7 nationwide NGO service provider making a positive difference in the lives of thousands of victims, Victim Support has much to contribute to policy and practice in the areas of victims' rights and support. It welcomes the opportunity to continue the close relationship with the Minister of Justice and officials.

The desire, and indeed the expectation, to exert some degree of influence over domestic policy making was strongly voiced by many of the victim support organizations examined across the nine jurisdictions. Victim Support Scotland, for example, identifies 'continuing to have a strong profile within the justice sector, contributing to policy development' (2006: 9) as a key component of its ongoing strategy. In Ireland, where the former national Victim Support group has recently splintered into a host of smaller organizations,[3] one of the key charities, Advocates for Victims of Homicide (AdVIC), states that as well as offering advice to the families of homicide survivors 'a further objective of AdVIC is to advocate for changes in our Criminal Justice system' (Advocates for Victims of Homicide (Ireland) 2010). A particularly close relationship seems to exist in The Netherlands between the Dutch Ministry of Justice and Victim Support Netherlands. When interviewed for this project, the Director of the NGO expressed great confidence in his 'outstanding relationship' with The Hague and that his organization was seen by the government as 'the experts' and 'a respected partner in business when it comes to new legislation or new organizations or policies'. Indeed, unique to all the countries under review in this volume, the Dutch Ministry of Justice was the only governmental agency to refer me directly to a non-government victim support organization when making initial enquires about this project. In England and Wales too, Victim Support has had a growing *political* presence. This has been demonstrated at the European level through the charity's involvement in drafting the 2001 EU *Framework Decision*, and domestically though the publication of a 'manifesto' (Victim Support England and Wales 2001). Significantly, Victim Support England and Wales has also been included on a list of 'Criminal Justice System Agencies and Partners' issued by the UK Home Office (2001a).

It is notable that all of the countries referred to in the last paragraph are jurisdictions where victim support schemes have traditionally adopted a less politicized stance.[4] Rock (2004) has noted in the English context how this transformation from an excluded interest group to what Maloney et al. (1994) call a 'core insider' to the policy making network in this area[5] was achieved though a long-term strategy of victim support workers removing themselves as far as possible from politics and concentrating on providing support services to victims in a neutral fashion. The other common feature of these victim support groups is their recent transition from a diverse collection of loosely associated charities to one large overarching organization. Such unification has occurred in Victim Support Netherlands (in 2005), in Victim Support Scotland (in 2007) and in Victim Support England and Wales (also in 2007).[6] The Director of Victim Support Europe relayed the importance of this development from the perspective of the Netherlands Ministry of Justice, stating that prior to unification: 'The Ministry of Justice said, look, we don't know who we're dealing with when we deal with Victim Support' (interview with the Director of Victim Support Europe 2009).

The Director had similar comments concerning the recognition of a newly unified Victim Support Europe by the European Commission. Unity then has facilitated the acceptance of some victim support schemes within the ambit of national and international policy making, although this is not always the case, as the situation in the Republic of Ireland demonstrates. Here, an initially unified Victim Support Ireland split apart in 2005, reputably owing to internal disputes over the use of government funding when this became available in the early 2000s. In an unusual step, the Irish Department of Justice, Equality and Law Reform sent auditors to examine the working of Victim Support Ireland which concluded (as a matter of public record) that the organization had become dysfunctional (interview with the Head of the Irish Victims of Crime Office 2009). The episode prompted a wide-ranging rethink about the provision of victim services in Ireland, leading to the instigation of a Commission for the Support of Victims of Crime to distribute public funding to individual victim groups. A new Victims of Crime Office was also created within the Department of Justice, Equality and Law Reform. As noted by this Director of the new Office: 'a lot of what we now have descends from Victim Support' (interview with the Head of the Irish Victims of Crime Office 2009). In this rather distinctive sense, the operation of NGOs has had an enormous impact on policy development in the Irish context.

In South Africa too there is evidence of significant involvement on the part of NGOs in the formation of the government's Victim Empowerment Programme. For example, in a document setting out the context of the South African Victims' Charter the Department for Justice and Constitutional Development recalls:

> The Victims' Charter was developed by a group of stakeholders, including government departments, Chapter 9[7] institutions (the Human Rights Commission and the Commission on Gender Equality) and NGOs in 2004. (South African Department of Justice and Constitutional Development 2008b: 5)

Furthermore, in a conference to mark 10 years of the South African Victim Empowerment Programme, a representative of the Department commented:

> Social Development[8] has consistently provided the space for NGOs and government departments to collectively translate the vision of our caring South African nation into a reality for victims. (Webster 2008b: 2)

It should also be noted that victim support NGOs also have a place on the management committee of the Victim Empowerment Programme, a move unparalleled even in England and Wales, where Victim Support England and Wales has achieved a particularly high level of acceptance by policy makers.

Of course, aspiring to exert genuine influence in policy making is quite different from actually achieving this in operational practice. In England and Wales, Victim Support claims many successes in influencing policy and it is true that, over the years, there has developed a certain degree of choreography between the issues raised by Victim Support and the actions of government policy makers. So, for example, it is notable that many (although not all) of the issues raised in Victim Support England and Wales' (2001) manifesto could subsequently be found in UK Home Office policy documents (2001a, 2001b). Similarly, when Victim Support England and Wales published its *No Justice Beyond Criminal Justice* (2002b) report on the plight of victims outside criminal justice this was swiftly followed by similar views being expressed in the Government's *new deal* outline of its reform agenda (UK Home Office 2003a).[9] In addition, one may note the active involvement of Victim Support England and Wales in drafting the 2001 EU *Framework Decision*, which was later implemented domestically in England and Wales though a statutory *Code of Practice for Victims of Crime* (Victim Support England and Wales 2002c) under the Domestic Violence, Crime and Victims Act 2004. In a similar vein, at interview representatives of Victim Support Europe provided extensive evidence of the influence exerted by that organization on public policy at the domestic and European levels:

> We made this manifesto in which we call members of [the European] parliament to see to it that in the next five year programme of the EU there should be a chapter or at least a paragraph on victim issues ... and I already know that the lights are green and that we have been successful with this. (interview with the Director of Victim Support Europe 2009)

In Ireland, the relatively new landscape of victim support NGOs and government departments makes it difficult to draw conclusions as to the former's place in the policy process. Nevertheless, the Director of the Victims of Crime Office did describe the significant plans of the Minister of Justice for consultation with such agencies, and how these had been initiated:

> The Minister organised to meet the 43 agencies that were funded ... I come in and say let's see the timetable. He was going to meet half the groups in one room and then he was going to meet the other half in another room. He wanted to hear their concerns, listen to them, engage with them. I said there's a problem here ... the Minister for Justice is not going to sit around for an hour listening to people talk to him, and then another hour for the next group. They said, no, this timetable was dictated by the Minster. He had decided he was going to spend a Friday afternoon listening to victims. (interview with the Head of the Irish Victims of Crime Office 2009)

There were clear distinctions between the countries discussed so far in this section (England and Wales, Scotland, the Netherlands, Ireland, and South Africa) and those where victim assistance groups have traditionally been more politicized (Canada, Australia, USA and New Zealand). Generally speaking, the relationship between government and victim support services in this latter set of jurisdictions was far more integrated, to the point where government departments rather than NGOs provided many of the services directly. One representative of Victim Support Western Australia interviewed for this research summed up her opinion that victim support in Australia tended to be more of a 'government thing' in that jurisdiction compared to the independent (albeit government-subsidized) NGO model utilized across much of Europe. It is true that in none of these jurisdictions was there an overarching politically independent and *national* organization lobbying for victims' rights and services enjoying the same level of government recognition and integration (at least in terms of policy participation) as Victim Support in England and Wales or The Netherlands. While all of Australia and New Zealand fell under the remit of Victim Support Australasia, no mentions of or attributions to this organization arose in any official policy documents or interviews with policy makers in these jurisdictions. In contrast, the contributions of such organizations in England and Wales, Scotland, Ireland, The Netherlands, and South Africa are frequently acknowledged.

This is not to say, of course, that victim support organizations have played no part in policy development within this latter group of jurisdictions. In Canada, for example, the Policy Centre for Victim Issues (a federal department) has acknowledged the lobbying efforts of several groups including Citizens United for Safety and Victims of Violence. In addition, Citizens Against Violence Everywhere Advocating Its Termination and Mothers Against Drunk Driving have both advocated the creation of federal legislation to guarantee victims' rights across Canada since the 1980s, as has the Canadian Police Association's Resource Centre for Victims of Crime. In the USA, while no truly unified national organization has emerged, NOVA is often commissioned to produce reports and recommendations for the federal Office for Victims of Crime.[10] In addition, we can note the impact of the group National Victims Constitutional Amendment Passage (NVCAP). NVCAP is a loose alliance of the key US victims NGOs, which campaigns for an amendment to the US Constitution guaranteeing victims' rights. While the proposed amendment itself has been debated at the federal level for over a decade, in 2004 NVCAP had an important role in drafting a federal Victims Bill offering various guarantees to victims across the USA including: protection, the right to confer with the prosecution, and the right to proceedings free from unreasonable delay. The Bill was passed by the United States Congress (by a vote of 96 to 1) in November 2004 as the Justice for All Act. While NVCAP's claim that this constitutes 'the most sweeping federal victims' rights law in the history of the nation' (Mothers Against Drunk Driving 2004) must be viewed with due caution, it does illustrate that NGOs have had a large influence at the highest level of the US system.

In sum, the lobbying of government actors for policy change by NGOs is pervasive, widespread, and sometimes successful even in jurisdictions still lacking a truly national victim support organization. The distinction lies rather in the fact that, in this latter group of states, there is less sense that any particular group(s) or organization(s) have been promoted to the level of a permanent 'core insider' at the policy making table. This is true both at the federal and (in Canada, the USA and Australia) state and territorial levels, where few references are made to NGOs *as stakeholders* in the policy process by government actors within published policy documents or on government websites. This is very different from the mentality exhibited in The Netherlands, for example, where one is automatically forwarded to Victim Support Netherlands for any discussion on victim policy.

What has been demonstrated by this discussion is that victim support NGOs constitute an active part of the policy process across most of these jurisdictions, albeit to different extents. Of course, this general conclusion may hide a more complex reality. Take for example England and Wales, where the acceptance of Victim Support by the government as a stakeholder in the policy process is *prima facie* among the most developed. It certainly seems to be the case that Victim Support England and Wales is now being consulted on almost all upcoming actions and reports relating to victims and witnesses.[11] Given such observations, it might be tempting to think of Victim Support as the logical driving force responsible for pushing government reforms on victims and witnesses. However, fundamentally, we can question the extent to which Victim Support England and Wales has been afforded the political ability to sway policy making. Indeed, despite adopting a more professionalized character in recent years, the charity has resisted any attempts to actively sway opinion on victims by commissioning research or holding independent conferences. In fact the role of Victim Support appears to be more consultative. The same is true in New Zealand, where Victim Support New Zealand openly refers to its 'no surprises relationship with the Minister' (2008: 2). Indeed, unlike other pressure groups (such as the Howard League for Penal Reform), Victim Support England and Wales has failed to establish any platform for itself (such as the courting of media interest) whereby it can criticize the government when its calls for reform are not heeded.

The conclusion to be drawn from this examination is that there is often a trade-off to be had between taking a politicized, critical stance of a government's policies, thereby effecting occasional major reform, and being less critical in exchange for a permanent seat at the table.

Victims and Policy Making

Certainly in the USA and Canada, many of the victim support NGOs remain considerably more vocal in their disdain for government action or inactions compared to the 'core insider' NGOs of Europe and South Africa. Take for example the US National Center for Victims of Crime's (2010: n.p.) public insistence that, despite all the work of the federal Office for Victims of Crime for the last 30 years, 'federal and state resources for victims of crime have been insufficient to meet the substantial and complex needs of crime victims'.[12] The above notwithstanding, the real issue is the extent to which government has truly ceded to governance in relation to victims of crime. While some theories of governance predict a loss of control of policy making by governments (Pearce and Mawson 2003), others maintain that governments in fact retain significant influence, especially over the composition of policy networks (Richardson 2000). As a general rule this appears to have been the case with victim support NGOs across the nine jurisdictions under review. While many such groups make strong claims to a permanent seat around the table of policy making, the fact remains that many are there on the invitation of government actors, and strictly on the terms of the latter.

Crime prevention initiatives and populist punitiveness

The serious academic study of crime prevention techniques is a relatively new field (Pease 1997). Similarly, the formulation of specific crime prevention policies by national governments is a recent development which broadly parallels the timescale of the development of victim policies. The two are linked by theories of victim-orientated crime prevention (Johnson and Bowers 2003) which broadly hold that, as the majority of victimization is centred on a relatively small percentage of the population, targeting crime prevention efforts at previous victims or those identified as potential victims can prevent a large proportion of crime (Riley and Mayhew 1980; Laycock 1984). The link between a desire to reduce crime and the formulation of policies which assist victims of crime is relatively clear at the national and international levels. Indeed, the 1985 UN Declaration was a product of the Seventh United Nations Congress on the Prevention of Crime and the Treatment of Offenders. As such, the Declaration itself has been read as requiring states to offer crime prevention advice to victims (Winkel 1991).

Advocates of the crime control agenda have continued to exert considerable influence over the development of victim policies in all nine countries under review and, as such, constitute another key

Victims in domestic policy making

component of the policy network in this area. Indeed, it will be noted later that in some instances this agenda has been pushed to such a degree as to arguably reflect an underlying populist punitiveness (Garland 2001).

Among the sample of jurisdictions under discussion in this volume, the development of victim reform was most clearly grounded on crime prevention concerns in South Africa. Here a representative of the Corrections Service interviewed for this research was very clear as to the origins of victim measures:

> I think it was primarily about preventing crime. It was about looking at the urgency around the fact that there was high crime at the time and there was an outcry, especially on crime that affected women and children. So it was more in terms of saying, we've got to bring the crime level down. One of the ways in which you can do that is to put in place programmes that actually allow victims to assist us in preventing crime. (interview with a representative of the South African Corrections Service 2009)

South Africa is the starkest example of this overlap between victim and crime prevention priorities, principally because the crime rate in that jurisdiction reached crisis point after democratization (Shaw 1997), although similar examples can be drawn from across the nine jurisdictions under review. For example, in one of the founding policy documents concerning victims and witnesses in England and Wales, the UK Home Office (2002: para. 0.3) set out its reform agenda in the following terms: 'Our programme of reform is guided by a single clear priority: to rebalance the criminal justice system in favour of the victim and the community so as to reduce crime and bring more offenders to justice'. In this construction, it would appear that reforms in favour of victims are grounded in a higher set of priorities to reduce crime and prosecute more offenders, both of which are consistently popular as political aims. The same may be said of Canada's federal initiatives, summarized by the Canadian Department of Justice (2008: n.p.) as follows:

> The federal government's initiatives to address victim concerns about the criminal justice system are designed to improve the victim's experience and to facilitate their participation in the criminal justice system. This approach complements the equally

important crime prevention and public safety initiatives with initiatives to address concerns of victims of crime (i.e., after the crime has occurred).

Crime prevention and victim support are therefore closely linked in Canada, and indeed are often organized at the provincial and territorial levels collectively under a combined Division of the Solicitor General.[13] Crime Prevention and Victim Services is also a combined Division of the Royal Canadian Mounted Police. In the USA too the need to tackle high crime levels has frequently been cited as one of the driving influences behind the growth of the victims' movement (Young 1997b). Indeed, the development of government interest in victims in the USA seemed to coincide with the findings from the first victimization surveys that crime was more widespread than had previously been thought. Indeed, one of the first US federal bills to pass through Congress relating to victims of crime was the Family Violence *Prevention* and Service Act 1984[14] (emphasis added). As in Canada, the New York State police are one of many forces across the USA which brackets victim assistance programmes under the umbrella of crime prevention. As summarized by Hindelang (1982: 151): 'In my view it is no accident that the explosion of interest in victims and victimization surveys developed simultaneously. Each has provided some stimulus for the other and each has the potential for providing benefits to the other'. This link between the advent of victimization services and government interest in victims more generally has also been drawn in the Australian context (David *et al.* 1990).

Of course, this correlation must not be taken too far or applied too laterally. In England and Wales for example crime rates have generally been *falling* since 1995. This coincides with the *growth* of the modern victim reform agenda, especially since the coming to power of the New Labour Government in 1997. In New Zealand too, victims of crime fall under the mandate of the government's wider Crime Reduction Strategy in so far as, when implementing this strategy, all government agencies must consider and address the needs of victims and potential victims of crime. In Australia, many states and territories have also amalgamated victim support policies with crime prevention initiatives, as demonstrated by this explanation from the Department of Justice and Attorney General of New South Wales (2009: n.p.):

> Even if we haven't experienced crime personally, the existence of crime can make us feel unsafe in our own communities. This is

particularly the case for people who have been victims of crimes themselves. Victims of crime often suffer physical or emotional harm, or loss or damage to property, as a result of a criminal offence. To address the problem of crime in a coordinated and strategic way, the Attorney General's Department has been given responsibility for the development of crime prevention strategies and for providing support and assistance to the victims of crime.

There was generally less evidence of a clear link between crime prevention initiatives and victim policies in the Irish and Netherlands contexts. In the former case this may again be due to the generally less developed nature of the policy scene in that jurisdiction given its recent reorientation. In The Netherlands however it is notable that, unlike most of the other jurisdictions under review, the Dutch have tended to favour social rather than situational crime prevention methods, addressing the perceived underlying societal causes of crime rather than individual victims[15] or offenders (Wemmers 1998). This of course is in keeping with The Netherlands' position as the only 'conservative corporatist' jurisdiction in this sample (Cavadino and Dignan 2007).

Naturally governments have both a political and a practical interest in reducing crime and, given the prevalence of repeat victimization, addressing the problem from the perspective of the victims themselves is logical. Indeed helping victims to avoid future crime is, according to Victim Support Australasia (VSA 2008), one of the core components of an integrated victim support service. To this end VSA has set its sights on the Commonwealth, advocating that 'responses to crime victims are integrated within Commonwealth crime prevention activities' (p. 2).

There is nothing necessarily problematic about victim policies being at least partly intended to cut crime. The difficulty comes when policies ostensibly presented as assisting victims in fact fail in this goal, or *increase* secondary victimization in pursuit of an alternative crime prevention agenda. Take as an example the issue of rape prosecutions. In a far-reaching study, Temkin (2002) has drawn examples from the UK, USA, Ireland, Australia, Canada and New Zealand which demonstrate how, despite recent changes apparently aimed at making the justice process less hostile to rape victims, states still essentially use rape victims as a prosecutorial tool to achieve convictions, often with little regard to their personal circumstances or feelings about the justice process. Cretney and Davis (1997) have

Victims and Policy Making

demonstrated similar trends regarding victims in domestic violence cases in England and Wales. While some jurisdictions, notably the USA (Ellison 2002), have attempted to address such problems through 'victimless prosecutions'. This tension between crime control and victim empowerment is a permanent dilemma for the victims' movement.

A victim reform agenda driven partly by crime control concerns clearly recalls Garland's (2001) view (discussed in Chapter 1) that such reforms derive partly from the perception (if not the reality) that the criminal justice system is unable to control crime. The clearest links between crime prevention and victim policies have also generally been uncovered where public concern about crime is greatest (USA, England and Wales, South Africa). Certainly in South Africa's case, this supports the hypothesis drawn in Chapter 1 that in this jurisdiction victim policies were driven by necessity, this being the necessity to control crime (especially crime against women) rather than the need to help victims for their own sake. While there is nothing objectionable about this on the face of it, it does raise the concern that at best such policies will not be tailored to maximize benefit to victims themselves (as has been shown with domestic violence and rape cases) and at worst victims may become a tool of populist punitiveness.

To expand upon the final point in the last paragraph, recent debates on criminal justice matters have become dominated by reference to punitive rhetoric, the 'politicization' of crime and the 'punitive populism' (Bottoms 1995) engendered by Garland's (2001) 'culture of control' (see also Downes and Morgan 2002; Young and Matthews 2003). While in more recent years mainstream political parties in most developed states have established a form of middle ground 'second-order consensus' on law and order issues (Downes and Morgan 2002), it seems that the punitive impetus remains (Young 2003). This has been the principle concern of Elias (1983, 1986) and Ashworth (1998, 2000) with the victim reform agenda in the USA and UK respectively. For Ashworth, allowing victims the right to participate in the criminal process presents an unacceptable risk of interfering with the rights of defendants. In particular, Ashworth (2000) argues forcefully that the involvement of victims in sentencing through victim impact statements has been used as a means of legitimizing a punitive stance against offenders. Many other examples, common to most of the nine jurisdictions under review, can be discussed in support of this punitive interpretation of the victims policy agenda. These include: limitations on defendant's questioning of (rape) victims; mandatory arrest policies in cases of domestic violence; and the anonymization of witnesses giving evidence in court. This latter development has attracted particular controversy in the USA (Parker 1981), the UK (Ward 2009), and Canada (Ferguson 2007).

We may be concerned then that pressure for increased crime control and punitive leanings, engendered by the politicization of crime, constitutes an unwelcome component of the policy network(s) surrounding victims within and between the nine jurisdictions under review. That said, Williams (1999b: 85) makes the point that such developments are not identical across all junctions, highlighting in particular the difference in approach between Canada and the USA:

> In the UK, the victims' movement has avoided becoming associated with those campaigning for stronger law enforcement. In the US the two issues have become intertwined and, to some extent, confused. In Canada a balance has been struck with a modified version of the American concept of zero tolerance: 'domestic' violence is taken seriously, and routinely dealt with as a criminal matter, but offenders are increasingly given treatment rather than punishment-orientated sentences.

Here Williams is referring to the restorative-based options utilized in such cases in Canada, and now also in The Netherlands and parts of Australia.[16] While it is arguable that the law enforcement aspect of the policy network has increased in prominence in both the USA and the UK since the author made this statement, it does demonstrate that such influences on policy are not equal across the nine jurisdictions.

The 'rights' agenda

The following section will consider the content and context of so-called 'victims' rights' now available in the countries under review in some detail. For the present purpose, this section seeks to emphasize the more general development of 'rights' and 'rights-language' across the nine jurisdictions and how the proponents of such rights play a large role in the policy networks surrounding victim issues in all the countries under review. Tracing back to the UN's *Universal Declaration of Human Rights* (1948), the development of 'rights' discourse has been an international, globalized, trend for the last 50 years.[17] As a consequence, the 'rights' label has been attached to a diverse range of groups defined in terms of gender, disability, age, cultural origin and sexuality among many others. This label has now also been applied to victims of crime in all the countries under review, a development supported by growing agreement in the academic literature that

> The legitimacy of a justice system lies in its ability to protect human rights. This is typically interpreted as the duty of the justice system to protect the rights of the accused. However, as T Hart (1994) points out, protection of human rights is much broader: it applies to all citizens, including victims of crime. Failure by authorities to address the position of the victim undermines the legitimacy of the justice system.' (Wemmers 1998: 73)

This view once again marries the development of victim policies to concerns about the perceived legitimacy of criminal justice systems, in accordance with Garland (2001) and Boutellier's (2000) constructions.

As might be expected, the influence of such rights discourse has been longest felt in those countries with a firm history of granting enforceable 'rights' to their citizens. Hence, the first US Victims' Rights Week was organized by the Philadelphia District Attorney in 1975. The notion of victims having 'rights' was also a founding concept for the 1982 Presidential Taskforce on victims, which would go on to recommend an amendment to the US constitution guaranteeing victims' rights.[18] As has already been discussed, NVCAP has been campaigning for such an amendment to provide meaningful and enforceable rights for crime victims since 1987. At the state level, Rhode Island became the first state to amend its constitution to guarantee victims' rights in 1986. Similarly, Rock (1983) discusses how the human rights agenda played a key role in the development of victim policies in the Attorney General's Office of Canada in the 1970s and 1980s. In 1988, prompted by the 1985 UN Declaration, all Canadian Ministers of Justice agreed to adopt a uniform policy statement of victims' rights that would be used to guide their legislative and administrative initiatives in the criminal justice sphere.[19]

In Europe, the notion of rights is traditionally a less engrained concept in many jurisdictions (Merrills and Robertson 2001). This is especially the case in England and Wales, where there is no written constitution (De Smith and Brazier 1998). Consequently, European nations were slower to refer to victims having rights in official policy documents than was generally the case in North America. Indeed this is a relatively recent development, following the proliferation of rights language in the 2001 EU *Framework Decision* and, before that, the introduction of the European Convention on Human Rights in 1950. Nor was this always a steady development in European jurisdictions. For example, government policy in England and Wales fluctuated from the language of 'rights' in their first Victims' Charter (UK Home Office 1990), following the UN in its preamble to the 1985 Declaration, to that of 'service standards' in the second Charter of 1995 and subsequently reverted back to 'rights' after the 2001 EU *Framework Decision*, by which time Rock (2004) confirms the prevailing influence of the human rights agenda on British victim politics. In The Netherlands too, while this jurisdiction (like England and Wales) has a relatively long history of affording victims services and even procedural involvement in the criminal justice system,[20] the Director of Victim Support Netherlands noted at interview that only now was a Bill going through the Dutch Parliament which expressly referred to the rights of victims (including the right to speak in court), although he did maintain that this was merely 'canonizing what is already common practice' (interview with the Director of Victim Support Netherlands 2009). The extent to which utilizing the *language* of rights is commensurate to the actual *granting* of genuine rights is an issue to be discussed in Chapter 5, although the example of The Netherlands clearly demonstrates that the 'rights issue' was influencing domestic policies well before the language was directly applied to victims in government circles.

The development of a human rights discourse has most recently begun to influence and drive victim reforms in South Africa. With universal rights being such a fresh concept in this country, representatives from the Department of Justice and Constitutional Development were clear that, as far as they were concerned, the new rights afforded to citizens automatically implied that rights should also be given to victims (among other groups):

> The constitution in 1996 was now formerly adopted, and although the constitution doesn't really mention victims, it's really all encompassing in the sense that everyone is entitled to rights, everyone is entitled to equality. So the constitution then formed the basis upon which a new thinking around the criminal justice system and rights within the criminal justice system. (interview with a representative of the South African Department of Justice and Constitutional Development 2009)

One distinctive characteristic of this process in South Africa is that, in this jurisdiction, victims' rights were being developed *at the same time* as many defendant rights, as opposed to being grafted on to an existing system.[21]

The creation of victim policies has therefore been intertwined with the development of rights in a broader sense across the jurisdictions under review. To some this is a controversial development, bringing concerns that to afford rights to victims of crime may reduce the rights of defendants (Ashworth 2000). In another sense, however, this can be viewed as one aspect of a general social phenomenon of modernity whereby rights are being applied to traditionally marginalized or vulnerable groups. Indeed, another important aspect of the policy network affecting victim reforms across jurisdictions has been the identification and recognition of specifically vulnerable groups of victims, which is discussed in the next section.

Vulnerable victims

Linked to the discussion of definitions in Chapter 2, it is clear that the victim policy agendas in all the jurisdictions under review have been given particular impetus by the increased recognition of specific groups of vulnerable victims, especially when they become involved in the criminal justice system as witnesses. As such, advocates for these groups form another important component of the overall policy network. This was a finding of Rock (2004) in the context of England and Wales, and one that can be applied in the other jurisdictions under review here. Evidence of this has already been discussed in the South African context, where representatives of the Executive were clear that addressing the needs of female victims of rape and domestic violence lay at the foundations of its wider Victim Empowerment Programme.[22]

In Chapter 2, a number of questions were posed concerning the implications of governments focusing attention on specific groups of vulnerable victims. In particular, it was questioned to what extent this might betray a preoccupation with a limited subset of ideal victims to the exclusion of the vast majority of (less ideal) victims. It was also noted that the suffering of such ideal individuals readily draws sympathy from the general public and, as such, governments can gain political capital when they are seen to address their needs. These principled arguments aside, the evidence remains that moves to assist victims as a whole have in most jurisdictions been partly driven by the perceived needs of such specific groups. Three groups of vulnerable victims have gained particular prominence in the policy agendas of all nine jurisdictions discussed in this volume: female victims of rape and sexual assault (including domestic violence); child victims; and victims of human trafficking. Each of these groups will now be examined in turn.

Female victims of rape, sexual assault and domestic violence

The victimological literature is fairly unanimous in its condemnation of the attitudes traditionally expressed towards female victims of rape and domestic violence by criminal justice actors in most of the countries under review. In New Zealand, Jordan (2001) describes the misogynistic practices of police officers as 'worlds apart' from the needs and expectations of female victims reporting sexual assault and rape. In Canada, reports indicate that the response of the police to domestic violence cases and their engagement with victims is still very inconsistent across the federal jurisdiction (Hannah-Moffat 1995). In The Netherlands, the Haaglanden Police (2005: 2) of The Hague acknowledge that in the past 'domestic violence has never before been treated as a crime' by their organization. Similarly, the Fawcett Society of England and Wales continues to produce reports which highlight what they present as a 'postcode lottery' governing the success or failure of rape convictions, pinning the blame on inadequate responses to female victims from across the criminal justice system (Coy et al. 2008). In Scotland too, the criminal justice system (as well as individual judges) frequently receive criticism from the media for 'betraying' those victims of rape who come forward (Harris 2009). Similar criticisms have been made in Ireland (Bacik 2002) and Australia (Australian Broadcasting Corporation 2007) where Rollings and Taylor (2008: 2) maintain that until the late 1980s 'police did not consider policing of family and domestic violence to be part of their job'. Prior to democratization it has been noted that the response of the South African criminal justice system to domestic violence was practically nonexistent, especially in the rural communities (Vetten 2005). In the USA, drawing from research carried out in North Carolina, Lord and Rassel (2004: 156) have argued that despite the recent changes in rape laws discussed in Chapter 2, 'Evidence [from across the USA] still suggests that victim credibility continues to be doubted and that this doubt prejudices sexual assault prosecutions'.

Poor treatment and general disbelief of female victims of domestic violence and sexual assault is therefore a recurring theme seen across the nine countries under review. Various theories have been put forward to explain this, most of them centring on the dominance of hegemonic masculinity in the police forces and other justice agencies of many jurisdictions (see Hodgson and Kelley 2004) as well as the male-dominated, adversarial trial system used in all these jurisdictions except for The Netherlands. Indeed, on this latter point, Sue Lees (2002) condemned criminal justice processes as constituting a 'secondary rape' for the victims of such crime. Such gendered debates will not be the topic of extended discussion here (see Wykes and Welsh 2008), but they do provide one possible framework by which female victims of sexual and familial violence have exerted influence over policy making in so many criminal justice jurisdictions.

The general impact of feminism and women's pressure groups on the growth of the victims' movement internationally has already been discussed in Chapter 1. Politically, the issue was galvanized in several of the jurisdictions under review by specific 'horror stories' of women brutally (re)victimized by an apparently unsympathetic criminal justice procedure. These include the case of Carol X, a Scottish prostitute labelled by prosecutors in 1981 as 'too unreliable' to give evidence against one of her clients in a rape case (Harris 2009). In England, one of the most influential cases was that of Julia Mason, a rape victim cross-examined for 6 days in 1996 by her rapist wearing the same clothes as on the day of the crime (Laville 2001). Referring to a much publicized rape case in New Zealand, Sankoff and Wansbrough (2006: 4) make the point that in this jurisdiction too: 'Calls for the better treatment of victims ring out frequently, with vows for change being especially popular after the conclusion of a major trial in which the victim was made to suffer in one way or another'. The point can be expanded to other victims, including children (to be discussed later) and the families of murder victims. One very influential example followed the murder of 21-year-old college student 'Marsy' in California in 1983. Sustained interest by the media in her case was compiled by the poor treatment of her family by the authorities, which eventually led to the passing of a constitutional amendment to facilitate victims' rights in California, known as 'Marsy's Law'.

Such reports have kept the issue of female victimization in particular at the heart of much of the policy movement in the countries under review. In Ireland, for example, 26 out of the 45 victim groups supported by government funds are domestic violence organizations (interview with the Head of the Irish Victims of Crime Office 2009). In addition, the first Irish Victims' Charter required criminal justice agencies 'to show special sensitivity in relation to sexual offences' (Irish Department of Justice, Equality and Law Reform 1999: 8). In a similar vein, it has been noted in the US context by Marlene Young and John Stein (2004: n.p.) (the former being a past president of NOVA) that: 'it is significant that of the three first victim programmes in the United States, all begun in 1972, two were rape crisis centres (in Washington, D.C. and the San Francisco Bay area)'.

Indeed, we saw in Chapter 2 how the plight of victims of sexual offences has prompted the most fundamental changes in the law of many states regarding rape and sexual assaults, both in Europe and in North America. Such reforms include *prima facie* limitations on the kinds of questions defendants and their lawyers can ask in cross-examination. In Ireland, the Sex Offenders Act 2001 goes so far as to require that separate representation be afforded to complaints in rape and other serious sexual assault trials when an application is made to adduce evidence or cross-examine on the subject of the complainant's past sexual history.[23] In addition, most jurisdictions recognize victims of sexual assault or rape as automatically entitled to the provision of facilities such as video-links and screens to assist them in giving evidence.

Governments across the nine jurisdictions have taken similar steps to confront the well known difficulties of tackling domestic violence in the courts.[24] These include the creation of specialist domestic violence courts. The earliest such court was constituted in Cook County, Illinois, in the early 1980s.[25] Canada's first specialist domestic violence court began operating in Winnipeg in 1990. Eley (2005) sites the first Australian domestic violence court in Joondalup (Western Australia) and the first comparable British system at Leeds Magistrates' Court the same year. Scotland has also been piloting a specialist domestic violence court in Glasgow since 2004. In The Netherlands, rather than developing specialist domestic violence courts *per se*, the government's Action Plan on Domestic Violence (*De volgende fase*) (Netherlands Ministry of Justice 2002) emphasizes the support of welfare initiatives like shelters and outreach programmes. The most significant legal change is the introduction in 2009 of 10-day restraining orders for perpetrators of domestic violence. The Irish Government is presently in a period of consolidation following the recent changes in the landscape of victim support and the establishment of a Victims of Crime Office. In 2007 the Irish National Office for the Prevention of Domestic, Sexual and Gender-based Violence was set up and is presently examining options for the enactment of new legislation and the introduction of court procedures to tackle domestic and sexual violence.

Much of the evidence suggests specialist domestic violence courts in particular have brought benefits to victims giving evidence through less obtrusive procedures, better training and an enhanced understanding of relevant issues from court staff (Stewart 2006; UK Home Office 2006). Conversely, however, there is relatively little evidence that such schemes work to actually *reduce* domestic violence. Scant indications of any such effect were found in the evaluation of the New Zealand specialist family violence courts set up in 2005 at Manukau and Waitakere. The report on the pilots also expressed concerns that, due to the unexpectedly high volume of cases, witness waiting rooms had become overcrowded and victims were obliged to wait with abusers (Knaggs *et al.* 2008). Domestic violence has also been tackled by clearer prosecution policies and by addressing police attitudes. In some jurisdictions this has led to zero-tolerance policies of mandatory arrest,[26] although once again the evidence that this approach reduces domestic violence has been mixed in all jurisdictions where it has been tried (Fritzler and Simon 2000).

It is clear then that female victims of rape, sexual assault, and domestic violence have been the subject of considerable attention by policy makers across all of the jurisdictions under review. What is perhaps more significant, however, is how the development of understanding surrounding these victims has informed wider debates and developments in relation to victimization as a whole, and the subsequent response of criminal justice systems. Young and Stein (2004) note a number of contributions made by the women's movement to the wider victims agenda across jurisdictions including. First, the recognition of emotional crisis as a critical part of the impact of crimes and, second, the opening of investigations into the nature of psychological trauma and methods to alleviate it. Similarly, the lessons learned from the streamlining of specialist domestic violence court proceedings can be applied to trials more generally which has been demonstrated by the publication of case management criteria in England (UK Home Office 2004b) and Canada (Office of the Attorney General of Ontario 2008).[27] In addition, moves to assist victims of rape or domestic violence evoke a general philosophy of helping victims deal with the practical consequences of rebuilding their lives rather than rely on a criminal justice system. Such a philosophy has seen restorative justice initiatives piloted across the nine jurisdictions under review.[28]

Child victims
As with victims of rape and domestic violence, there has been a growing recognition that children often constitute invisible victims, principally because the special difficulties they face giving evidence

in courtroom traditionally meant such evidence often went unheard (Hoyano and Keenan 2007). South Africa has faced particular problems in this regard, and consequently the reduction of childhood victimization in that jurisdiction has been touted as a priority aim since the publication of the 1996 *South African National Crime Prevention Strategy* (Raunch 2001). The issue was given particular impetus when research began to suggest that many child victims (of other crimes) were also sexually assaulted. Meek (1999: 12) explains the scale of the crisis facing South Africa's new democratic Government after 1994:

> Although the need to prevent and combat crimes against children was identified in 1986, it was not until 1996 that the police were able to begin to collect comprehensive data on crimes committed against children. A study conducted by the Human Science Research Council (HSRC) over 1993–1995 found that the number of cases of crimes against children was increasing by an average of 28 per cent per year.

In the USA too, crime figures have consistently demonstrated that children are particularly vulnerable to sexual and violent crime, with one study from the US Department of Justice reporting that 1 in 18 victims of violent crime in that jurisdiction are under 18 (Wilson 2000). In Canada, Trocmé *et al*. (2003) discuss how relatively few reports of child abuse were received by the authorities up until the late 1980s, and ascribe this to the particular difficulties children face when giving evidence, as well as the prevailing assumption by the criminal justice system that the evidence of children was unreliable. Indeed, major changes to the legal positions of child witnesses did not arrive in Canada until the Badgley Committee of 1988 made recommendations to this effect. The formation of the Committee itself was prompted only by a flurry of adult survivors of childhood sexual assault coming forward (Lowman 1986). Similarly, in New Zealand government action was prompted largely by reports from adults about the experiences of their children or about their own experiences as children (Maxwell and Carroll-Lind 1998). As with female victims of rape, media reports of high-profile cases, such as the murdered toddler James Bulger in England and Wales in 1993 and Australia's notorious 'baby–dingo' case of 1980[29] instilled child victimization into national and international consciousness. Particular mention should also be made of the Irish context, where systematic and very long-term abuses orchestrated against children by members of the Catholic Church has again focused considerable attention on the issue of childhood victimization and the response of the criminal justice system, the government and of wider society (Irish Office of the Minister for Children and Youth Affairs 2009).

To some extent the challenge faced by criminal justice actors in all nine jurisdictions under review when dealing with child victims has been cultural rather than practical. In Australia, for example, Richards (2009) has emphasized that the failure of measures designed to assist child victims to achieve all the results promised by government reforms is principally due to the obstructive exercise of judicial discretion, and the fact that lawyers are not putting principles into practice. There has also been a degree of residence (at least initially) from the legal professions in most countries to the use of video-linked or recorded evidence (Davies 1999).[30] As noted earlier, most of these countries also have a tradition of excluding child evidence by reason of its presumed unreliability. All nine jurisdictions under review have had to address the issue following the UN Convention on the Rights of the Child, Article 12(2) of which guarantees that children 'shall in particular be provided the opportunity to be heard in any judicial and administrative proceedings affecting [them]'. As such, the latest Canadian Federal Evidence Act of 2005 sets down a presumption that children are competent to give evidence in court (s.16.1). England and Wales has similar provisions in the form of s.53 of the Youth Justice and Criminal Evidence Act, making *all* witness *prima-facie* competent to give evidence. Most jurisdictions have adopted similar mechanisms by which individuals (including children) are judged on a case-by-case basis as to competence, rather than drawing arbitrary age cuts offs. This principle was established in the USA in 1985 in *Wheeler* v *United States*[31] where the Supreme Court ruled that competency was a matter of whether a child has the relevant cognitive capacity to be a useful witness and whether he knows the difference between telling the truth and telling lies. On the latter point, Canadian law has moved away from arduous or abstract questioning specifically on this issue (Harvey 2002).

As with female (adult) victims, discussion and reform of how criminal justice systems approach children has raised wider questions about the needs of victims in general. In particular, childhood victimization has prompted considerable work on the lasting impacts of crime. Such impacts include not only the long-term psychological impacts of such experiences (Morgan and Zedner 1992), but also the propensity of such childhood victims to become involved in violent crime in the future as victims and/or offenders (see Widom 1995). Such findings have forced states to take action or face significant criticism from their own citizens and from the wider international community. One example of the latter is the recent report of UN Committee on the Rights of the Child on The Netherlands' implementation of an optional protocol to the *Convention on the Rights of the Child on the Sale of Children, Child Prostitution and Child Pornography*. Here the Committee expressed marked concerns regarding the lack of resources available to the Dutch police for the investigation of such crimes, as well as the lack of adequate response to tackle the issue of child sex tourism within the jurisdiction (ECPAT The Netherlands 2009). Such cases provide stark examples of the pressures faced by governments across the nine countries under review following revelations as to the true scale of child abuse and childhood victimization of all kinds occurring within their jurisdictions over the last 20 years.[32]

Victims of human trafficking
As with childhood victimization, the scope of human trafficking has only recently become clear across all nine jurisdictions under review. Again, such developments constitute recognition of a group of victims who were previously all but invisible to the authorities and policy makers in most countries, save perhaps when they became defendants in visa and exportation proceedings. Indeed, drawing on a UK[33] initiative, campaigns to raise awareness of the issue often utilize the symbol of a blue blindfold in England and Ireland, with moves afoot to introduce the emblem across Europe.[34] The nature of the crime and associated activities has naturally made it a particular focus for international instruments, which we saw in the last chapter. Certainly the problem of trafficking is heavily steeped in wider social and political changes at the global level. For example, echoing Rijken (2003), Segrave *et al.* (2009: 16) describe how 'the re-emergence of trafficking in persons on the international agenda coincided with the fall of the Berlin Wall and a period of increased mobility from the Global South to the Global North'.

Indeed, when interviewed for this study, the representative of the Irish Department of Justice, Equality and Law Reform principally responsible for this area immediately ascribed her government's interest in the issue to the measures taken by the UN and the EU discussed in the last chapter. Certainly in many of the countries under review there was a sense throughout this project that policy makers are rapidly trying to catch up with the pace of developing knowledge in this specific area of victim reform. The Irish policy maker, for her part, discussed how she had only just been given a statutory definition of the problem to work with: 'We didn't before June of last year [2008] have a proper definition in this jurisdictions of what constituted human trafficking' (interview with a representative of the Irish Anti-Human Trafficking Unit 2009).

The legislation referred to here is Ireland's Criminal Law (Human Trafficking) Act 2008, which broadly reflects the definition of trafficking laid down in Article 3 of the UN Protocol.[35] Following this the Irish Immigration, Residence and Protection Bill will provide victims of human trafficking with a 60-day recovery and reflection period in the state, extendable to six months if they choose to assist the Gardi with a prosecution. This model is very similar to that employed recently in Australia (see Chapter 2). Notably, both systems require an initial labelling of individuals as victims of human trafficking by the police which in the Irish context has caused considerable problems given that policy makers themselves were only just becoming clear on what constituted a 'trafficked' individual. The question of definitions has also caused difficulties in Canada, where the first convictions for trafficking under the Immigration and Refugee Protection Act of 2002 have been the subject of protracted appeals on the grounds of vagueness in the legislation (Raaflaub 2006).

Human trafficking, and specifically sex trafficking, has been a particular concern for the Dutch Government, where the recent relaxing of laws pertaining to prostitution and brothels[36] has sparked some criticism both within and outside The Netherlands (US Department of State 2008).[37] This being the case, the Dutch Government has been keen to demonstrate its serious response to human trafficking, and has publicized its prosecutorial successes in the area on a global scale (Associated Press 2006). In 2000 The Netherlands also became the first country in the world to establish an independent National Rapporteur on Human Trafficking. The Netherlands also named human trafficking as one of its main priorities during its Chairmanship of the Organization for Security and Co-operation in Europe (OSCE) in 2003 and also proposed making the subject a major theme at the Economic Forum of the OSCE of the same year (see Everts 2003). As with other areas of victim reform, the UK has also been instrumental in promoting the issue of human trafficking in Europe. The year 2002 saw the publication of the *EU Proposal for a Council Directive on Short-term Residence Permit Issues in Relation to Victims of Action to Facilitate Illegal Immigration or Trafficking in Human Beings*. The following year, the UK Home Office funded the pilot 'Poppy' projects to provide shelter and basic services to such victims. The chain of causation actually becomes cyclical at this point as following this the UK made human trafficking a priority during its tenure as president of the G8 and the Council of the European Union. This facilitated the adoption of an EU action plan on this issue in December 2005 (Ferrero-Waldner 2006) and the launch of a consultation on a domestic action plan, covering both England and Wales and Scotland, in early 2006 (UK Home Office and Scottish Executive 2006).

The impetus of governments from all jurisdictions to take action on human trafficking has been very much galvanized by transnational and international pressures, not least because the US Department of State produces a yearly *Trafficking in Persons Report* (TIP) in which jurisdictions are rated according to their adherence with US recommendations on the issue. The report is mandated under the key US legislation on human trafficking, the Trafficking Victims' Protection Act of 2000, the stated aim of which is to: 'raise global awareness, to highlight efforts of the international community, and to encourage foreign governments to take effective actions to counter all forms of trafficking in persons' (US Department of State 2008).

Lee (2007) explains that a poor rating in the report can lead to a withdrawal of all non-humanitarian aid from the USA and the denial of funding for anti-trafficking initiatives from international donors and NGOs. Both The Netherlands and New Zealand, along with several Australian jurisdictions, have received criticism in the TIP for their partial decriminalization of prostitution which is viewed in the report as incompatible with a robust policy to fight trafficking (US Department of State 2009).[38] This is despite the fact that all three countries are rated 'Tier 1' in the 2009 Report, indicating full compliance with the US guidelines. Such criticisms are in fact obligatory for the compilers of the TIP following a US policy decision taken in December 2002 that

> the U.S. government opposes prostitution and any related activities, including pimping, pandering or maintaining brothels as contributing to the phenomenon of trafficking in persons. According to the Trafficking in Persons National Security Presidential Directive of February 2002, U.S. policy is that these activities are inherently harmful and dehumanizing and should not be regulated as a legitimate form of work for any human being. (US Department of State 2009: n.p.)

This of course raises interesting questions concerning the impact of policy decisions (and, indeed, moral positions) taken by governments on the evaluation of such measures.

Two of the nine countries under review in this volume were ranked Tier 2 in the most recent TIP: Ireland and South Africa. Tier 2 indicates a 'watch list' of borderline cases. In the case of Ireland, the report predates the recent legislative initiatives noted earlier and, for this reason, it can be presumed that the country will be upgraded in future reports. In the case of South Africa, while the report notes that the authorities are making 'significant efforts' to tackle trafficking, the compilers of the TIP were frustrated by a lack of information provided by that jurisdiction on police investigations, prosecutions, or convictions. Like Ireland, South Africa lacked any specific in force or planned legislative framework directed at trafficking until the recent publication in May 2009 of the Prevention and Combating of Trafficking in Persons Bill. The Bill adopts a model of specific offences for the perpetrators and support measures for victims similar to that introduced in other jurisdictions, including a 90-day reflection and recovery period. The scale of the trafficking problem in South Africa is thought to be considerably greater than in any of the other countries under review, which partly explains the difficulties experienced by both the legal authorities and policy makers in tackling the issue (Delport et al. 2007). Furthermore, and as indicated previously, when interviewing representatives of the South African Department for Justice and Constitutional Development there was a definite sense that the issue of domestic violence and sexual assault against women was at present monopolizing much of the Department's time and resources.

In sum it is clear that, perhaps to a greater extent than most other aspect of victim reform, human trafficking is an area of policy that has been greatly spurred on by transnational and international and pressures. Following the UN protocol, it is also an issue where most jurisdictions have adopted a very similar (globalized) model of legislation to address the problem. Of course, initiatives to fight human trafficking also constitute part of most governments' wider crime prevention strategy as the links between this activity and other criminal networks (drugs; weapons profits funnelled into other criminal activities; car theft rings; terrorist groups) is well documented (Delport et al. 2007). As in other areas, NGOs have played a considerable role in drawing attention to this hitherto ignored category of victimization although, unlike other vulnerable groups, victims of human trafficking have not always provoked unanimous public sympathy. This may be due to perceived links with 'deviant' actives such as prostitution and with illegal (or indeed legal) immigrants/asylum seekers. As such, in Australia it has been noted that these victims can often be labelled as 'undesirables' (Marmo and La Forgia 2008).[39] Addressing such barriers is far from straightforward, prompting Lee (2007) to advocate the basing of principles of justice in immigration matters on a doctrine of 'hospitality' whereby, following Benhabib (2005), such hospitality can only be denied to immigrants, including victims of human trafficking, if they prove dangerous to the fundamental rights of existing residents.

Vulnerable victims: tools of the state?

On one level it comes as little surprise that such pronounced attention has been paid in all the countries under review to victims who appear especially vulnerable and for whom the impacts of crime and the trauma of being involved in the criminal justice system are particularly great. Of course, this is not to assume that such close scrutiny is always best for the vulnerable victims themselves. Indeed, I have argued elsewhere that any *de facto* blanket requirement that all children give evidence through special facilities like video-links can be detrimental (Hall 2009a).[40] This notwithstanding, the real difficulty again comes with the understanding that the vulnerable groups discussed in this section still represent a small minority of victims of crime. The point is illustrated by Victim Support Scotland (2006: 2) in the following terms: 'The public perception of crime against children and young people tends to be centred on child abuse and bullying; While these crimes do happen, young people can be affected by many other types of crime'.

For McBarnet (1983), victimologists themselves are partly to blame for this state of affairs. By concentrating their attention predominantly on traditional notions of victimhood (with particular emphasis on rape victims) the author argues that researchers in the field have somewhat played into the hands of governments wishing to derive political capital from victims, and from punitive criminal justice responses:

> Indeed, *politically*, victimology has contributed to the strengthening of the state's role. It has set itself up as engaging not just in academic debate but in 'affirmative action for the victims of crime', and, like traditional criminology before it, its too-ready acceptance of official definitions of criminal and victim have reinforced rather than questioned the status quo. More specifically, its moral indignation has provided an apparently liberal, humanitarian gloss for less liberally based campaigns to reduce defendants' rights and strengthen the powers of the state. (p. 302, emphasis in original)

It has been demonstrated in this section how, in accordance with such views on the politicization of victim issues (Elias 1983), concerns about especially vulnerable victims have indeed led to reforms in most jurisdictions which arguably extend state power whether by promoting arrests or by limiting the types of evidence defendants are allowed to elicit in court.[41] Such criticisms have been made in all the jurisdictions under review, with one particularly emotive example coming from Wright's (1998: 3) article in the US *Journal of Prisoners on Prisons*:

> The political use of the victims' rights movement is seen by the rise of this movement as part of the overall trend towards increased state repression that began in 1968 but which accelerated markedly with the Reagan presidency. Virtually all the well funded victims' rights groups receive substantial portions of their funding directly from law enforcement agencies or groups linked to such agencies. The result, intended or not, is that these groups tend to parrot the party line of more police, more prisons, more punishment, more draconian laws.

As the words of a former prisoner, turned noted advocate for prisoner rights, this extract demonstrates the depth of frustration felt from the defence perspective with the focus on so-called ideal victims. While some jurisdictions, notably Queensland in Australia, have published policies on 'vulnerable persons' in general within the criminal justice system (Queensland Department of Justice and Attorney General 2006)[42] the issue of vulnerable *defendants* has been largely absent from the policy agenda in most countries. This is a noteworthy oversight, given that studies show that defendants too can often demonstrate vulnerabilities, particularly social and psychological problems as well as language and communication difficulties (Cavadino and Dignan 2007). Consequently, while invariably giving impetus to reforms and developments of knowledge and practice which benefit victims more generally, the centrality of 'vulnerable victims' within the policy discourse of all nine jurisdictions under review serves to accentuate perceived (and perhaps false) distinctions between strong, bad offenders and weak, innocent victims.

Efficiency and monetary concerns

All criminal justice systems, whether adversarial or inquisitorial, require witnesses to come forward to provide the evidence on which prosecutions can be based. This is particularly important in the case of victims, who often provide the most directly applicable evidence and in many cases are the only witnesses available. As such, the governments who fund and (to varying degrees) administer criminal justice agencies have an inherent interest in ensuring their citizens are disposed to work with the system and are capable of providing clear, detailed evidence when they do so. The meeting of such goals brings increased efficiency in the criminal justice system, reduced delays and, ultimately, a saving of public funds. Pressures to reap these benefits have constituted another important element of the policy network in all nine jurisdictions under review.

The link between victims of crime and efficiency concerns within criminal justice is most clearly demonstrated through attempts by governments in all nine jurisdictions to address the issue of domestic violence. At the heart of the difficulty faced by criminal justice systems when dealing with such crimes the low reporting rates and the fact that, even when victims do come forward to the authorities, the perception is that complainants in such cases have a tendency to retract their initial police statement at a late stage and become unwilling to give evidence in court. Such difficulties have been well documented and are demonstrable across England and Wales (Cretney and Davis 1997; Ellison 2003); the United States (Hanna 1996); Canada (Canadian Department of Justice 2000); Australia (Laing 2002) and New Zealand (Wurtzburg 2003). Jurisdictions utilizing an inquisitorial justice model are not immune to these problems. In The Netherlands, for example, it has been reported that only 12 per cent of domestic violence cases are reported to the police and that '75% of the severest domestic violence cases remains beyond the scope of social workers' (Netherlands Ministry of Justice 1997). Understanding the complex interactions of pressures behind this situation is an ongoing effort for commentators and practitioners in all countries (see Davis 2007).

The financial costs of victims of domestic violence withdrawing their evidence from criminal procedures have been variously estimated across the nine countries under review. One research project carried out in British Columbia put the annual costs of domestic violence trials in that province at roughly 39 million Canadian dollars, with charges being withdrawn in 25 per cent of those cases. In the US state of Tennessee, the Economic Council on Women published a figure of US$49.9 million being spent on processing domestic violence court cases that year, with trials failing to proceed in roughly 37 per cent of those cases (Tennessee Economic Council on Women 2002). The issue has also been examined in Greater London, where it is estimated that failed domestic violence trials in the region cost the taxpayer around £9 million annually (Greater London Authority 2005). Only a crude comparison of these figures across jurisdictions is possible due to differences in classifications and counting methods. Nevertheless the point is clearly made that difficulties associated with bringing domestic violence cases to court have significant financial implications for all criminal justice systems. Of course, this itself is only a small percentage of the total cost of domestic violence for society as a whole. Indeed, the situation is perhaps best summarized by the Inter-American Development Bank (1997: n.p.), which operates across the region of Latin America and the Caribbean: 'Although the numbers are incomplete, their message is clear: domestic violence costs the region's economies many millions of dollars in health care, police and court costs, and lost productivity'.

Domestic violence is a clear and widely researched example of the wider point that, by introducing reforms which successfully address the needs of victims, governments themselves benefit from a more efficient criminal justice system where less time is wasted preparing and running trials which ultimately fail due to witness reluctance, intimidation or alienation from the process. As a 1991 report on victim service provision in Australia makes clear that 'the lack of co-ordination of services and the lack of the sharing of information concerning both existing services and the needs of victims of crime impede the efficient and effective utilisation of the available scarce resources' (David *et al.* 1990: 21). As such, the development of victim policies seen in most jurisdictions has been accompanied by the formation of schemes intended to promote efficient case handling. Indeed, in a report prepared on behalf of the British Columbia Justice Efficiencies Project Criminal Justice Reform Secretariat, the authors neatly summarize the pervasiveness of the 'efficiency' issue across many criminal justice systems in recent years:

> The question of how to reduce system inefficiencies is getting a new momentum. This is true in Canada, in several provinces and at the national level, as well as in Australia, New Zealand, England, Scotland, Europe, and several jurisdictions in the United States. The Council of Europe, in particular, has established the European Commission for the Efficiency of Justice (CEPJ) which has taken a systematic approach to the issue and has framed some of the questions outside of the narrow framework of common law.' (Dandurand 2009: 4)

As such, in the year 2000 the US Department of Justice became interested in commissioning a report from the National Institute of Justice on the timeliness of criminal trials across nine states (Ostrom and Hanson 2000). This report was produced in the context of the Sixth Amendment to the U.S. Constitution, which guarantees the fundamental right to 'a speedy and public trial'. The Canadian Charter of Rights and Freedoms similarly has a provision guaranteeing defendants the right 'to be tried within a reasonable time' (s.11(b)). Other examples include the 2003 introduction of the *Criminal Case Management Framework in England and Wales*. At courts, the *Framework* encompasses the Effective Trial Management Programme which is designed to promote efficient use of court time and the speedy disposal of cases. The following year, the Irish Joint Committee on Justice, Equality, Defence and Women's Right published a report on the criminal justice system which made recommendations for increasing speed and efficiency. That report initially cites the problems faced by victims when the criminal justice system works too slowly, but then proceeds to emphasize the strain put on judicial and physical resources (Joint Committee on Justice, Equality, Defence and Women's Rights 2004).

One of the key implications of this new drive for efficiency has been a greater utilization of performance targets for criminal justice agencies which have been rolled out in all nine jurisdictions. To give a typical example, in Ontario the Ministry of the Attorney General published its *Justice on Target* strategy in 2008 setting out its key goals as follows: 'Ontario will achieve faster, focused justice by targeting 30 per cent reductions in the provincial average of days and court appearances needed to complete a criminal case. The province plans to meet its target in four years' (Office of the Attorney General of Ontario 2008: 25). Such targets can be quite specific such as those set by the New Zealand Ministry of Justice for limiting time delays between committal proceedings and the commencement of jury trials (126 days for standard cases and 154 days for complex ones) (New Zealand Ministry of Justice 2004). The setting of targets by governments has become a common phenomenon across many public services in the jurisdictions under review, and further afield.[43] Indeed, in England and Wales the then New Labour Government received some criticism for the proliferation of so-called Public Sector Agreement (PSA) mandates and the establishment of a 'target culture' across many areas of public service, including education (Gorard *et al.* 2002), health (Greener 2004), and the economy (Dorey 2004). The *English Criminal Case Management Framework* applies this mentality to the criminal justice system, setting strict target times for case disposals and minimizing delays and inefficiencies (UK Home Office 2004b).

In the criminal justice sphere victims have often been presented as the ultimate beneficiaries of these targets as in the following press release from the Attorney-General of Australia on the publication of plans to give victims veto powers over plea bargaining:

> Attorney-General of Australia, John Hatzistergos, yesterday announced the Government planned to review its Charter of Victims' Rights which protects victims of crime and sets out how government agencies should treat and assist them. Mr Hatzistergos said he was considering giving the charter bite, with performance standards and time limits built in to give victims more weight. (Fife-Yeomans 2009: n.p.)

Clearly, however, there are considerable benefits to be gained by the criminal justice system if such targets are successfully met. This point is made explicitly in the following extract from a report into court performance in Minnesota:

> Besides keeping track of the average length of days cases take to resolve, the court also keeps track of the average number of appearances that are necessary to dispose of cases. Each appearance includes a judge, at least two attorneys, the defendant, and possibly other system players such as probation officers, psychologists or social workers. Clearly, the more useful appearances are the more cost effective the whole system becomes for everyone. (Minnesota Judicial Branch 2004: 11)

For their part, most of the governments in the jurisdictions under review have been similarly upfront in admitting that, to some extent, by helping victims they are helping themselves. The point is made succinctly in the 2001 report of the Victim Services division of the Department of Justice of Newfoundland and Labrador in Canada (2002: 2): 'While such services assist victims, they also promote greater efficiency and effectiveness in criminal justice system operations'. Similarly, a report from a survey of witness satisfaction carried out in Gauteng, South Africa, notes:

> Underpinning this concern is a belief that witnesses [including victims who are witnesses] should be supported in participating in the criminal justice system, not only because they have needs

and concerns, but because this will serve the cause of improving the effectiveness and efficiency of the criminal justice system in its task of bringing offenders to justice. (Bruce and Isserow 2005: 45)

Returning for a moment to the issue of populist punitiveness and its role in shaping victim policies, it is telling that this extract cites increased convictions as the ultimate aim of the exercise. This notwithstanding, the quotation demonstrates the equally important point that the goals of reducing delays and time wastage themselves bring benefit to victims, especially when waiting around to give evidence in court. Indeed, the efficient handling of cases is a pledge made to victims themselves in most of the victims' charters introduced across the nine jurisdictions.[44]

To some extent then victims have much to gain from increased criminal justice efficiency. Nevertheless, we can express concern that policies claiming to assist victims are in fact not designed around these purposes, not least because, under this construction, efficiency goals often trump the meeting of victims' needs. A clear example came in England and Wales in October 2003 with the introduction of a consultation paper, *Securing the Attendance of Witnesses in Court* (UK Home Office 2003b). This document invited consultation on the proposed resurrection of witness orders to compel witnesses' attendance at Crown Court and summary trials. These proposals illustrate the fact that, while improving victim and witness satisfaction and making them feel more at ease with their role in the criminal justice system is presented as the headline policy, these aims are still connected with the less personal goal of getting witnesses (not victims) to come to court and thus improving the operation of the system. The consultation paper itself points out the possible conflict of policy:

> Ensuring that witnesses attend court ... is directly relevant to the delivery of the Government's Public Service Agreement (PSA) targets on bringing more offences to justice and increasing confidence in the criminal justice system. However, it is possible that introducing a greater element of compulsion [through witness orders] might have a negative effect on the confidence PSA (particularly the witness satisfaction element of this target). (UK Home Office 2003b: 3)

The proposed renewal of witness orders was eventually dropped. Nevertheless, the publication of this consultation suggests that policy makers were, in this instance, willing to trade victim satisfaction for increased efficiency. This indicates a very different set of priorities than those implied by the pledge made by many governments to put victims and witnesses at the heart of the criminal justice system, or the apparent moves from an institutional-based to a citizen-based criminal justice system (Tapley 2002; Goodey 2005). Instead, it reminds us that governments are still very concerned with efficiency and the associated low public confidence (and escalating costs) in the criminal justice system, and that these concerns have a large influence on measures incidentally benefiting victims and witnesses. This has significant implications for our understanding of victim policies, as it downgrades the benefits brought to victims to the level of pleasing by-products of a wider efficiency-driven agenda. In Canada, for example, Wemmers (2008: 8) observes of restorative justice schemes: 'Although these programs often boast restorative values, they typically owe their existence to efficiency concerns and an overburdened criminal justice system'. Furthermore, writing in the Australian context, Douglas and Laster (1994: 5) predict that, in the new era of prioritizing efficiency in the criminal justice system, victims will ultimately lose out: 'Cases have become "units" to be processed as expeditiously as possible. If victim involvement in any part of the process interferes with the dictates of efficient case-flow, it is likely to encounter considerable resistance'. If this is true, and efficiency must indeed be prioritized above all else, then this also has implications for our evaluation of victim measures. As such, the same authors have criticized the use of the victim impact statements in Victoria for being inconsistent with the Australian criminal justice system's commitment to efficiency. In sum, while the dual goals of promoting victim needs and system efficiency to some extent go hand in hand, there is real potential for the two to come into conflict.

Customer-orientated criminal justice

The final distinct influence on victim policy development to be discussed in this chapter is the extent to which criminal justice systems have become service-orientated, with victims and the general public cast as the consumers of a service (Zauberman 2002). This is a change facilitated principally by the publication of service charters for victims in all nine countries under review.[45] These documents all guarantee victims certain minimum standards of service from criminal justice agencies. Victims are cast as the recipients of services not just from independent assistance organizations and other NGOs, but from the formal criminal justice system and, ultimately, the state. Discussion as to the extent to which such charters can be said to afford victims actual 'rights' will be left for the following chapter. For present purposes this section will focus on the implications of this new consumer status of victims.

First, and linked to the points raised in the last section, treating victims as consumers of criminal justice has required agencies in many jurisdictions to meet service delivery targets. In the last section it was pointed out that targets relating to efficiency and speed of case disposal benefit the agencies themselves, and the governments who fund them, at least as much as individual victims of crime. Nevertheless, in England and Wales the government has gone so far as to set down specific targets relating to the time witnesses (including victims who are witnesses) should be kept waiting in court on the day of a trial. These targets dictate that in magistrates' court proceedings 60 per cent of witnesses should not wait more than one hour, 80 per cent should not wait more than two hours and the average waiting time should not exceed 1.5 hours. In the Crown Court 60 per cent of witnesses should not wait more than two hours and the average waiting time should not exceed 2.5 hours. In the statutory *Code of Practice for Victims of Crime in England and Wales* these targets are truncated into a pledge that victims should not have to wait more than two hours in court. The accompanying Witness Charter guarantees that waiting times should not exceed two hours. Most other jurisdictions have shown reluctance to be this specific, as illustrated by the Justice Department of Quebec (2010: n.p.) in its advice to witnesses attending court: 'As mentioned earlier, it is practically impossible to predict how long proceedings will take. You must remain at court until you have testified or until the judge authorizes you to leave, which will generally be after you have testified'.[46]

In the Australian territory of New South Wales, the Audit Office produced a report in 1999 detailing its support for the introduction of realistic targets for witness waiting times but conceded that, in practice, these may be unachievable:

> Time targets are unlikely to be fully effective, unless there is a high level of certainty that trials or other hearings will occur when scheduled. Adjournments at the request of the parties may be outside the control of the court and may occur when the parties are not ready or a witness is not available. Adjournments

may also occur at the request of the court because of such factors as overlisting. (Audit Office of New South Wales 1998: 46)

Certainly, achieving the specific waiting time targets for victims and witnesses set down in England and Wales has been problematic. In 2009 a joint thematic review of the experiences of victims and witnesses in the criminal justice system recorded an average wait of 1 hour 10 minutes in the magistrates' courts and 3 hours 46 minutes in the Crown Court among the witnesses.[47] The report goes on to question the utility of the targets as presently conceived:

> The firm commitment given about witness waiting times in the Witness Charter is supported by generic courts charters for the magistrates' courts and Crown Court respectively which state 'You shouldn't have to wait more than one/two hours from the time you are asked to attend to when you are called to give evidence'. However, the targets adopted demonstrate an acceptance that the average wait can be above the Charter commitments and that 40 per cent of witnesses can wait longer than the commitment. Inspectors question whether the targets adopted ensure that the Charter commitments are met. (Criminal Justice Joint Inspection 2009: para. 77)

The second major implication of the customer focus on victims is that it has brought with it a need for justice agencies in all jurisdictions to *measure* their performance, not just through numerical targets for the benefit of state administrators or accountants, but also through gathering feedback from victims and witnesses themselves. This has led to the widespread use of victim and witness surveys in most jurisdictions.

In South Africa, surveys of witnesses carried out by the Centre for the Study of Violence and Reconciliation (Vetten 2005) and the Public Service Commission (Bruce and Isserow 2001) provide insights into witnesses' views about the court process and their place within it, revealing that such views are heavily affected by waiting times and by the treatment received from criminal justice personnel. The design of these surveys was based on an even more extensive English programme of research, for which national Witness Satisfaction Surveys were carried out in 2000 and 2002. These research instruments have since been supplanted by the more sophisticated Witness and Victims Experience Survey (WAVES).[48] In the USA too, courts users' surveys have become common since a major study conducted in Wisconsin courts in 1996 (Voelker and Kritzer 1997). In this report, the authors again describe a new public service ethos in criminal justice and specifically refer to court users as 'consumers'. Unlike the South African or English surveys, the US equivalents tend to focus more on users' perceptions of fairness and physical access to the court, rather than on wider victim and witness issues *per se*. That said, in California the Superior Court of Stanislaus regularly asks users what they found most frustrating about their court experience and allows users to classify themselves as witnesses.[49] In any event, the customer-orientated focus remains prevalent.

Given the pace of development across jurisdictions in recent years, it is perhaps easy to overlook the significance of criminal justice agencies spending time and money on ascertaining the views of victims and witnesses at all. Rock (1990) has noted how many of the early reforms pertaining to victims of crime in England and Wales and Canada were implemented without any consultation with victims or victims groups. This change may reflect wider moves seen in most developed jurisdictions towards 'rational' or 'evidence-based' policy making (Lawrence 2006). This trend has placed the emphasis on 'what works' (Shaxson 2005), although Sanderson (2003) notes the frequent difficulties experienced in establishing this across many policy areas.

Williams (1999a: 392) has expressed a note of caution regarding the construction of victims as consumers of criminal justice: 'Victims of crime are at best reluctant consumers of criminal justice services, and to characterise what expectations they have of such services in the language of consumer rights is misleading'. The substantive point behind Williams's argument is that victims have no *choice* but to utilize the criminal justice system provided by the state. It is therefore wrong to view victims as consumers, because they are unable to switch allegiance to a different 'product'. Nevertheless, the problems associated with low reporting rates for domestic violence cases indicates that victims do at least have the option of not going to the criminal justice system at all, and in this sense may be said to exert real consumer power. This academic argument aside, another criticism of the notion that victims are now the consumers of criminal justice is that, as demonstrated earlier, most of the survey instruments utilized across the jurisdictions under review are actually designed to elicit the views of *witnesses*, some of whom will be victims, rather than victims *per se*. Needham (2009) has commented that while the UK Government has increasingly drawn upon consumer terminology in reference to other areas of public service, this tendency has been less developed in the criminal justice sphere. Needham's argument is therefore not intended to deny that this terminology has been applied in this area, but rather that it has been utilized in a restrictive way:

> Where the term customer was used by the [UK] Home Office, it was applied to all users of the service. However, it was clear that 'law-abiding citizens', particularly victims and witnesses, would be the priority customers of the service. This finding is consistent with the victim orientation anticipated by hypothesis. (p. 1).

This point returns us to the argument that the new consumers of criminal justice may in fact be ideal, law-abiding victims rather than crime victims as a whole.

Victims of crime: a transnational and international policy network

The goal of this chapter has been to demonstrate the complex interaction of influences driving victim reform in the countries under review. While this has inevitably been a far from comprehensive overview, what is clear is that the reforms are grounded in a variety of different influences comprizing a complex policy network of interest groups. It is also clear that common influences are being felt across these nine jurisdictions despite their differing social and political contexts and histories. These of course have combined with the influences discussed in the last chapter to produce a truly transnational and international policy network of actors, organizations and interests groups.

It has also been confirmed that victims are a highly emotive and politicized issue. This is again demonstrated by the following extract from questions to the Irish Minister of Justice, Equality and Law Reform in the Irish Parliament:

> The Minister has outlined a very comprehensive list of legislation and procedures. However, would he not agree that victims, who are often witnesses in criminal cases, are central to the good operation of the criminal justice system and that all the information from recent high profile cases indicates they are totally alienated from the criminal justice system? (*Irish Parliamentary Debates*, Volume 584, 05 May 2004: para. 3)

In the face of such criticisms, governments from across the world have been forced to act and act quickly: not least because of growing sympathy for these victims, and the worry that crime is rising and that the criminal justice system is ineffective. This to some extent bears out the theories of Boutellier and Garland set out in Chapter 1.[50] Yet this chapter has also uncovered a number of other influences common to many of the countries under review. The interest of the media in specific high-profile cases, for example, has galvanized government action in a number of situations and a number of jurisdictions. In addition, academics themselves exercised influence both through their concentrating on specific kinds of victims and through the development of new ways to expose the level of victimization felt by marginalized or otherwise invisible groups.

The breadth of actors and issues contributing to the development of these policies lends much credence to the notion of policy networks and the development of governance, and its relevance to victims, discussed at the start of this chapter. There, it was noted that any generalizations to be drawn between jurisdictions must be subject to the highest scrutiny. Certainly the above discussion has uncovered differences as well as similarities between the jurisdictions under review, particularly in terms of the impact of law enforcement agendas, the position of NGOs, and the imposition of specific targets. What can be said with confidence however is that victim policies in all these jurisdictions came about as a result of a complex interaction of national, transnational and international influences rather than a simplistic governmental pronouncement to 'do right' by victims of crime. It has been shown that this complexity has sometimes required compromise, as well as bringing benefits to victims themselves.

Notes

1 For the sake of brevity, this volume will ordinarily refer to 'policy networks'. See Atkinson and Coleman (1992) for a full analysis and comparison of this differing terminology.
2 Space restrictions require me to circumvent the considerable debate surrounding the meaning of this term, except insofar as to acknowledge Scholte's (2000: 41) observation that 'the only consensus about globalizaton is that it is contested'.
3 See below.
4 See Chapter 1.

5 See also Tisdall and Davis (2004).
6 Victim Support Scotland and Victim Support England and Wales remain separate organizations, although they maintain close links.
7 Chapter 9 of the South African Constitution established several so-called 'State Institutions Supporting Constitutional Development'.
8 The Department of Social Development is another key player in the formation of the Programme.
9 Which in turn was followed that same day by a statement from Victim Support England and Wales applauding the government for adopting its ideas so quickly.
10 The federal Office for Victims of Crime also provides partial funding for NOVA's annual conference.
11 Indeed, this is made clear though its Annual Reviews (Victim Support England and Wales 2009). Victim support schemes also had representation on the JUSTICE Committee (1998).
12 See also, for example, the mission statement of the Canadian Resource Centre for Victims of Crime: http://crcvc.ca/en/about/leg_priorities.php.
13 For example, in British Columbia. See: http://www.gov.bc.ca/pssg/.
14 On the initiative of another self-described 'grassroots' NGO, the National Coalition Against Domestic Violence.
15 Although this is not to say The Netherlands has not experimented with victim-orientated crime prevention (Winkel 1991).
16 See Chapter 6.
17 Although of course the history of human rights development is much longer. See Steiner and Alston (2000).
18 See Chapter 1.
19 This was updated in 2003.
20 In the form of the *partie civile* model. See Chapter 5.
21 The same can be said of the International Court of Justice.
22 See p. 98.
23 s.34, amending the Criminal Law (Rape) Act 1981.
24 See Alexander (2002) and below.
25 Subsequently in Philadelphia in 1990. This was a misdemeanour court. The first felony Domestic Violence Court in the USA became operational in Brooklyn, New York, in 1996.
26 The first being initiated in New York State in the mid 1990s (Cavadino and Dignan 2007).
27 See below.
28 See Chapter 7.
29 The eventual acquittal of Lindy Chamberlain for the murder of her nine-week-old child has also made this latter case synonymous with poor police practices and media bias impacting upon trials (see Marcus 1989).
30 See p. 45.

31 159 US 523 (1985).
32 A development which itself owes much to the advancement of sophisticated means to count crime in the same period (Maguire 2007) and the rise of evidence-based policy making (Shaxson 2005).
33 Human Trafficking has tended to be addressed at the national level in the UK, with the Scottish Government subscribing to the UK Home Office Action Plan on the issue (UK Home Office and Scottish Government 2006). That said, there have been some indications that the problem of trafficking is disproportionately high in Scotland compared to the rest of the UK (Lebov 2009).
34 According to one interview respondent in the Irish Department of Justice, Equality and Law Reform interviewed for this research. The Blue Blindfold campaign received praise in the latest *Trafficking in Persons Report* produced by the US Department of State (2009). This report is discussed in more detail later.
35 'The recruitment, transportation, transfer, harbouring or receipt of persons, by means of the threat or use of force or other forms of coercion, of abduction, of fraud, of deception, of the abuse of power or of a position of vulnerability or of the giving or receiving of payments or benefits to achieve the consent of a person having control over another person, for the purpose of exploitation. Exploitation shall include, at a minimum, the exploitation of the prostitution of others or other forms of sexual exploitation, forced labour or services, slavery or practices similar to slavery, servitude or the removal of organs'.
36 In a bid to assist police in the protection of those involved in the sex industry (Daalder 2007).
37 See below.
38 Austria, Belgium, France, Italy, and Switzerland are all criticized for the same reason.
39 This may in part constitute fallout from the Tampa crisis of 2001 (see Lee 2007).
40 In England and Wales, such a policy recently led to the controversial questioning of a four-year-old witness in London's Central Criminal Court (Hall 2009c).
41 Chapter 5 will examine in more detail the contention that increasing victims' rights has compromised the rights of defendants.
42 Which emphasizes 'the need to ensure justice for victims and defendants' (p. 13).
43 For example, a recent report from the Auditor General of Tasmania (2008: 1) criticizes magistrates' courts in the jurisdiction for failing to set targets, stating that 'the Magistrates' Court's strategic plan was out of date needing targets and measures relating to timeliness'.
44 See Chapter 5.
45 In the USA (Wisconsin) in 1980; The Netherlands in 1986; England and Wales in 1990; Ireland in 1999; Australia (New South Wales) in 1996;

New Zealand in 2002; South Africa in 2004; Scotland in 2005 and Canada (as part of the National Victim Services Program) in 2007.
46 See http://www.justice.gouv.qc.ca/english/publications/generale/temoins-j-a.htm.
47 Research carried out in South Africa indicates that 53 per cent of witnesses feel they should be able to give evidence as soon as they arrive in court and 68 per cent feel no more than a one-hour wait is reasonable (Bruce and Isserow 2005).
48 In a speech delivered in January 2010, the Lord Chancellor and Secretary of State for Justice, Jack Straw, noted that the WAVEs survey indicated that '90 per cent of victims and witnesses now say they are satisfied with the way they are treated by criminal justice staff – an all time high' (n.p.). Text of the speech available at: http://www.justice.gov.uk/news/speech270110a.htm.
49 See http://www.stanct.org/Store/Forms/SurveyWebEngl.pdf.
50 See pp. 10–11.

Chapter 5

Victims' rights: an international review

In the last chapter it was argued that the development of a human rights discourse across the nine countries under review has had a significant impact on the formation of policies relating to victims of crime within these jurisdictions. The present chapter will focus on the conceptualization of victims' rights, exploring their content, their basis in statutory charters, and their implementation in both domestic and international courts. Despite the ongoing development of the international victims' movement, it will be demonstrated that victims' rights have yet to be made judiciable within the criminal justice process of any of these jurisdictions. While this position might bring the enforceability of such rights into question, it will be argued that the inclusion of victims within statutory charters has exerted a powerful influence over the occupational practices of judges in most countries, to the point where consideration of victims by criminal courts is arguably becoming normalized. In contrast to traditional notions of defendants' rights, the rights of victims are gaining authority not through the enforcement of specific legal sanctions but via a gradual acceptance by legal practitioners that the concerns, expectations, and even opinions of crime victims are legitimate and merit due consideration. In addition, by highlighting the similarity of the provisions adopted in each of the nine countries under review, it will be argued once again that such developments are becoming globalized.[1]

Victims and Policy Making

Theorising victims' rights

The provision of rights to victims is a controversial issue, provoking significant conceptual debates in the literature. Most such discussions have been primarily concerned with the degree to which victims can be permitted to influence decision making within a criminal justice system while still safeguarding defendants' right to due process. For Ashworth (1998) the key distinction to be drawn is between so-called 'service rights' for victims and 'procedural rights'. The service rights Ashworth has in mind include: respectful and sympathetic treatment, support, information, the provision of facilities at court and compensation from the offender or state. For Ashworth (2000), victim participation should never be allowed to stray beyond this and into the domain of 'public interest'. Falling within this latter category, Ashworth is particularly concerned with the possibility of victims exerting influence over sentencing decisions through victim impact statements. In support of his position, Ashworth cites the inability of the court to test robustly the accuracy of the information contained within such statements. In addition, he argues that it is unjust to allow unforeseen, unpredictable, or unusual impacts of crime on victims to affect sentence. As such, for Ashworth (1993, 2000) the international spread of victim impact statements constitutes a means of legitimizing a punitive stance against offenders. Such a position resonates significantly with the points raised in Chapter 4 concerning the influence of populist punitiveness on victim policy development in all the jurisdictions under review.[2]

Expanding upon Ashworth's notion of procedural rights, Edwards (2004: 973) labels 'participation' 'a comfortably pleasing platitude' which is rhetorically powerful but conceptually vague. In his analysis, Edwards describes four possible forms of victim participation in criminal justice. The most significant casts victims in the role of *decision makers*, such that their preferences are sought and applied by the criminal justice system. Less drastic would be *consultative* participation, where the system seeks out victims' preferences and takes them into account when making decisions. Edwards sees the traditional role of victims as one of *information provision*, where victims are obliged to provide information required by the system. Finally, in a system of *expressive* participation victims express whatever information they wish, but with no instrumental impact. Both Ashworth (2000) and Edwards highlight the danger of victims being given the impression that their participation in the criminal process will have a genuine impact on decision making when this is not in fact the case as this

Victims' rights: an international review

will raise their expectations unduly and ultimately lead to reduced confidence in the criminal justice system.

Edwards's typology of participation is a useful tool for assessing and comparing the provision of rights in different jurisdictions: although there is a sense that for Edwards these are all or nothing categories. As such, he does not examine how such categories might be combined in operational practice. The notion that some types of decision making on the part of victims may be less significant than others[3] is similarly not considered. Edwards (2004) also fails to elaborate on how different forms of participation impact on other actors in the process (such as defendants), which for Ashworth is the key issue. These criticisms notwithstanding, it will be demonstrated later how, in effect, Edwards's concept of consultative participation has been applied in most of the jurisdictions under review.

A new dimension to these debates is introduced by Sanders and Young (2000: 51), who argue that both service and procedural rights fail to cater for the interests of victims: as does the traditional 'due process verses crime control' dichotomy. The authors disagree with Ashworth's view of service rights as a solution to victims' grievances because they feel that such rights can also marginalize victims when they are poorly implemented. As an alternative, Sanders (2002) suggests an inclusive victims' rights approach combined with inquisitorial-style systems in the short term, moving towards restorative justice in the future. This model rejects any notion of victims being endowed with decision-making power within the criminal justice system on the basis that this:

> Would fuel the 'us' and 'them' non-relationship and therefore social exclusion ... The aim would be to listen to victims' information and their views, but decision making would be based on clear objective criteria derived from inclusive approaches such as the 'freedom perspective'. (Sanders 2002: 218)

The 'freedom perspective' referred to here is an attempt by Sanders and Young (2000) to replace the service/procedural rights dichotomy with a more sophisticated tool. Unlike Ashworth, Sanders and Young propose a mechanism whereby the rights of victims and defendants are balanced, by maximizing the net *freedom* within the system. Sanders (2002) illustrates this perspective by arguing that the provision of *information* to victims within a criminal justice system increases the freedom of victims without reducing the freedom of defendants. Conversely, Sanders and Young contend that if victims' opinions are permitted to sway decision making then this will reduce the freedom of offenders more than it increases the freedom of victims, and hence constitutes an unacceptable 'right'. Consulting victims on the discontinuance of their cases is however justified provided the final decision is made by the UK Crown Prosecution Service based on an objective evaluation of the balance of freedoms (Sanders and Young 2000). The notion of balancing the rights of victims, and in particular their views and expectations, alongside other factors relevant to decision making has been influential in the courts' handling of victims in a number of the jurisdictions under review. Indeed, Jackson (1990) has remarked on the dominance of 'balance' rhetoric within the transnational and international criminal justice discourse generally, and in relation to victim and offender rights specifically (Jackson 2004). Such developments will be highlighted later in this chapter with specific reference to relevant case law from the nine jurisdictions, and from international courts.

Not all commentators have argued so fervently against a more active form of procedural involvement for victims within criminal justice. In the USA, Edna Erez (1994, 1999, 2000) has advocated victim impact statements as a means of affording victims participation rights.[4] In challenging Ashworth's warnings, Erez (1999, 2004) begins by conceding that these statements have little impact on sentencing (see also Morgan and Sanders 1999). Nevertheless, for her this is a product of the resistant cultures of practitioners and their widely held view that only 'normal' levels of impact should affect sentences (Erez 1999). Conversely, Sanders et al. (2001) see victim impact statements as fundamentally flawed because they rarely contain unexpected information.[5]

Central to Erez's argument is the understanding that victims derive therapeutic benefit and vindication from expressing information about the impact of crime during the sentencing process, which in turn boosts satisfaction with the criminal system and may achieve restorative ends (Erez et al. 1997; Erez 2004). Her argument is therefore that normative issues matter to victims, which is also the conclusion of Tyler (1990; Tyler and Huo 2002). On a similar point, Shapland (1990) notes that one of the key benefits afforded to victims from having a judge order an offender to pay them compensation is that such action constitutes official acknowledgement of their pain and suffering or, as Miers (1980) puts it, a recognition of their victim status.

Whether through compensation orders or wider sentencing, Erez (1999, 2000) argues that what little influence victim impact statements have is on the *proportionality* of the sentence. Erez's contention is based on studies from the USA and Australia (Erez and Rogers 1999) which seem to confirm that victim impact statements are generally not used as a vehicle for communicating vindictive opinions to the court (Hoyle *et al.* 1999). As such, she suggests a VIS can influence sentences in either direction such that the two cancel each other out and obscure the affect on sentencing in the statistical analyses:

> Some changes in [sentencing] outcomes do occur, but they are hidden as in the aggregate they offset each other. Without victim input, sentences might well have been too high or too low. (Erez 1999: 548)

Sanders *et al.* (2001) heavily dispute the notion that victim impact statements can actually reduce sentence severity (see also Giliberti 1991). Although the authors are unable to prove statistically that Erez's argument is incorrect, they advise caution on the interpretation of her findings and note that there were no comparable findings in the English pilot of victim impact statements (Morgan and Sanders 1999) or in a study carried out in New York by Davis and Smith (1994). Erez also appears to base her conclusion on the word of practitioners, notwithstanding the fact that 'what they say and what they do are not always the same' (Sanders *et al.* 2001: 449).

On the issue of vengefulness, Erez's general perspective has recently been supported by evaluations of restorative justice initiatives in Northern Ireland (Doak and O'Mahony 2006) and in Britain (Shapland *et al.* 2006). These studies indicate that when victims are given the opportunity to speak about sentencing matters they do not tend to advocate excessively harsh punishments, but instead suggest resolutions aimed at reducing the chance of the offender reoffending.[6] The point is a significant one given the proliferation of restorative justice and restitution schemes across the nine countries under review.[7] The 1998 *British Crime Survey* also indicates generally non-punitive attitudes among victims, along with their acceptance of restorative principles. The same report also offers evidence to the effect that the more informed about the criminal justice system the general public are, the less punitive they become (Mattinson and Mirrlees-Black 2000). That said, Sanders *et al.*'s argument is not so much that victims in general are vindictive and punitive, but 'simply that non-punitive victims rarely make a VIS' (2004: 104). Sanders *et al.* (2001: 450) also dispute the therapeutic benefits of victim impact statements on the grounds that they 'add another layer of depersonalised disempowering procedures which do little to ease secondary victimization for many, and add to it for others'.

An appraisal of theoretical positions

No conception of victims' rights has yet to win universal recognition and all can be subject to criticism. While Ashworth's views have been influential (see Zedner 2002), he offers no mechanisms for resolving the conflict he identifies between victim and offender rights. His position is therefore premised on notions of a zero sum game whereby to afford rights to victims is to restrict the rights of defendants. For this reason, Sanders *et al.* (2001) classify Ashworth's argument as a normative defence of the due process approach.[8] Sanders and Young (2000) present the freedom perspective as a solution to this dilemma, but give no indication as to how or by whom net freedom within the system is to be balanced. Erez takes a more positive view on victim participation rights (at least in relation to sentencing) but has failed to fully convince strict adherents of the due process model.

Both Erez and Sanders and Young agree on the point that a tradeoff between the rights of victims and defendants is not inevitable. For Erez, procedural rights afforded to victims through victim impact statements do not unjustly affect defendants, but improve sentence accuracy and promote therapeutic benefits. For their part, Sanders and Young would wish to maximize the 'freedom' of all sides. Garland (2001) has also questioned the assumption of a conflict between victim and defendant rights. For him, notions of a zero sum game are the products of a punitive ethos espoused by governments in the USA and England and Wales in an effort to deny the failure of their justice systems to reduce crime. This position is supported by Hickman (2004: 52):

> Fairness to victims is not a zero sum game. It can be achieved without detracting from the rights of the defendant. The fact that this government wishes us to think otherwise is a profoundly political matter.

Even if one accepts the contention that a zero sum game can be avoided (or does not really exist) none of these theories directly address how the rights of victims can be *enforced* in any given jurisdiction. Jackson (2003: 319) emphasizes the importance of this issue if victims are to achieve genuine acceptance in criminal justice procedures: 'One of the problems with putting obligations on criminal justice agencies, however, is that they are unlikely to be taken seriously unless consequences attach to non-compliance'.

The difficulty of enforcing the rights afforded to victims in international instruments has already been discussed in Chapter 3. The remainder of this chapter will demonstrate how similar problems can be indentified on the domestic level in the countries under review. Despite this, it will also be shown that both domestic and international courts are beginning to take account of the rights of victims in their judgments. This represents a challenge to Jackson's view that criminal justice actors and agencies must face the genuine threat of official reprimand when victims' rights are breached in order for such rights to be guaranteed. As such, this chapter will conclude with a discussion of how victims' rights may achieve instrumental effects in the criminal justice system through other means.

The formal rights of victims within national jurisdictions

The concept of victims' rights has the potential to encompass the vast majority of the domestic measures and reforms discussed in this volume. As such, this section focuses specific attention on the principle statements of such rights held up by governments from each jurisdiction which principally take the form of statutory and non-statutory charters or service standards. This section will examine the content of such documents and, following on from the previous discussion, consider their enforceability across the nine jurisdictions. This will be followed by a comparison of relevant case law from each country and from international courts, and an evaluation of the influence exerted by such rulings on the understanding and application of victims' rights in different jurisdictions.

Victims' charters

The majority of the countries under review have relied on combinations of minimum standards and 'legitimate expectations' (JUSTICE Committee 1998) as a means of affording rights to victims within their criminal justice systems, although we will see that the degree to which the term 'rights' is employed to describe such provisions varies between jurisdictions. The exception to this general rule is the USA, where individual states have been more inclined to incorporate victims of crime within state constitutions, or to produce separate victims' bills of rights. The extent to which such bills are in practice different or more enforceable than the charters used elsewhere is however open to dispute. In most jurisdictions these charters[9] are based in statute, either because their formation is mandated under primary legislation (as with the *English Code of Practice for Victims of Crime*[10]) or because examples of best practice are set down in statute (as is the case in most of the Australian charters[11]).

Among the earliest and most influential of these documents was the so-called *Vaillant Guidelines* of The Netherlands. This was published in 1985 following the reports of three separate committees into the role of victims in Dutch criminal justice (Wemmers 1996).[12] The guidelines placed statutory obligations on police and prosecution authorities to keep victims informed at all stages of the process; to include notes on the impact of crime on victims in the prosecution portfolio; and, if the victim wished it, to pursue restitution from the offender. The rules were augmented in 1988 by the *Terwee Guidelines*, which are heavily based on Council of Europe Recommendation 85(11).[13] In particular, these new rules place even greater emphasis on the criminal justice process to facilitate mechanisms of restitution to victims. The *Terwee Guidelines* were recognized as a source of law by the Supreme Court of The Netherlands in 1990[14] and were extended across the Dutch criminal justice system in subsequent years, eventually being rolled out nationally in 1995. The *Guidelines* have received significant media attention within The Netherlands, which Brienen and Hoegen (2000) suggest have made them difficult for authorities to ignore.[15] The significance of this observation lies in the fact that many jurisdictions have struggled to ensure that the principles espoused in their victims' charters are transferred into operational practice (see van Dijk *et al.* 2008). From a reformers' perspective the difficulty here lies in the fact that, in most cases, the provisions of such charters are not law in themselves and direct legal sanction cannot result from their breach. This is true even when the charters purport to ground themselves in some higher authority, such as the South African Charter, which is said to reflect the broader rights to which victims (as citizens) are entitled under the national constitution. Hanly (2003) has made similar observations in relation to victims' rights in Ireland, where the Irish Victims' Charter refers to the UN Declaration of 1985 in its preamble.[16]

It is apparent that most of the victims' charters examined across the nine jurisdictions under review constitute not only a list of services and/or rights for victims to expect, but also an official acknowledgement of their traditional neglect and dismissal at the hands of criminal justice actors. Hence, all such documents affirm a new commitment to approaching victims, in the words of the Irish Charter, with 'empathy, courtesy and respect' (Irish Department of Justice, Equality and Law Reform 1999: 6) or, as the Australian model Charter maintains: '[A] victim should be dealt with at all times in a sympathetic, constructive and reassuring manner and with due regard to his or her personal situation, rights and dignity'.[17] Such pronouncements should not be dismissed as incidental. Joutsen and Shapland (1989) have emphasized the significance attributed by victims of crime to basic courtesy and respect from legal practitioners and court staff. Similar findings have been replicated in the US (Tyler 1990; Bazemore 1998) and The Netherlands (Wemmers *et al.* 1995), as well as by the *International Crime Victimization Survey* (van Dijk *et al.* 2008) and the *British Witness Satisfaction Surveys* (Angle *et al.* 2003b). As such, the basic right to be treated with respect and sympathy by the criminal justice system is among the most significant guarantees afforded to victims across these jurisdictions, reflecting victims' *stated* needs, as opposed to their *presumed* expectations of the criminal justice process.[18]

Generally speaking, the other rights found in the various forms of victims' charter adopted across the nine countries under review fall within four broad categories: information provision, protection, compensation/restitution,[19] and consultation. Numerically, a content analysis of the charters reveals that the vast majority of such rights (in general and in individual documents) involve providing information to victims. Typically such information includes the progress of cases, the outcome of proceedings and appeals, and the reasons why decisions have been made. A number of the charters go further to emphasize that *explanation* as well as *information* must be provided. For example, the *Scottish National Standards for Victims of Crime* assure victims that they are entitled to *understand* the information being presented to them (Scottish Executive 2005: 3). The English and Welsh and Irish charters also make provision for prosecutors to meet with victims personally, prior to court proceedings, to offer explanations and answer questions.[20] Elsewhere, charters set down time limits by which victims must be updated on the progress (or lack of progress) in a case, with the Australian Capital Territory model service charter stipulating monthly communication between police and victims as a minimum. In addition, England and Wales, Scotland, Western Australia, and New Zealand have all introduced enhanced victim notification schemes for victims of serious crimes. Typically such schemes are set up on an opt-in basis and offer additional information to victims concerning offenders in custody including: information about parole hearings for the offender in their case; information about temporary release of such offenders; and (in the case of New Zealand) notification of an offender's escapes or absconding. It is notable that other charters, including those of South Africa and Ireland, provide such information to *all* victims in relevant cases without the need to opt in to a separate scheme.

The Irish Charter is interesting for the further reason that, alone of all the charters reviewed for this project, it contains a greater number of provisions relating to the protection of victims than the provision of information. Protection here includes the provision of special facilities to assist vulnerable and intimidated witnesses to give evidence at court; the avoidance of unnecessary contact with the defendant at court; the security of victims' personal data; and the provision of health, social and counselling services. The Irish Charter goes into some detail: guaranteeing victims of rape access to a doctor of the same gender; a pro-arrest policy in cases of domestic violence;[21] and special measures to protect homes in cases of elderly victims. The level of detail in the Irish Charter may in part derive from the particularly strong concerns voiced in that jurisdiction in recent years over the response of authorities to high levels of domestic violence (Bacik 2002). By comparison, other charters set down much broader provisions. Examples include the *Canadian Statement of Basic Principles of Justice for Victims of Crime*,[22] which maintains that 'the safety and security of victims should be considered at all stages' (Canadian Department of Justice 2003: principle 4) and the South African Charter, which refers to a right to protection. The New Zealand Charter is distinguished by its lack of any specific protection provisions.

Most of these charters also contain provisions concerning victims' receipt of compensation from either the state or the offender (usually termed 'restitution') or both.[23] The English and Welsh version is particularly detailed as to the standards victims should expect from the state compensation system, including set time limits for the communication of decisions and appeals. The South African Charter places a general duty on the courts to ensure compensation (here restitution) orders are enforced against offenders. Restitution is also mentioned in the English and Welsh, Irish, and Dutch charters. For example, in relevant cases police are obliged in England and Wales to pass on the details of victims to Youth Offending Teams for the purposes of including them in restoration or restorative justice initiatives. The YOTs themselves are obliged elsewhere in the Charter to consult victims and involve them in that process. The South African Charter provides a right to restitution, listing restorative justice as one of its guiding principles, and the Irish Charter places an obligation on courts to ensure restitution is directed at the victim. As noted above, the Dutch *Terwee Guidelines* were specifically intended to develop mechanisms of restitution (see Malsch 1999). In particular, these latter guidelines introduced restitution orders, whereby a court can order an offender to pay restitution to victims, either alone or together with any other sanction, with no set upper financial limit.[24]

So far, all of the rights discussed above would fall into the category of service rights, as none provide for any degree of participation[25] in the sense of victims exerting influence over decision making. Nevertheless, most of these charters do provide for a limited degree of participation for victims in the criminal justice system, mainly through an obligation placed on criminal justice actors to *consult* victims when making specific decisions. In some cases these obligations are phrased widely. For example, the South African Charter speaks of a victim's general right to offer information. Similarly, Scottish national standards promise victims 'consultation on decisions affecting you at all times' (Scottish Executive 2005: 4).

Other charters are more specific, setting out particular areas and decisions on which victims can expect to be consulted. On the matter of prosecution decisions, both the Irish and the Dutch charters suggest that victims' views should be taken into account when making this determination. The same is true in England and Wales, although here the relevant provisions are in the separate Prosecutor's Pledge (UK Crown Prosecution Service 2005) and in the Code for Crown Prosecutors (UK Crown Prosecution Service 2004). In all cases such expectations are however tempered by clear statements to the effect that victims will not be permitted to dictate prosecution decisions:

> The [UK] Crown Prosecution Service does not act for victims or the families of victims in the same way as solicitors act for their clients. Crown Prosecutors act on behalf of the public and not just in the interests of any particular individual. (UK Crown Prosecution Service 2004: para. 5.12)

Similarly, the *Prosecution Guidelines of New Zealand* list the 'attitude of the victim of the alleged offence to a prosecution' as a matter which 'may arise for consideration' (New Zealand Crown Law Office 2010: para. 3.3.2(m)) but emphasize that such attitudes will not necessarily be determinative. In The Netherlands, the criminal code affords the state a complete monopoly over prosecution.[26] Anyone with an interest in the prosecution has the right to complain to the Court of Appeal when a prosecution is not pursued in a given case. This prompts an examination of how that decision was made, during which the victim has a right to have his opinion presented to the court. That said, while the Court can order the prosecutor to review the decision, in practice such orders are seldom made (Wemmers 1996).

Most significantly, and despite Ashworth's misgivings discussed earlier, all the charters examined for this project contain provisions affording victims the opportunity to communicate the effects of a crime to the court through victim impact statements.[27] Only the Irish Charter expressly notes that such information will be taken into account by sentencers, the Scottish Standards makes the general point that victims' views will be respected and the Canadian Statement maintains that 'the views, concerns and representations of victims are an important consideration in criminal justice processes and should be considered in accordance with prevailing law, policies and procedures' (Canadian Department of Justice 2003: principle 8). Another key area in which victims can expect to be consulted in a number of the jurisdictions under review[28] is that of parole and the temporary release of offenders. Such consultation often occurs in conjunction with the enhanced victim notification schemes discussed earlier.

Consultative participation on various decisions therefore features as a legitimate right in all the victims' charters produced by the countries under review. Nevertheless, the practical operation and the impact of such consultations – whether on prosecution decisions, sentencing, or other matters – are frequently left vague. Indeed, similar observations can be made of a number of the charters more generally. By far the most detailed is the English and Welsh Code of Practice for Victims of Crime, which meticulously sets out the expectations of all the separate bodies within the criminal justice system in their dealings with victims. By contrast, the South African Charter refers to very few specific organizations and speaks instead of victims' general rights at all stages of the justice process.

A further observation to be made of the victims' charters from all nine jurisdictions is their lack of any form of robust (legal) enforcement mechanisms, which Jackson (2003) argues are necessary in order to make such rights functional. In The Netherlands, for example, judicial control of the authorities' adherence to the *Terwee Guidelines* is limited to the judicial review procedure (Brienen and Hoegen 2000). In England and Wales, the Prosecutors' Pledge contains no specific provisions detailing the options open to a victim who finds its targets are not met. Presumably this would involve approaching the CPS through its standard internal complaints procedures. The *Code of Practice for Victims of Crime in England and Wales* itself is based in statute, which is significant, although its provisions are not law and its enforceability again remains with the complaints procedures of individual criminal justice agencies. The difference is that under the *Code* victims who remain dissatisfied with the outcome of a complaints procedure can report the matter to their member of parliament, who can refer it to the Parliamentary Commissioner for Administration (the Ombudsman) for investigation (UK Home Office 2005: para. 1.4).[29] A new Victims and Witnesses Commissioner is charged with monitoring the operation of the *Code*, although it has not been said that discontented victims can complain directly to her.[30] It is envisaged that victims can take their complaints to a statutory Victims' Advisory Panel but neither the Panel nor the Commissioner have powers of investigation or redress,[31] although the Commissioner is being touted as a 'champion' of victims' rights (UK Home Office 2006). Without exception all the charters reviewed for this project rely on similar mechanisms for their enforcement, which in practice are mainly limited to the complaints procedures of individual justice organizations.

It is telling that most of these charters do not explicitly refer to victims having rights at all. The only exception is South Africa where, as noted earlier, the prevailing view is that the Charter represents a specific application of rights found under the constitution rather than a source of new rights *per se*. Many of the charters are also marked by the absence of any specific obligations placed on the judiciary, the expectation being the requirement already described in the Irish Charter to take account of the impact of crime on victims. The New Zealand Charter also requires the court to take account of victims' views when granting bail in cases of serious crime.

Victims' charters (as opposed to legislation and case law) constitute the most easily accessible statements of victims' rights in the jurisdictions under review, most having been produced specifically for a lay audience. Nevertheless, the lack of judiciable enforcement mechanisms in any of these documents calls into question the progress made towards the *effective* introduction of victims' rights across these nine jurisdictions. As such, to uncover the true extent (or lack thereof) to which victims can now be said to have rights (even service rights) in any of the jurisdictions under review it is necessary to look more closely at primary sources of law.

Victims in national legislation

The drawing of clear distinctions between the rights afforded to victims in charters on the one hand and in primary legislation on the other is complicated by the considerable overlap between the two in most jurisdictions. This is especially the case in The Netherlands, where it has been noted that the *Terwee Guidelines* are considered law by the Supreme Court.[32] As discussed previously, most of the charters reviewed earlier are grounded to varying degrees in legislation. For example, the New Zealand Victims' Rights Act of 2002 sets down most of the provisions published as the New Zealand Victims' Charter,[33] with the same broad categories of rights (information, protection, compensation/restitution and participation in the form of consultation on the impact of crime, prosecution decisions, bail and parole). The Act offers more procedural detail than the Charter produced for the public, but essentially takes these basic rights no further. This is equally true of the enforcement mechanisms available for victims who feel they have been denied their rights, which are covered in s.49 of the Act. Here the legislation makes it clear that the primary mode of redress should be a complaint to 'the person who, under the relevant specified provisions, appears to be required to accord the victim or person the right' (s.49(1)(a)). Failing this, the victim can turn to an Ombudsman, the Independent Police Conduct Authority or to New Zealand's Privacy Commissioner. Nevertheless, the degree to which these authorities may offer any form of redress to aggrieved victims is unclear, especially in light of the stipulation in s.50(2) that no financial redress can be ordered for breach of the principles listed in s.49:

> No person (for example, the Crown in right of New Zealand) may be required (for example, by any court, tribunal, or other body) to pay any money (whether by way of damages, compensation, or otherwise) to any other person just because of a breach of any of the specified provisions.

A similar variety of provision is found in the English Domestic Violence, Crime and Victims Act 2004. While refraining from setting down the exact contents of a charter, this legislation mandated the creation of the *Code of Practice for Victims of Crime in England and Wales*. Section 34(1) of the Act expresses the effect of non-compliance with the Code in the following terms: 'If a person fails to perform a duty imposed on him by a code issued under section 32, the failure does not of itself make him liable to criminal or civil proceedings'.

As with the charters discussed in the last section, the enforceability of the rights set down in national legislation remains an issue of conjecture in all the countries under review. The Australian state and territorial charters are all grounded in state/territory-level legislation, based on original principles set down in the Australian Capital Territory (ACT) Victims of Crime Act 1994, and adopted by the Australian Standing Committee of Attorneys-General[34] in 1996. However, the ACT legislation offers little by way of clarification as to how victims' rights may be enforced, except in so far to create a post of Victims of Crime Coordinator, charged with 'investigating ... conduct in the administration of justice which the Coordinator believes on reasonable grounds involves a breach of the governing principles referred to in [this Act]' (s.9(2)). The coordinator must report the findings of any such investigation to the relevant minister (s.9(2)), although he or she is afforded no power of redress, but is merely authorized to 'do all things necessary or convenient to be done in connection with the performance of the Coordinator's functions' (s.10). These methods of enforcing the legislation have been reproduced in other Australian states and territories. Hence the South Australian Victims of Crime Act 2001 creates a post of Commissioner for Victims, but again his or her powers of redress are restricted to '[giving] notice in writing to the public agency or official, recommending that the agency or official issue a written apology to the relevant victim' where their rights have been breached (s.16A(2)). The Victorian Victims' Charter Act of 2006 is even less robust in regards to the enforceability of victims' rights: simply requiring the relevant agency to 'inform [the victim] about the processes available for making a complaint' (s.19) and offering no guidance or guarantees as to how that complaint will be dealt with.

In sum, in most of the countries under review victims' charters do not attain any greater level of enforceability, or indeed offer a great deal more in terms of individual rights, when they are traced back to their parent legislation. However, as a discussion of the USA will illustrate, the difficulties of enforcing the rights of victims remain equally unsolved in jurisdictions where victims have prompted constitutional change.

In the USA, all 50 states have implemented statutes detailing victims' rights, 33 having amended their constitutions to include such provisions by the end of 2007 (Human Rights Watch 2008). California made this 34 in the Crime Victims' Bill of Rights Act of 2008.[35] With these rights now comprising part of the State Constitution, the Californian Attorney General's office describes their enforceability in the following terms:

> A victim, the retained attorney of a victim, a law representative of the victim or the prosecuting attorney upon request of the victim, may enforce the rights enumerated in subdivision (b) of Section 28 of Article I of the California Constitution in any trial or appellate court with jurisdiction over the case as a matter of right. The court shall act promptly on such a request. (Office of the Attorney General of California 2010: n.p.)

This does appear to impose a mandate on the courts to enforce victims' rights, although it is telling that the victim's representative apparently has to ask for such enforcement rather than it being the duty of the court to routinely enquire whether these rights have been adhered to. In contrast, the Attorney General's Office of Arizona has created a post of Victims' Rights Enforcement Officer, who will adopt '*proactive* and *reactive* approaches' in ensuring victims' rights laws are adhered to (Office of the Attorney General of Arizona 2009: n.p., emphasis in original). Specific roles attributed to the Officer include: acting as an ombudsman for crime victims; addressing victims' complaints of criminal or juvenile entities; and conducting inquiries into alleged violations of victims' rights laws. There is little information given as to any powers of compulsion or redress the Officer may have although presumably, as constitutional amendments, the rights found in both California and Arizona could be enforced by State Supreme Courts. Such an action has however yet to be taken in the United States concerning state level legislation on victims' rights. The Supreme Court of New Mexico has issued what it calls Court Orders on Victim Standing, which purport to grant victims legal standing to assert their rights,[36] although it is noted that these Orders are not controlling precedence and are offered for informational purposes only.

At the federal level, the US Justice for All Act of 2004 has been heralded as a major breakthrough by proponents of a more judiciable form of victims' rights (Doyle 2008), introducing such rights into the US penal code.[37] The Act restates standard service rights of information protection and compensation, as well as a procedural right for victims 'to be reasonably heard at any public proceeding in the district court involving release, plea, sentencing, or any parole proceeding'.[38] The most significant feature of the legislation, however, is the enforcement mechanisms it creates. Here, individuals or the federal government may assert victims' rights at the District Court level. If the victim or the government are still not satisfied with the enforcement of these rights they may file a petition with the Court of Appeals for a writ of mandamus. A court's decision to deny any of these rights may be asserted as an error by the prosecution in the case. Even more significantly, in limited circumstances a victim may move for a new trial on the basis of the denial of their rights[39] (see Doyle 2008).

The Justice for All Act does not apply to the states, as it is not an amendment to the Bill of Rights in the US constitution. Nevertheless, the Act was incorporated into the Federal Rules of Criminal procedures, which is followed by all judges in federal criminal cases, in April 2008. The Act does not give victims the right to sue the federal government for breach of their rights, but remains the most robust system of right enforcement for victims seen in any of the jurisdictions under review. That said, the question of enforcement of victims' rights in the United States is far from settled. It was noted earlier that at the state level enforcement mechanisms still tend to be rather vague and ultimately non-compulsive. At the national level, Human Rights Watch (2008: 12) concluded in a review of the development of victims' rights in the United States that there was still much to do in this regard: 'More attention needs to be paid to enforcing the victims' rights laws that already exist so that violations of victims' rights are prevented and, when violations occur, victims have a remedy'.

Beyond 'victim-centred' legislation and charters

As noted at the start of this chapter, the rights afforded to victims in all these jurisdictions go beyond those specifically articulated in the principle legislation or charters. Indeed many of the reforms discussed throughout this volume could be construed as creating new rights for victims of crime even when they are not expressly presented under this banner.

In particular, a large percentage of criminal justice reforms seen in these jurisdictions over recent years have been partly concerned with bolstering victims' rights to protection from revictimization and secondary victimization. In England and Wales, for example, the Youth Justice and Criminal Justice Act 1999[40] falls within this category through its statutory grounding of special measures provisions to assist vulnerable and intimidated witnesses to give evidence in court. Similar provisions were introduced in Ireland in the same year[41] and in Scotland in 2004, under the Vulnerable Witnesses (Scotland) Act. All these pieces of legislation offer guarantees of access to special measures facilities in particular to child witnesses and to complainants in cases of sexual assault and rape (subject to their availability at specific courts).[42] Protection is also afforded to victims giving evidence via the enactment of 'rape shield' laws to prevent cross-examination by defendants in sexual cases. Such provisions were first enacted in Michigan in 1974 and had by the mid-1980s been implemented in most of the countries under review (see Fitzgerald 1984).[43] Indeed, in Ireland the Sex Offenders Act 2001 goes so far as to require that separate representations for victims be provided in rape and other serious sexual assault trials where an application is made to the court in the course of the proceedings to adduce evidence or cross-examine on the subject of the complainant's sexual history.[44]

Similarly, the right of victims to be consulted on various matters goes well beyond the specific victims' charters or victims' rights legislation in the nine countries under review, and in fact predate these developments. Hence, Ireland's Criminal Justice Act of 1993 contained provisions required courts to take into account any effect (whether long term or otherwise) of a sexual offence on a victim six years before that 'right' was reproduced in the Irish Victims' Charter. In the same vein, the first Australian state or territory to legislate on Victim Impact Statement was South Australia in 1989, five years before the Australian Capital Territory Victims of Crime Act.

Victims in national legislation: an interim conclusion
In sum, charters and legislation purporting to introduce rights for victims in the criminal justice process have featured in all the jurisdictions under review over recent years. Given the long history of the victims' movement[45] and related policy development[46] in all of these jurisdictions, it is important to appreciate that in none of these documents were the so-called legitimate expectations of victims being articulated for the first time by policy makers or legal practitioners. As noted in the last chapter, common practice in the criminal justice system of The Netherlands, for example, had for some time afforded victims various 'rights' of respect, information, and consultation despite the fact that legislation specifically mentioning the victim is only now working its way through the parliamentary system.[47] Similarly, in the guidelines accompanying the South African Charter it is explicitly stated that nothing within its provisions should be considered new:

> The Victims' Charter contains seven rights which are contained in existing legislation (the Constitution, the Criminal Procedure

Act, the Access to Information Act and other legislation). For example, the first right of the Victims' Charter is [the right] to be treated with fairness and with respect for your dignity and privacy. Section 10 of the Constitution guarantees the right to dignity. The Victims' Charter aims to provide easy reference to existing rights so that victims are not re-victimized by the criminal justice system. (Webster 2008: 3)

As such, the goal of the South African Charter is one of expression and clarification, allowing victims to know their existing rights, and also to set these out clearly for practitioners, rather than creating new ones. This may in part explain the lack of specific enforcement mechanisms found in this and other charters, or in relevant legislation from the nine jurisdictions. Rather than being legally prescriptive documents *per se* (with significant, instrumental impacts for those who breach them) their purpose may be to foster a change in the occupational culture of practitioners and the judiciary towards better treatment of victims and sensitivity to their needs. This contention will be expanded upon in the following discussion on court judgments concerning victims' rights.

Victims' rights in domestic courts: a question of balance?

The position of victims of crime within the criminal justice process has been addressed in a number of contexts by courts across most of the jurisdictions under review. The main exception to this is South Africa, where the issue of victims' rights has not yet reached the Supreme Court or indeed received much formal judicial attention elsewhere.[48] The judiciary of The Netherlands, coming from a civil law background, have also been relatively silent on this issue except to confirm that the statutory guidelines discussed earlier should be regarded as a source of law.[49] In other jurisdictions the courts have tended to deal with victims in a somewhat piecemeal fashion, giving opinions on specific issues as they arise. In Canada, for example, the Supreme Court has exerted a marked influence over the development of rape shield laws,[50] passing several judgments concerning the impact of such legislation on a defendant's right to make 'full answer and defence' under the Canadian Charter of Rights and Fundamental Freedoms (s.11(d)). In early cases, the Court sought to restrict the scope of these laws (*R v Seaboyer*; *R v Gayme*[51]), even striking down one such (common law) regime as unconstitutional (*R v O'Connor*[52]). A revised version of the rape shield was inserted into the Canadian penal code in Bill C-46 of 1997 which, owing to the inclusion of increased safeguards, was deemed to meet constitutional standards in *R v Mills*.[53] In coming to this judgment the Court set out the conflict between a defendant's right to be heard and a victim's right to privacy in the following terms:

> Equality concerns must also inform the contextual circumstances in which the rights of full answer and defence and privacy will come into play. An appreciation of myths and stereotypes in the context of sexual violence is essential to delineate properly the boundaries of full answer and defence. An appreciation of the equality dimensions of record production in cases concerning sexual violence highlights the need to balance privacy and full answer and defence in a manner that fully respects the privacy interests of complainants' (*R v Mills* 1999: n.p.)

Case law from the United Kingdom (*R v T; R v H*[54]), Australia (*M*[55]), and the USA (*People v MacLeod*[56]) has similarly emphasized the need for balance and the exercise of discretion on a case-by-case basis where sexual history evidence is adduced, as opposed to imposing blanket rules.[57] In the case of rape shields, this reliance on judicial discretion has led some commentators to predict that, given their overriding mandate to ensure fair proceedings, judges will feel compelled to exercise their discretion to allow such evidence relatively freely (Temkin 2002).

Another issue prompting the development of its own body of case law in most jurisdictions[58] is that of the victim's role in sentencing decisions, and specifically the submission of information concerning the impacts of crime at the sentencing stage. In England and Wales, for example, it has been well established by the courts that judges should ordinarily seek out the impact of offending on victims.[59] This might suggest that victims have a right to provide such information personally.[60] By comparison, in an early New South Wales case the Court of Criminal Appeal expressed dissatisfaction with the convention in place in most Australian states and territories of having victim impact statements compiled by other agencies (usually the police, based on interviews) with the finished version never actually being seen by the victims themselves before being submitted for consideration by the court:

> [A] serious weakness in the present system is that [victim impact statements] are not signed or even acknowledged as accurate

by the victims concerned and, at best, reflect the attitude and impression of the police officer preparing them. (*R* v *Nicholls*[61], cited in Erez *et al.* 1996: 209)

The US courts have also emphasized the right of victims to convey the impacts of crime to sentencers. In the first test case following the Justice for All Act 2004, the US Court of Appeals for the Ninth Circuit ruled that a trial judge had erred in law when he refused to allow victims to speak in court concerning the impact of money laundering and fraud.[62] This followed the major US Supreme Court judgment in *Payne* v *Tennessee*[63] where the court reversed two of its previous judgments in ruling that the use of victim impact statements in capital cases was constitutional. This position has recently been affirmed in the joint cases of *Douglas Oliver Kelly* v *California* and *Samuel Zamudio* v *California*.[64] The significance of these rulings lies in the fact that it is the *indirect* victims of murder (friends and family of the victim) being permitted to submit a VIS in all three cases. Although not all jurisdictions under review are prepared to accept victim impact statements from indirect victims (New South Wales being one such example), it is clear that the use of such statements, from direct and indirect victims, is expanding in all nine jurisdictions.

The above examples demonstrate that domestic courts across the nine jurisdictions under review[65] have begun to acknowledge the participation of victims within the criminal justice process. Indeed, in the second major case concerning the Justice for All Act the US Supreme Court notes that the legislation had been enacted to make crime victims full participants in the criminal justice system.[66] That said, it is clear that such participation is still largely restricted to consultation, with courts in most jurisdictions resisting any attempts by victims to exercise real decision-making power in the criminal process. In Ireland, for example, the Supreme Court has articulated the relative position of the state and the victim in prosecution decisions as follows: 'Although the bringing of a prosecution may undoubtedly be central to vindicating the rights or interests of crime, the interests of the People in bringing a prosecution is, in the interest of society as a whole, of wider importance'.[67]

Similarly, in *R v Secretary of State for the Home Department and another, ex parte Bulger*[68] the Divisional Court of England and Wales held that the family of a murder victim did not have standing to seek judicial review of any tariff set in relation to the murder. Furthermore, in a recent practice direction issued by Lord Justice Judge the UK House of Lords[69] confirmed that any opinions as to the 'correct sentence' expressed in victim personal statements or family impact statements should not have any effect on sentencing in English courts.[70] The High Court of New Zealand took a similar line in *A v New Zealand Parole Board and Peter Mana McNamara*[71] when a victim argued that in releasing her rapist on parole, after what she considered a short term in prison, the Board had failed to give due weight to a submission made by her opposing such a decision. The Board was required to do so under the Parole Act 2002 s.7(2)(d).[72] The court dismissed the petition and, in coming to its decision, made it clear that just because a victim has the right to make a submission to a criminal justice agency, that submission does not automatically carry superior weight in comparison to other relevant considerations:

> The need for the Board to give 'due weight' to what a victim says cannot create an ability in a victim to expand the relevant considerations simply by raising them. 'Due weight' must include the concept of relevance vis a vis the statutory obligations and considerations that regulate the Board's decision making functions. (para. 17)

In other words, the victim's view could not supersede a careful consideration of all relevant matters.[73] As with the use of sexual history evidence in the precedents discussed earlier, the victim submission is viewed as one of many considerations for the Board (and therefore, the court) to take into account. Inherent to this position is the idea of balancing 'relevant'[74] information from different sources. Indeed, the use of balance rhetoric has become a consistent theme in the court rulings of all the countries under review when dealing with victim issues as demonstrated by the extract from the Canadian Supreme Court reproduced on p. 155–156.[75] This seems to reflect a general principle, adopted in most jurisdictions, of leaving it to the discretion of judges in individual cases to determine the proper weight to be given to information obtained from victims in various court decisions. As a general rule, the courts have in turn sought to avoid being overly prescriptive on such matters. For example, in the case of *Angus Sinclair v Her Majesty's Advocate*,[76] heard by the Scottish High Court of the Judiciary, the court specifically declined to comment on the Crown's argument that 'the right of an accused to a fair trial under Article 6 might require to be balanced against the rights of victims or their relatives to have effective proceedings brought against persons accused of serious crime. It might on the other hand be that victims' rights could be encompassed within the scope of a "fair trial"' (para. 9).

In sum, it is clear that victims have attained a new prominence in judicial decisions in most of the countries under review over the last 20 years, adding judicial weight to the rights set down in charters and legislation. It has been demonstrated that this applies particularly to rights of consultation and privacy, although the courts' consideration of victims does not end there. For example, the Canadian Supreme Court has stated in *R v R.E.M.*[77] that providing *explanations* to a victim of crime as to why a conviction is or is not entered is 'no less important' than a trial judge giving reasons for his or decisions to defendants. This reflects the victim's right to information and explanation discussed earlier in this chapter. In addition, the English cases of *R v Billam*[78] and *R v Millberry*[79] both acknowledge that the sentencing discount to be expected by defendants who plead guilty prior to a trial in cases of rape is partly based on the fact that victims will be spared the distressing experience of giving evidence in open court about what had happened to them, even where their identities were protected. This demonstrates judicial application of the victim's right to protection from undue distress and intimidation. Finally, it is clear from a number of Irish Supreme Court judgments that victims in that jurisdiction have a right to make an allegation of criminal activity affecting them to relevant authorities.[80] Such victims do not have the right to expect such complaints to result in a full criminal investigation, charge or prosecution, but capricious decisions to drop such cases can be the subject of review by the courts.[81]

Judges then are taking note of the principles espoused in victims' charters and associated legislation, despite the absence of formal enforcement mechanisms from most of them. What this suggests is that the occupational culture and practices of judges can be influenced by less formal mechanisms which brings us full circle back to Brienen and Hoegen's (2000) point that the Terwee Guidelines have been publicized to the point that they can no longer be ignored by the authorities. This notion of victims' rights being facilitated through changes in occupational *cultures* in the criminal justice system of the nine jurisdictions under review, rather than changes in law or legal precedent, will be returned to in Chapter 7.

Victims' rights in international courts

We may now be moving closer to a stage where 'victims' rights' are clarified and documented within international statutes and case law which also provide firm enforcement mechanisms. This is particularly apparent across Europe where the *Maria Pupino*[82] and *Katz*[83] rulings from the European Court of Justice regarding the impact of the 2001 EU *Framework Decision* have already been discussed.[84] In addition to this, several rulings from the European Court of Human Rights (ECtHR) now appear to offer victims giving evidence in court a degree of protection from undue intimidation. For example, the cases of *Baegen* v *Netherlands*[85] and *Doorson* v *Netherlands*[86] confirm that keeping witnesses (including victim witnesses) anonymous in order to reduce intimidation and enhance protection does not breach a defendant's Article 6 rights under the Convention[87] to a fair trial, provided their evidence can still be effectively challenged. In addition, the case of *Sn* v *Sweden*[88] confirms that Article 6 does not grant the defence an unlimited right to secure the appearance of witnesses in court (Ellison 2003). The *Sn* case also maintains that witnesses can give evidence through recorded interviews without breaching Article 6. Doak (2005) further contends that victims might also find favour under Articles 3 and 8 of the Convention if they are treated in a degrading manner by the criminal justice system or the state fails to protect their rights to privacy when giving evidence. As with the domestic courts, however the ECtHR has resisted interpretations of the Convention which afford victims more explicit influence over decision making in sentencing, although in *T and V* v *UK*[89] the parents of a young murder victim were allowed to make representations to the Court.

On a wider scale, Oda J. of the International Court of Justice has referred to the notion of having victims having rights in his dissenting opinion in the case of *LaGrand (Germany* v *United States of America)*. The case concerned an application on the part of Germany to delay the execution of one of its nationals (Walter LaGrand) by the State of Arizona following his conviction for murder. In his critique of the majority opinion to grant the order, Oda J. puts forward the argument that: '[If] Mr. Walter LaGrand's rights as they relate to humanitarian issues are to be respected then, in parallel, the matter of the rights of victims of violent crime (a point which has often been overlooked) should be taken into consideration'.[90]

Victims' participation rights have also been recognized in the first criminal trial of the International Criminal Court, where 93 victims were permitted to present impact statements. These victims were mainly children enlisted as soldiers by the defendant, Thomas Lubanga, as a rebel leader in the Democratic Republic of the Congo. Nevertheless, McDermott (2009) has criticized the manner in which these statements were dealt with and, in particular, the fact that they contained information about war crimes not listed in the official indictment.

The 'normalization' of victims' rights?

It is clear from the above discussion that, as highlighted in Chapter 3, the rhetoric surrounding victims' rights has taken a firm hold in all nine of the jurisdictions under review in this volume. Generally speaking, such rights as have been afforded to victims tend to conform to a fairly standardized list of service rights, reflecting expectations found within international instruments such as the UN *Declaration* of 1985 and the 2001 EU *Framework Decision*. This includes rights to information, protection, compensation and/or restitution, and more general guarantees concerning sympathetic and respectful treatment from all criminal justice actors. As noted earlier, this is quite in keeping with the findings of much of the research into victims' expectations across multiple jurisdictions, which suggests that victims of crime generally do not expect or desire to exert significant control over decision making in the criminal justice system (Shapland *et al*. 1985). Nevertheless, it is evident that participation rights for victims, in the form of *consultation* on specific decisions, have likewise become the norm in all these countries, with victims' views typically being sought on prosecution decisions; sentencing (with regards to the impact of crime); and parole decisions (sometimes as part of enhanced information schemes). Importantly, however, in none of these jurisdictions are the views of victims binding on criminal justice professionals, but rather constitute one of many factors to be considered and balanced alongside other relevant information. Clearly this reflects the concerns voiced by proponents of the strict due process approach to criminal justice that to extend victims' participation and influence within the system will have a detrimental impact on the rights of defendants. The existence of a zero sum game between victim and defendant rights continues to be debated, although arguments to the effect that the relationship is not as straightforward as this label might suggest have been discussed earlier. The arguments put forward by Sanders and Young (2000) and Erez (1999) attempt to chart ways around this perceived conflict of rights, although no universally accepted solution has been forthcoming.

The fact that similar types of rights have been uncovered across the nine countries under review is testament to the globalized nature of the victim issue. Indeed, in England and Wales the JUSTICE Committee has pointed out that modern debates on victims' rights tend to concern themselves less with the content of those rights and more with mechanisms for delivery and accountability (JUSTICE Committee 1998). On this point, it has been shown that the enforcement of victims' rights in these jurisdictions tends to be placed outside the formal criminal process, in separate complaints mechanisms or in references to ombudsmen and their equivalents, who tend to lack specific powers of compulsion or redress. The apparent lack of enforcement provisions is a significant issue and, following the arguments of Jackson (2003), could be said to negate any claim that victims are indeed being afforded genuine rights whether these be classified as service rights or rights of participation. While most countries have now grounded victims' rights in statutory charters, neither the charters themselves nor their governing legislation tend to offer detailed enforcement mechanisms other than those described earlier. That said, clearly the grounding of such rights in statute is significant, and a positive development from previous efforts to introduce charters and lists of service standards with no basis in legislation at all. Indeed, the significance of this development from non-statutory to statutory charters is acknowledged by Victim Support Australasia (2009: para. 4.3) in the following terms:

> Victim Support Australasia Inc views legislated obligations couched in terms of 'rights' as carrying more authority, symbolism, acknowledgement and enforceability. An administrative charter 'is a form of quasi-legislation embodying rules which are not directly enforceable in civil or criminal proceedings'.

Despite these sentiments, this analysis raises real questions as to whether this new statutory basis does much in practice to enhance the enforceability of these charters in any of the countries under review. As late as 1993, three years after the Dutch Supreme Court had recognized the Terwee Guidelines as a source of law, Swart (1993) was still able to convincingly argue that, in practice, victims had no rights in the Dutch criminal justice system. One possible answer to this is that, while strictly speaking these enforcement mechanisms lack legal power, the impact of such statutory provisions has been an increased acknowledgement of victims' rights (including participation rights) by judges in all the jurisdictions under review. As such, while little official action within the justice process can result from the breach of these rights, their symbolic impact upon the occupational practices of the judiciary (as well as the rest of the legal professions) has been quite extensive both in national and international courts.

Fundamentally, this analysis indicates that the concept of victims' rights is becoming normalized across these jurisdictions both as a matter of policy and as a matter of judicial and legal practice. By contrast, until relatively recently victims' rights have been viewed as unusual and novel compared with defendants' rights: which are considered sacrosanct and inherent to the criminal justice process. Hence, while Ashworth (2000: 189) refers to the "normal" rights' of defendants both this author and Edwards (2002) have objected to any 'common sense' grounding of victims' rights. Speaking in the Irish context, Hanly (2003: 8) has criticized this tendency to conceptualize victims' rights as unusual and in need of extra justification, even when they are being supported: 'The promotion of human rights should not require any utilitarian justification. We do not feel the need to justify the protection of the defendant's fair trial rights by reference to some other objective'. Here, Hanly grounds his argument on the notion that victims' rights are an application of broader human rights, which has also been the position taken by the South African Government[91]. Although the author acknowledges that the focus of national and international human rights instruments on the rights of the defendant 'is not without justification' (p. 11) (owing to the inequalities of resources available to the state to prosecute defendants and to the defendants to mount their defence), his basic position remains that both victim and defendant rights constitute human rights and should be approached with similar standards.

In sum, the real impact of this move towards the statutory grounding of victims' rights may lie not so much in their increased judiciability but in their normalization of victims' rights as a concept that the courts feel able to openly reflect on and apply. To some advocates of victims' rights this compromise will no doubt be unsatisfactory, and in particular there is a concern that rights understood on this basis are doomed to ambiguity and inconsistent application. At worst such rights may be reduced to mere rhetoric. On this point, a recent report from the European Commission criticizes the 2001 *EU Framework Decision* on the basis that while the document promises victims 'a real and appropriate role in criminal proceedings' (Art.2(1)), no indication is given of what this might mean. In a similar vein, the South African Department of Justice and Constitutional Development (2008: 4) has admitted that due to the vagueness of the South African Victims' Charter government departments initially applied its principles 'sporadically'. On the other hand, it has already been noted how victims' rights have developed through judicial interpretation in the short time they have been addressed directly by national and international courts. As such, the argument that victims' rights may become robust and *in effect* judiciable through changes in judicial culture, as opposed to the imposition of legal rules and enforcement mechanisms, still holds some currency.

Notes

1. As hypothesized in Chapter 1.
2. See pp. 102–107.
3. For example, giving victims the choice over whether or not to give evidence over a video-link may be relatively uncontroversial compared to affording them influence over prosecution or sentencing decisions (see Hall 2009).
4. See also JUSTICE Committee (1998).
5. Erez maintains that exposure to victim impact statements will give practitioners a more realistic impression of 'normal' levels of impact (Erez 1999; Erez and Rogers 1999).
6. Although it is unknown whether a disproportionate number of 'ideal' victims or potential victims tend to participate in such studies and therefore whether such results reflect the views of atypical victims of crime.
7. See Chapter 7.
8. A similar argument has been taken up taken up by Cape (2004).
9. For simplicity the term 'charter' will be used in this section as an all-purpose descriptor of the various codes, guidelines and service standards used in the nine jurisdictions under review with comparable legal force.
10. Required under the Domestic Violence, Crime and Victims Act 2004.
11. Based on the Australian Capital Territory Victims Act 1994.
12. For 'serious crimes'. The guidelines were expanded to all crime the following year.
13. See p. 71.
14. 19 June 1990, *Nederlandse Jurisprudentie* 1991, nr. 119.
15. Unlike the *Vaillant Guidelines*, which were unknown to many police officers (Wemmers 1996).
16. See pp. 62–66 for a discussion of the enforceability of the Declaration.
17. Australian Capital Territory Victims of Crime Act 1994, s.4(a)).
18. See Rock (1990).
19. Which will be the subject of more in depth analysis in Chapter 7.
20. Although in England and Wales this is limited to family and partners of homicide victims.
21. See p. 113.

22 At the federal level. Individual territories and provinces have their own charters generally modelled around this document.
23 The exceptions here being the New Zealand Charter and the *Canadian Statement of Basic Principles of Justice for Victims of Crime.*
24 Despite the significance of this development we should note the findings of Wemmers (1996) that restitution is still quite rare in the Netherlands criminal justice system.
25 With the possible exception of Edwards's (2004) 'information provision' category of participation.
26 In all other jurisdictions under review in this study private prosecutions are possible but very rare.
27 Which are called Victim Personal Statements in England and Wales and Scotland.
28 England and Wales, South Africa, New Zealand and Australia (New South Wales).
29 The New Zealand Charter also provides for victims to take concerns to an ombudsman.
30 The actual appointment of such a Commissioner (Louise Casey) did not occur until March 2010. In the interim, Sara Payne, the mother of murdered schoolgirl Sarah Payne, was appointed 'independent Victims' Champion' in January 2009 with a mandate to 'act in an advisory role on victims' issues'. See http://www.justice.gov.uk/news/newsrelease260109b.htm and http://www.justice.gov.uk/ news/newsrelease300310b.htm].
31 The Parliamentary Commissioner can *recommend* that agencies provide redress.
32 See p. 144.
33 Replacing the Victims of Offences Act 1987 which, though less detailed, was still essentially a charter of service rights based on the 1985 UN Declaration.
34 Consisting of the Attorneys General from all seven states and territories.
35 Known as 'Marsy's Law'.
36 *Nasci* v *Pope*, Supreme Court of the State of New Mexico, 8 November 2006, no. 29878.
37 18 USC 3771.
38 18 USC 3771(a)(4).
39 18 USC 3771(d)(4).
40 As amended by the Coroners and Justice Act 2009.
41 Criminal Justice Act 1999.
42 With provisions relating to child witnesses previously being clarified in the Children Act of 1997. See pp. 45–47 for more discussion of the roll-out of special measures provisions in the countries under review.
43 Discussion of judicial reactions to such laws in domestic courts can be found on pp. 155–156.
44 s.34, amending the Criminal Law (Rape) Act 1981.

45 See Chapter 1.
46 See Chapter 4.
47 See p. 38.
48 This was confirmed for the purposes of this research by correspondence with representatives of the South African Department of Justice and Constitutional Development.
49 See p. 144. Technically the opinions of the Supreme Court of The Netherlands are non-binding on lower courts, although in practice its judgments do tend to be followed (Tak 2003).
50 Laws to restrict the circumstances in which the defence can cross-examine a victim of rape as to his or her past sexual history.
51 [1991] 2 S.C.R. 577.
52 [1995] 4 S.C.R. 411.
53 [1999] 3 S.C.R. 668.
54 [2002] Crim. L.R. 73.
55 (1993) 67 A Crim R 549.
56 Colorado Supreme Court. No. 06SC705. 4 February 2008. Lawyers USA No. 9939305.
57 The Court applied the same logic to victim impact statements in *R v Swietlinski* [1994] 3 S.C.R. 481.
58 See pp. 155–160.
59 *Attorney General Reference No.2 of 1995 (R v S)* [1995] Crim. L.R. 835. See Shapland (2002).
60 The *Code of Practice for Victims of Crime* now refers to a victim's 'right' to make a victim personal statement.
61 (1991) 57 A Crim R 391 (NSW CCA).
62 *Kenna v United States District Court for the Central District of California* 435 F.3d 1011 (9th Cir. 2006).
63 501 US (1991).
64 555 US (2008); Nos. 07–11073 and 07–11425.
65 With the possible exception of South Africa.
66 *United States v Wood* Nos. S-08-0195, S-09-0196, 2009 WL 2517175 (Wyo. Aug. 19 2009).
67 *SH v DPP* [2006] 3 IR 575, per Murray C.J.
68 [2001] All E.R. 449.
69 Now the Supreme Court.
70 [2009] WLR (D) 155. One anomalous case discussed by Edwards (2002) is that of *R v Perks* [2000] All ER (D) 763 in which the court seemed to be indicating that a sentence could be moderated if it aggravated the victim's distress or the victim's forgiveness indicates that his or her psychological or mental suffering must be very much less than would normally be the case. Thus, in certain circumstances, the victim's choice to forgive a defendant becomes relevant to sentencing.
71 HC WN CIV 2007-485-2809 [9 July 2008].
72 Which requires that the Board ensures 'that the rights of victims (as defined in s.4 of the Victims' Rights Act 2002) are upheld, and submissions

by victims (as so defined) and any restorative justice outcomes are given due weight'.
73 A fact reflected in most policy documents on the issue from across the nine jurisdictions. For example, the principle Canadian federal strategy for victims is entitled *Victims' Rights: A Voice Not a Veto*.
74 The concept of 'relevance' is a familiar tenant of the law of criminal evidence in most common law jurisdictions (Ho 2008).
75 And, according to Jackson (1990), in criminal justice policy rhetoric in general.
76 [2007] HCJAC 27.
77 [2008] 3 S.C.R. 3, 2008 SCC 51.
78 [1986] 8 Cr. App. R. (S) 48.
79 [2003] 1 Cr. App. R. 25.
80 *R v Dytham* Q.B. 722 (an English precedent) applied by *DPP v Bartly Criminal Liability* (Dublin 2000).
81 *Fowler v Conroy* [2005] IEHC 26.9.
82 Case C-105/03 *Maria Pupino*.
83 Case C-404/07 *György Kaz v István Roland Sós*.
84 See pp. 76–77.
85 Application No. 16696/90, 26th October 1995.
86 [1996] 23 EHRR 330. Although in June 2008 the House of Lord's judgment in *R v Davis (Iain)* seemed to restrict the use of anonymous evidence in British courts. The government responded by swiftly changing the law to reverse the ruling by rushing through the Criminal Evidence (Witness Anonymity) Act in July of the same year. The relevant provisions are now found under the Coroners and Justice Act 2009.
87 Convention for the Protection of Human Rights and Fundamental Freedoms, Rome, 4.XI.1950.
88 Application No. 34209/96, 2 July 2002.
89 [2000] Crim. L.R. 287.
90 I.C.J. Report-1 999 (I): p. 18, per Oda J.
91 See pp. 154–155.

Chapter 6

Compensation, restitution and restorative justice

In examining the provision of compensation and restorative justice to victims of crime in the nine countries under review, this chapter encompasses what may be seen as both the earliest and the most recent developments in policies impacting upon such victims. This is so because such provisions generally began in these and other jurisdictions with the accordance of some form of (state-based) compensation to victims of specific types of (usually violent) crime. Young (1997b) has therefore listed the establishment of state compensation as an important factor in the development of the international victims' movement and Rock (1986, 1990) presents compensation as a key influence on the development of victim policy making in England and Wales and Canada specifically. Over the years such moves have expanded with the introduction of offender-based compensation, 'restitution' scheme[1], and the establishment of victims' funds financed by surcharges imposed on offenders. Most recently, all nine jurisdictions under review have experimented with various forms of restorative justice. This chapter will therefore examine and compare the development and provision of state compensation, restitution and restorative justice to victims of crime in the nine countries under review. The goal of this analysis will be to gauge the significance of theses issue within the wider policy network[2] of victim reform found within and between all these jurisdictions, along with their relative impact.

State compensation schemes

Justifying state compensation

In 1951, English activist Margaret Fry presented the argument that the state should provide some degree of compensation for the personal injuries suffered by victims as a result of violent crime. Fry's conception of such a system was that it would be based around the existing industrial injuries scheme in operation in England and Wales (now known as Industrial Injuries Disablement Benefit), and grounded on the same welfare principles. The scheme eventually introduced in England and Wales in 1964[3] eschewed this route in favour of a system based on common law damages. Nevertheless, as Miers (1997: 10) points out, in so doing the UK Government failed to set out any clear theoretical basis on which the scheme was to be constituted, and indeed has since never truly 'come to terms with what was being contemplated by the introduction of the scheme; namely, the creation of a system of state funded compensation for victims of intentional torts to the person'.

Similar observations can be made in other jurisdictions. For example, the Californian government code which provides the legal basis for California's state compensation scheme justifies the scheme's existence in the following (abstract) terms: 'The Legislature finds and declares that it is in the public interest to assist residents of the State of California in obtaining compensation for the pecuniary losses they suffer as a direct result of criminal acts'.[4] The same observations have been made in New Zealand, the site of the world's first state-based compensation scheme for victims of crime, where a recent report from the Law Commission in that jurisdiction concludes that developments in compensation provision have generally been ad hoc and pragmatic: 'They have been introduced in a piecemeal fashion without much regard to any underlying principles about where the burden of harm resulting from crime should fall' (New Zealand Law Commission 2008: para. 1.2).

In the case of The Netherlands, when contacted for this research on the question of justifying state-based compensation, a representative of the Dutch state compensation scheme (*Schadefonds Geweldsmisdrijven*) listed the following eclectic mixture of justifications for that system's existence:

– The victim should not only be reliant on his civil rights claims to get reimbursed.

– To the offender, the victim and the community, a more direct relationship between damage and restoration is a desirability, from a standpoint of conflict resolution.
– The Ministry of Justice has an important account [sic] in the context of the overall welfare.
– There should be more focus on victims. Previously, in criminal law and criminal sciences practice the focus was more on the offender.
– The community has a special responsibility to the victims of crimes, and violent crime in particular. (2009)

There is a strong emphasis on welfare concerns in this response, as well as the collective responsibility of the state and the community to care for victims. There is also a recognition that state compensation to some extent acknowledges the victim in a way the criminal justice system previously did not.

As such, Rock (1990) has observed that, in England and Wales and elsewhere, the introduction of state compensation was largely based on a presumption that victims wanted it, and indeed might turn to vigilantism without it. The implications of this are that compensation originally surfaced on the policy scene in a most ad hoc manner, far removed from the modern focus on evidence-based policies discussed in Chapter 4 and witnessed across all jurisdictions in more recent years.

The literature in this area offers a number of well-rehearsed positions from which state compensation can be justified. The most common of these portrays such schemes as an extension of the welfare state.[5] This ties well with van Dijk's (1983) discussion of a care ideology as one possible basis for victimogogic measures more generally.[6] Alternative justifications place liability for criminal injuries with the state by reason of a perceived breach of the social contract in allowing crimes to occur; in effect a form of torteouse negligence on the part of the government (Edelhertz and Geis 1974). Other arguments favour the redistribution of the costs of crime to the masses and, more recently, the notion that compensating victims will lead to increased satisfaction and cooperation with the criminal justice processes has gained prominence. In Texas, for example, the Attorney General's office presents the primary purpose of the state's Crime Victims Compensation Program as 'encouraging greater victim participation in the apprehension and prosecution of criminals' (Office of the Attorney General of Texas 2009: n.p.). Miers (1991, 1997) has expanded at length on the view that each of these justifications are 'for various reasons and to varying degrees unconvincing' (p. 3). Both Miers and Elias (1983) emphasize the heavily political character of state compensation as a concept. This echoes the earlier statements of Harland (1978), writing from a US perspective, to the effect that state compensation programmes are often grounded in the contemporary emotional and political climate, created in the wake of tragic and dramatic events or victim rallies:

> The reality of state-funded victim compensation seems to be that it is an extremely limited service available to only a minute proportion of those who suffer loss or injury as a result of crime. Too often, however, this reality is cloaked in a political show of concern for victims, while the underlying fears of costs continue to emerge in the form of programme restrictions. (p. 213)

Or, as Miers (1997: 10) describes:

> One of the most notable features of the introduction of criminal injury compensation schemes in common law jurisdictions has been that they have often been immediately preceded by the commission of a particularly serious crime of violence against a vulnerable or altruistic victim, which in turn occasioned a public campaign in favour of 'doing something' for victims of crime.

Clear examples and comparisons of the mediatized effect Miers and Harland have in mind can be drawn from the USA and the UK following the compensation schemes set up in the aftermath of the terrorist attacks in New York and London in 2001 and 2005 respectively. As noted in Chapter 1, the former scheme received criticism for the large amount of money it paid out (put at over US$38 billion in total), whereas the latter scheme provoked criticism regarding the perceived low level of payments.[7]

State compensation systems were introduced in all the jurisdictions under review, with the exception of South Africa, between 1963 and 1976.[8] In South Africa, interviews with representatives of the Department of Justice and Constitutional Development indicated that the possibility of introducing such a scheme had been investigated in 2006. The Department had dismissed the idea mainly on the grounds that, given the nature and level of crime in South Africa coupled with the likely popularity of such a scheme, state compensation was not financially viable.

Victims and Policy Making

All such schemes introduced in the countries under review maintain that their existence in no way amounts to an acknowledgement of liability on the part of the state for criminal injuries. For example, the Irish scheme justifies itself in the following terms:

> The necessity for such a Scheme arose from the fact that perpetrators, as a general principle, do not have sufficient funds to pay the level of damages that would be awarded by the courts under the Civil Liability Act 1961. In effect, the victims of crime had no legal remedy available for their injuries ... Under the Scheme the State takes the place of the offender in terms of compensating the victim. The State, however, does not accept liability for the offence in which the victim suffered injury. (Irish Criminal Injuries Compensation Tribunal 2009: 1)

This justification essentially grounds compensation on common law damages as a solution to the frequent problem of offenders having less financial resources with which to compensate individual victims directly[9] (see Nagin *et al*. 1995). Early schemes in Canada followed similar reasoning. This is demonstrated by a 1968 report advocating the introduction of state compensation for victims of violent crime in Alberta:

> We are in an era when society recognises many new obligations; for example, the care of victims of cancer and tuberculoses. A closer parallel is that of compensation when a person is injured from the negligence of car drivers as provided in the unsatisfied Judgment Fund. (Institute of Law Research and Reform 1968: 3)

Nevertheless, a review of such schemes reveals that they often contain provisos to the effect that they are not intended to *match* the levels of common law damages that might be expected from taking action against offenders, but should be viewed more as a symbolic gesture. This perspective is demonstrated by the system in operation in Queensland since 2005, which was revised in December 2009:[10]

> The purpose of the COVA [Criminal Offence Victims Act 2005] scheme is to recognise the impact of crime on victims and help with the financial cost of injuries. However, as in all other jurisdictions, it is not intended to reflect the amount of compensation a victim may receive at common law. (Queensland Department of Justice and Attorney General 2009: 13)

Similarly, the Dutch scheme makes the following stipulation:

> The Fund does not pay full compensation, but rather an allowance for personal injury. The amount of this one-off payment may therefore differ from the actual amount of damage you suffer. (Schadefonds Geweldsmisdrijven 2008: 6)

Of course, such disclaimers are partly intended to ensure that the costs of these schemes do not escalate out of control. This has been a considerable problem for most state compensation systems since their inception (Rock 1986) which, as noted earlier, prevented South Africa from introducing such a system from the offset. This issue will be returned to later.

Returning to the justifications of such schemes, from the US perspective Edelhertz and Geis (1974: 110) categorize early state-based compensation programmes in California (introduced in 1965)[11] and New York (introduced in 1967) as 'welfare-orientated'. It is notable however that in more recent years both these schemes have become part funded by surcharges placed on offenders and by the proceeds of fines, rather than wholly state or federal monies. As a consequence, the schemes have grown more akin to restitution than state compensation.

In New Zealand, the world's (first) state compensation system for victims of crime, as originally conceived, appears to have been based on the philosophy of spreading the costs of crime around the community (New Zealand Law Commission 2008). The present legislation also refers to 'enhanc[ing] the public good and reinforc[ing] the social Contract',[12] although here the New Zealand Law Commission (2008: para. 4.3) has recently called for a major rethink of the groundings of the system:

> Victims' compensation schemes cannot be justified on the basis of abstract notions about the social contract between state and citizen. Furthermore, while some initiatives may be able to be justified on a cost-benefit analysis, it is generally difficult to justify special treatment of crime victims on grounds of social utility. Accordingly, should any changes be considered desirable, they are likely to be justified primarily by the need to maintain public confidence in the justice system and their symbolic value and an expression of public sympathy to crime victims.

This singling-out of confidence in the criminal justice system by the New Zealand Law Commission as a principal justification for such schemes is in keeping with discussions in Chapter 4 relating to the growing importance of this issue in the policy network as a whole across jurisdictions. It also resonates with Garland's (2001) and Boutellier's (2000) conception of victim reform as a means of legitimizing the criminal justice system, though such schemes are usually independent from the formal criminal process itself. Again this construction dismisses any direct liability on the part of the state for criminal victimization, whether on the basis of a social contract or on other grounds. The extract also raises what has become a key question in such debates: that of why victims of *crime* should be singled out for special attention, assistance, and (public) funding compared to victims of other social misfortunes.[13] Again the history of most state compensation systems betrays confusion on this point as demonstrated by the further reasoning of the 1968 Alberta report:

> Why should victims of crime be singled out for assistance from the public purse? We base our recommendation on the plight of the victims and the fact that his injuries have arisen from the wrongful acts of an element in society. There is a connection between the social breakdown manifested in crime and injury to innocent citizens. (Institute of Law Research and Reform 1968: 3)

As might be expected, this report presents the familiar disclaimer that its recommendation for the introduction of a state compensation scheme 'does not rest on the argument that the machinery of law enforcement has broken down, or on the proposition that the state is under a duty to compensate' (p. 3). In so doing, the above comment is rendered markedly obscure.

Of course the question of why victims of *crime* are so important also recalls some of the earliest debates of the victims' movement prior to the widespread focusing of victimology on victims of crime specifically.[14] In New Zealand this dilemma is circumvented (although only rhetorically) by including criminal victimization under the definition of an accident. Hence victims fall within the scope of the wider Accident Compensation Scheme set out in the Prevention, Rehabilitation and Compensation Act 2001.

In sum, most of the state compensation systems in the jurisdictions under review continue to rely on traditional and vague statements of their theoretical justification. Notions of 'welfare', 'spreading costs', and 'recognition of victims' suffering' are touted widely, although increasingly concerns regarding public satisfaction with the criminal

Compensation, restitution and restorative justice

justice system and governments' handling of victims more generally are coming to the forefront. The more substantive point to be drawn from this is that the development and implementation of state-based compensation systems seems to reflect wider debates and influences on the national, transnational and international policy network(s) as a whole. These include: the special position of crime victims (and their suffering) in the national and international consciousness, and the use of victims to legitimize, promote, and assist the state's efforts to tackle crime.

State compensation: a review of the schemes

While the state-based compensation schemes available to victims of crime in the eight relevant jurisdictions[15] vary in terms of the detail provided in their constituting documents,[16] most follow a similar model of eligibility and payments, again suggesting a degree of globalization to such provisions. One characteristic of all these schemes is that they are relatively restrictive in terms of the scope of victimization and the impacts of crime they cover. As such, they are all principally aimed at victims of violent crime who suffer physical injury. Both the English and the New Zealand systems employ the term 'personal injury' which encompasses physical and mental injury, although eligibility to claim for the latter category is typically more restricted in all jurisdictions.[17] The Irish scheme refers to 'personal injury where the injury is directly attributable to a crime of violence' (Irish Criminal Injuries Compensation Tribunal 2009: para. 1) and indeed it is clear that a link between the compensated harm and a violent crime (or at least an attempted violent crime) must usually be present in all these schemes. North American state-based compensation schemes in both Canada[18] and the USA (Californian Victim Compensation and Government Claims Board 2009) tend to be especially prescriptive in this regard, providing extensive schedules of specific 'qualifying offences',[19] most of which are crimes of violence or sexual crimes (the latter often being classified as a constituent of the former). The New Zealand system has a similar list. This approach can be compared to the one seen in many Australian jurisdictions, and in particular New South Wales, where the relevant legislation[20] provides lists of *injuries suffered* as opposed to *crimes committed*.

One common exception to the rule that a (potential) crime of violence must be involved in order for victims to receive state compensation relates to the provision of compensation for victims who attempt to assist police officers in arrests or to prevent crimes themselves. The

Irish and UK models both compensate victims for injuries 'arising from the action of the victim in assisting or attempting to assist the prevention of crime or the saving of human life' (Irish Criminal Injuries Compensation Tribunal 2009: para. 1) *without* specifying that the relevant crime or attempted crime be one of violence. The Quebec provincial compensation programme similarly compensates victims injured 'while lawfully preventing or attempting to prevent the commission of an offence or suspected offence, or assisting a peace officer preventing or attempting to prevent the commission of an offence or suspected offence'.[21] The scheme in operation in New South Wales also compensates those who try to prevent crime, although here eligibility is once again limited to the prevention of crimes of violence. That said, it is significant that this latter scheme also provides compensation for those *witnessing* a crime of violence (provided they too have suffered a 'compensable injury')[22] as does the scheme in Victoria.[23] A further (unique) exception to the general requirement in such schemes for there to be a connection between a compensable injury and a crime of violence is found in the UK system where victims suffering personal injury as a result of the offence of trespass on a railway can also claim compensation. This provision was made part of the UK system in response to a particular problem in that jurisdiction of train drivers and operators suffering extensive and long-term mental injuries as a result of unavoidably colliding with trespassers on the railway lines (see UK Department of Transport 2004).

All the state-based compensation schemes under review extend to offering compensation to the families of those suffering fatal injuries as a result of crime. The Californian scheme refers to such claimants as 'derivative victims' who are legally dependant on the (primary) victim at the time of the crime and include (but are not limited to) a victim's children (including unborn children), domestic partner, spouse and any incapacitated, dependent adult. In Canada, the Quebec system is even wider in this regard, providing compensation to 'close relations' of the deceased, which are very widely construed under the Quebec Crime Victims Compensation Act 1996:

> For the purposes of this section, 'close relation' means the victim's spouse, the victim's father or mother or a person standing in loco parentis to the victim, the victim's child or the victim's spouse's child, the victim's brother or sister, the victim's grandfather or grandmother or the child of the spouse of the victim's father or mother. (s.1(c))

and

> For the purposes of subparagraph 1 of the first paragraph (1) 'close relation' also means any other significant person in the victim's life, chosen by the victim. (s.5.1(1))

Generally speaking the schemes in all eight relevant jurisdictions cover similar lists of dependants in fatal cases: called 'family victims' in the Australian Northern Territories scheme.[24] However, some schemes are more restrictive as to the scope of this group than others. For example, the UK system restricts compensation in fatal cases to children, spouses, partners and parents of the deceased. In contrast, the corresponding Dutch list excludes the parents of the victim.

In theory, none of the state compensation systems reviewed for this project requires a conviction to be achieved against a perpetrator, or indeed for any perpetrator to be identified, in order for a victim to receive compensation. Among the Australian states and territories, Queensland has until recently been a notable exception: where prior to December 2009 applications were normally made through the court. The state's newly revised system now explicitly dismisses any requirements for a conviction to be achieved (Queensland Department of Justice and Attorney General 2008). In New Zealand, a similar philosophy has been advocated by the courts, where it has been asserted that the civil standard of proof is sufficient to award victims compensation under the state compensation system:

> A key feature of s.21 [of the Injury Prevention, Rehabilitation and Compensation Act 2001] is that a person is entitled to cover for any act falling 'within the description of these offences'. Cover is not dependent upon whether or not a person has been charged or convicted of that offence. The section clearly envisages situations where the perpetrator of the act or acts in question cannot be identified or located, or otherwise charged with the offence. It also extends to situations where there has been an acquittal or where the offence is not capable of proof beyond reasonable doubt, but may still be proven to the civil standard for the purposes of the Act.[25]

Similarly, s.13 of the 1996 Crime Victims Compensation Act of Quebec states that an application may be made for compensation 'whether or not any person is prosecuted for or convicted of the offence giving rise to material damage, injury or death'. The UK (UK Criminal Injuries Compensation Authority 2008) and Irish (Irish Criminal Injuries Compensation Tribunal 2009) models have similar rules. However, in other cases the lack of a requirement for a conviction is less clear cut. For example, while the Californian scheme has no such direct requirement it is noted that:

> Significant weight may be given to the evidence from and conclusions of a law enforcement agency after investigation of the qualifying crime when determining whether or not a qualifying crime occurred. (Californian Victim Compensation and Government Claims Board 2009: para. 649.38)

This implies that a decision not to proceed with a prosecution from the District Attorney may exert a marked influence on the determination of any victims' compensation claim.

While primarily focused on physical injuries resulting from violent crime, all the schemes reviewed make some provision for mental injuries suffered as a result of crime. In most cases it is envisioned that such mental injury will have occurred *in addition* to some form of physical injury, preserving the essential violent crime/physical injury core to these schemes, although there are limited circumstances where mental injury alone can be compensated. In the UK, such compensation may occur when a victim is put in reasonable fear of immediate physical harm to his or her own person, or had a close relationship of love and affection with another person at the time when that person sustained physical and/or mental injury and either witnessed said injuries or was closely involved with the aftermath.[26] It should be noted that this provision still effectively links the compensable injury closely to incidents of violent crime and (the apprehension of) physical injury. Most other schemes from across the eight relevant jurisdictions have similar provisions, with the New Zealand system being slightly more restrictive in limiting compensation for mental injuries alone to cases of sexual offences.[27] Another distinctive example is that of the Irish scheme, which is fairly vague as to what is meant by 'injury' and is not specific as to how mental injuries will be assessed. Where mental injuries are compensated, all these schemes require the onset of an actual medically diagnosed condition, as opposed to mere upset or distress, although the Dutch scheme does offer a one-off payment for 'mental suffering inflicted on victims provided that the victim has also suffered a 'serious' physical and/or mental injury' (Schadefonds Geweldsmisdrijven 2008: 2).

Compensation, restitution and restorative justice

As noted earlier, most state-based compensation schemes make it clear that they are not intended to provide full monetary compensation for all losses incurred by qualifying victims or their families. Most of the schemes employ a system of assessing each case individually (within certain predefined limits) and base the amount of compensation awarded on equivalent civil damages. For example, the Irish scheme refers to the Irish Civil Liabilities Act 1961.[28] Other schemes are more prescriptive. This is particularly the case in the UK, where compensation payments are based on a fixed tariff: matching monetary awards to specific descriptions of injuries in what Easteal (1998: 200) calls a 'Table of Maims'. No discretion is preserved to vary such awards in individual cases. For example, a standard lump sum payment of £11,000 is paid in all cases where the primary victim has died as a result of criminal injuries. Queensland and New South Wales have employed similar tables. The Dutch system too makes a standard payment of €10,000 in cases of death,[29] which at interview representatives of Victim Support Netherlands described as symbolic. Nevertheless, even where cases are dealt with more individually, the schemes all impose arbitrary maximums in different situations. Furthermore, with particular reference to the Australian schemes, there is a growing sense that *monetary* compensation is less important than offering victims access to counselling and rehabilitation through state-based compensation mechanisms.[30] As such, schemes in Victoria, Queensland, New South Wales and New Zealand have all recently placed greater emphasis on such services (Easteal 1998). Similarly, the UK scheme has recently focused attention on helping victims through the criminal justice process:

> We have introduced new ways of working in the [UK] Criminal Injuries Compensation Authority (CICA). In July 2008, we moved to geographically focused teams in order to improve partnerships with local criminal justice agencies and a new case-working model for claims, which places greater emphasis on supporting victims through the process. (UK Ministry of Justice 2009: 51)

Two points can be made about these recent developments in the philosophy of some state-based compensation schemes. First, by focusing less on monetary awards, such changes inevitably cut costs. Second, particularly with regard to the earlier UK Ministry of Justice statement, there is a sense that the ostensibly separate state compensation systems is being utilized as a tool for facilitating victims' cooperation and support for criminal justice processes.

To continue on the last point, recent developments in Australia and the UK notwithstanding, state compensation systems in all jurisdictions have long been concerned with compensating only those victims that are deemed 'deserving'. Acquiring this status usually requires that victims cooperate with the authorities, are in no way responsible for their injuries, and are generally free of past criminal convictions. Hence, the Dutch system requires that victims 'bear no guilt' (Schadefonds Geweldsmisdrijven 2008: 3) for injuries, whereas the Californian system stipulates that

> A victim or derivative victim who knowingly and willingly failed to reasonably cooperate with a law enforcement agency in the investigation of the qualifying crime and the apprehension and conviction of any person involved in the qualifying crime is not eligible for assistance. (Californian Victim Compensation and Government Claims Board 2009: para. 649.52)

The Californian scheme itself is more liberal in relation to previous convictions:

> Neither that the applicant is presently incarcerated nor that the applicant has been convicted of a felony and has not been discharged from probation or released from a correctional institution and discharged from parole shall be reason for the VCP [Victim Compensation Panel] to refuse to accept an application. (Californian Victim Compensation and Government Claims Board 2009: para. 649.4)

This can be compared to the following, very wide, provision in the Irish scheme, which effectively allows compensation to be denied based on a victim's 'way of life':

> No compensation will be payable where the Tribunal is satisfied that the conduct of the victim, his character or his way of life make it inappropriate that he should be granted an award and the Tribunal may reduce the amount of an award where, in its opinion, it is appropriate to do so having regard to the conduct, character or way of life of the victim. (Irish Criminal Injuries Compensation Tribunal 2009: para. 14)

As has previously been discussed in Chapter 2, the overriding impression given by a review of the state-based compensation mechanisms in operation in the countries under review is that they are aimed at the ideal victim and at stereotypical notions of suffering. The other key issue is that of costs: which all state compensation schemes have struggled to keep under control. As early as 1968, for example, the Institute of Law Research and Reform argued in the US context that:

> Many States are facing serious budgetary problems and are finding it difficult to continue to fund, or to start to fund, victim compensation programs. For instance, the Washington program is not providing compensation to individuals injured on or after July 1 1981. (Institute of Law Research and Reform 1968: 1)

Rock (1986, 1990) has pointed to similar problems in Canada and the UK, while in Australia Freckleton (1998: 201) notes how the popularity of such schemes has raised costs beyond all predictions: 'The gloomy truth is that the success of statutory criminal injuries compensation schemes has made the initiatives of New Zealand and Victoria in dramatically curtailing financial awards highly likely to be adopted elsewhere'. In this context, it is not unreasonable to question whether periodic government rumblings in the UK to cease payments for non-serious injury (UK Home Office 2005a) have more to do with the financial cost of the scheme than with benefiting victims directly. The most recent proposal of this kind (UK Home Office 2005a) claimed the new system would reflect the practical and emotional support victims say they need in the British Crime Survey, although the survey has never actually asked victims whether they would prefer such practical support to small amounts of compensation. The Dutch system too requires that injuries be 'serious' in nature and, on this point, in interviews with Dutch victim service providers it was suggested that take up rates for state-based compensation systems were relatively low in that jurisdiction precisely because most criminal injuries were not serious.[31]

In sum, the development and implementation of state compensation systems in the eight relevant jurisdictions[32] again reflects some of the key elements of the policy networks discussed in Chapter 4. These include: the increased concerns about public satisfaction with the criminal justice system; the focus on ideal victims; and the financial concerns associated with growing costs. The cost issue has in turn led to further restrictions or proposed restrictions in such schemes, and has arguably fuelled a renewed focus on rehabilitation, counselling and on *offenders* footing the bill for compensating victims. We will turn to the latter development in the next section.

Restitution

As a general trend, in recent years all the jurisdictions under review have turned increasingly to offenders to provide monetary compensation to victims, either directly though the imposition of court-based compensation orders or through the establishment of victims' funds maintained by offender surcharges and fine payments. Such a move is well supported by the established literature, which consistently holds that payments from offenders themselves carry greater symbolic value to victims of crime than monies allocated from taxation. Hence, Shapland (1990), having interviewed victims directly on this question, concludes that victims feel their pain and suffering has been duly recognized by the judge when offenders are ordered to pay compensation or, as Miers (1980) put it, recognition of their 'victim status' (see also Wright 1998).

As such, restitution has become an integral, and indeed mandatory, component of many of the criminal justice systems under review. For example, in Canada the courts have established in cases such as *The Queen v Zelensky*[33] and *Re Torek and The Queen*[34] that compensating any victims of crime is an object of the sentencing exercise. The Canadian criminal code allows courts to make restitution orders at the time of sentencing an offender.[35] Such orders can be made on the application of the prosecutor or on the court's own motion, and can require an offender to make restitution to the victim to cover the latter's monetary losses or damage to property caused by the commission of the relevant crime.[36] Similarly, in the USA the national Mandatory Restitution Act 1996 makes it a requirement that courts impose restitution orders on offenders in most cases of violence and property crime, irrespective of the offender's ability to pay. Notably, it is clear from the 1996 Act that the purpose of such restitution is not merely symbolic, but in the words of the Californian scheme is intended: 'To help victims recover from any financial hardship caused by a criminal activity' (Californian Department of Corrections and Rehabilitation 2009: n.p.). Hence, restitution in the USA has frequently been based around instrumental considerations rather than the symbolic recognition of victims' suffering, as noted in the advice given to victims in the state of New York: 'Restitution is *not*

Compensation, restitution and restorative justice

for payment of damages for future losses, mental anguish or "pain and suffering"' (New York State Crime Victims Board 2008: 1). Such a position does however raise a conceptual difficulty here given that in most cases offenders will be unable to provide an amount of money which fully or even substantially compensates for the financial hardship of the victim. Such small payments as many offenders can afford can only in reality be symbolic, despite the wording of the 1996 Act. The situation in many US states can be contrasted to the system of compensation orders in operation in Victoria, where offenders can be made to compensate 'pain and suffering and related expenses' under s.74 of the Victims Support and Rehabilitation Act 1996. In The Netherlands, compensation orders can similarly be used to compensate victims for both material and immaterial damages (Malsch 1999).

In South Africa the passing of compensation orders against offenders dates from before the advent of democracy, and was legislated for in the Criminal Procedure Act 1977. A victim's right to both compensation and restitution have more recently been set down in the South African Victims' Charter.[37] Here the term 'compensation' is taken to mean financial payments from offenders for 'loss or damage to property' (South African Department of Justice and Constitutional Development 2008a: 13). 'Restitution' in this instance means the return or repair of property by the offender 'in order to restore you [the victim] to the position you were in prior to the commission of the offence' (South African Department of Justice and Constitutional Development 2008: 15). This was also the rationale given for the introduction of compensation orders in The Netherlands in the Terwee Act 1995. In South Africa, it is notable that neither the governing legislation (s.300 of the 1977 Act) nor the Victims' Charter itself include crimes of violence and the associated medical costs under the headings of restitution or compensation, as is the case with the US and Canadian schemes. As in all jurisdictions the point may however be somewhat academic given the limited means of many offenders, particularly in South Africa. Notwithstanding this, interviews carried out at the South African Department of Corrections revealed a significant commitment to the philosophy that: 'The only way of compensating victims is to make those who perpetrate crimes compensate them' (interview with a representative of the South African Department of Corrections 2009).

One of the most extensive and wide-ranging systems of offender-based restitution is found in New Zealand where, as in the USA and Canada, the Sentencing Act 2002 includes a strong statutory presumption in favour of restitution, and a judge must give reasons as to why such restitution has *not* been ordered in specific cases. Under the legislation, such reasons must demonstrate that the imposition of an order would 'result in undue hardship for the offender or the dependents' or that 'any other special circumstances would make it inappropriate' (s.12(1)). The New Zealand Law Commission has pointed out that, unlike the US system, this latter provision means that an offender's lack of earnings can be used to justify a refusal to make an order.[38] The same is true in England and Wales, where the Powers of Criminal Courts Sentencing Act 2000 requires courts to give reason when an order is not made (s.130(3)), but there is no specifically stated presumption in favour of granting restitution of the kind found in the USA and Canada.[39] For example, in California the discretion of courts to refuse to grant an order is extremely narrow:

> All persons who suffer losses as a result of criminal activity shall have the right to restitution from the persons convicted of the crimes for losses they suffer. Restitution shall be ordered from the convicted persons in every case, regardless of the sentence or disposition imposed, in which a crime victim suffers a loss, unless compelling and extraordinary reasons exist to the contrary. (Art.1(28)(b) of the Constitution of California)

In contrast, in England and Wales the only specific guidance given as to the factors a court must take into account when determining whether or not to make an order is the means of the offender (s.130(11)) meaning that, as in New Zealand, a lack of means can be sufficient reason for the purposes of s.130(3). A very similar (although more generally worded) model is used in the Irish Criminal Justice Act 1993 where a court may impose a compensation order 'unless it sees reason to the contrary' (s.6(1)) and in making this determination the only specific factor given for consideration is the offender's means (s6(5)(a)). One more distinct example is that of New South Wales where the Victim Support and Rehabilitation Act 1996 does not require the court to have regard to an offender's means, but it must have regard to any behaviour, condition, attitude or disposition of the 'aggrieved person' (the victim) which may have contributed to the injury suffered. This again seems to promote ideal notions of victimhood, albeit to a lesser degree than the provisions found in the state-based compensation schemes discussed earlier.

In addition to compensation orders, where specific offenders are ordered to pay money to the victims affected by their crimes, a number of jurisdictions have also introduced levies on all offenders to be paid into general victims' funds.[40] Such funds in turn are typically used to pay for services and support mechanisms for victims as a whole or, in some cases, provide a pot of money to which individual victims can apply for payments. In the USA, such funds are often combined with state-based compensation monies in a single fund, hence the Californian Victims Compensation Program is funded by 'restitution fines and orders, penalty assessments levied on persons convicted of crimes and traffic offenses, and federal matching funds' (Californian Department of Corrections and Rehabilitation 2009: n.p.). Under the Californian constitution, restitution fines (as opposed to restitution orders, which are broadly equivalent to compensation orders in other jurisdictions) are imposed in all cases of conviction for a felony or a misdemeanor in the state.[41] In England and Wales too, under the Domestic Violence Crime and Victims Act 2004 (s.14) a court must impose a flat £15 surcharge on offenders in cases where it also imposes a fine and/or a compensation order. This money is paid into a victims' fund which is then used to finance services and support mechanisms for victims. A separate but similar fund has recently been set up in Scotland, although this is funded entirely by charitable donations and other fund-raising activities (Victim Support Scotland 2009). In New South Wales, Part 5 of the Victim Support and Rehabilitation Act 1996 Act requires a levy of either AUS$30 or AUS$70 (depending on the mode of trial) to be imposed on offenders convicted of imprisonable offences. The levy is paid into a similar kind of fund. The levy can only be waived if the offender is less than 18 years of age and, as is the case in England and Wales, takes precedence over any other financial payment imposed on the offender by the court.[42] This can be contrasted to the system in Ontario where, under the Provincial Offences Act 1990, a victims' surcharge is based on the amount of fine payable but such fines take precedence over the surcharge itself.

Given the understanding in most jurisdictions that state-based compensation is not intended to fully recompense victims for their losses as a result of crime, but rather acts as a symbolic recognition of their suffering, the notion of shifting more of this financial burden to offenders themselves makes sense. It has been noted already that victims themselves feel that payments from offenders have even greater symbolic value. Furthermore it is clear that, as offenders are being required to foot the bill for victims' funds which are also contributed to by taxation, the distinction between state-based and offender-based compensation is blurring. For example, in the

Domestic Violence, Crime and Victims Act 2004, the UK Government introduced provision to allow the Criminal Injuries Compensation Authority (the state-based compensation system) to reclaim money from offenders.

These benefits notwithstanding, restitution in the form of compensation orders or levies paid into victims' funds also bring their own difficulties. In the USA, for example, authorities have faced considerable problems in *enforcing* restitution fines and orders since the enactment of the Mandatory Victims Restitution Act of 1996. As such, one set of figures puts the amount of uncollected federal criminal restitution debt as having reached US$50 billion by the end of 2007 (Criminal Justice Transition Coalition 2009). In addition, much depends on the cultural attitude taken by the courts to the notion of compensating crime victims in individual jurisdictions. For example, in England and Wales it has been noted that judges and magistrates often seem unwilling to impose these orders as a single penalty or to combine them with custodial sentences (UK Home Office 2004a). Difficulties also persist with prosecutors lacking enough information to judge how much compensation they should be seeking. This can lead to very small amounts being requested, or no request being made at all, in which case magistrates in turn are reluctant to make awards at their own discretion (Newburn 1988; Moxon *et al*. 1992).

It is submitted that there is little coincidence in the fact that moves towards restitution (and restorative justice) have largely coincided with the realization that state-based compensation systems are a permanently growing expense for all jurisdictions. Ironically, as such schemes become more and more popular (as all such schemes have done with the exception of The Netherlands[43]) they face greater danger of becoming financially unsustainable. This clearly reaffirms the relevance of financial concerns to the policy network discussed in Chapter 4, along with concerns about how the state is *seen* to be reacting to victims and their suffering. Nevertheless, it is also arguable that restitution approximates something closer to what victims themselves say they want as opposed to state-based compensation schemes which for the most part were introduced without victim consultation (Rock 1990). The next step in this development may lie with the roll-out of restorative justice programmes in all the jurisdictions under review, to which this chapter now turns attention.

Restorative justice

Restorative justice has been variously defined during the course of its development at the academic and policy levels, and across different jurisdictions. The most frequently cited definition from the literature is that of Tony Marshall (1999: 5), who conceptualizes restorative justice as: 'A process whereby parties with a stake in a specific offence collectively resolve how to deal with the aftermath of the offence and its implications for the future'. This is a forward-looking definition which focuses principal attention on the harms caused by offending rather than the offending itself. The Marshall definition has been widely used both by academics (Zebr and Mika 2003) and policy makers (United Nations Office on Drugs and Crime 2006) in recent years, and while alternative understandings exist (see Miers 2001) most such definitions still remain grounded in the *harm* caused by offending. For example, in the Scottish Government's guide to *Restorative Justice Services* (2008: 5) the term is understood as

> primarily designed to address the harm caused by identifiable action(s), rather than (merely) to address the underlying causes of harmful behaviour or patterns of such behaviour; although it can and generally does have the effect of reducing the level of harmful behaviour.

Similarly, in Ireland official understandings of restorative justice again tend to revolve around addressing the *impacts* of crime:

> Restorative justice is an umbrella term that describes a variety of means of bringing victims, offenders and the wider community together to collectively resolve the impact and consequences of crime. (Irish National Commission on Restorative Justice 2008: para. 7.1)

Such definitions are of course in keeping with the general theme emerging throughout this volume of defining victimisation by reference to the harm suffered (either directly or indirectly) as opposed to relying on complex, legalistic definitions.

It is not the purpose of this section to evaluate the definition and goals of restorative justice in great detail, although a succinct presentation of the latter is put forward by the UN in the following terms: 'Restorative justice programs can be used to reduce the burden on the criminal justice system, to divert cases out of the system and to provide the system with a range of constructive sanctions' (United Nations Office on Drugs and Crime 2006). This section will also bypass any lengthy description of the various forms restorative justice can take.[44] Typically the term is said to encompass victim–offender mediation schemes (whether direct or indirect), family group conferencing, community conferencing, restitution panels, sentencing circles and problem-solving initiatives designed to address conflicts between citizens. This list is, however, far from exhaustive and fails to convey the wealth of debate, overlap, and conjecture concerning what does and does not count as restorative justice.[45] What is clear however is that policy makers in all the jurisdictions under review have purported to adopt some form of restorative justice within their criminal justice process, often linking this development with the wider network of victim reforms. Academics too have frequently argued that restorative justice may hold the key to many of the problems faced by victims in traditional justice systems (Dignan and Cavadino 1996; Braithwaite and Parker 1999; Dignan 2002a, 2002b; Young 2000). For Dignan (2005) this is because policies and practice relating to victims of crime within the criminal justice systems of most jurisdictions have led only to their partial enfranchisement within that process.

Like other areas of victim reform, the international recognition and development of restorative justice owes much to the work of international organizations, including the UN and the EU. In the case of the former, the Vienna Declaration on Crime and Justice of 2001 encouraged the 'development of restorative justice policies, procedures and programmes that are respectful of the rights, needs and interests of victims, offenders, communities and all other parties' (para. 28). In 2002, the United Nations Economic and Social Council adopted Resolution 2002/12, which called upon all Member States implementing restorative justice programmes to draw on a set of *Basic Principles on the Use of Restorative Justice Programmes in Criminal Matters*. In 2005, the declaration of the Eleventh United Nations Congress on the Prevention of Crime and the Treatment of Offenders similarly urged the development of restorative justice initiatives and in 2006 the *Basic Principles* noted earlier were augmented by a new *Handbook on Restorative Justice* (United Nations Office on Drugs and Crime 2006). In Europe, restorative justice is also mentioned in the 2001 *EU Council Framework Decision on the Standing of Victims in Criminal Proceedings* discussed in Chapter 3. Here Article 10 contains the following requirement: 'Each Member State shall seek to promote mediation in criminal cases for offences which it considers appropriate for this sort of measure'.

On this point, it is notable that when interviewed for this project policy workers at the European Commission were not unanimously in favour of restorative justice as a primary tool for meeting victims' needs:

> I spend a lot of time listening to people who work in this field and they say to me two things. One is, most victims don't want it. It's something that offenders are asking for or probation officers are asking for on behalf of offenders and the victims don't really want it. The second thing is it's incredibly expensive. All forms of mediation are expensive in terms of money, human resources and time. What victim support specialists say is that that time, money and human resources is better spent doing something else. (interview with a representative of the European Commission 2009)

In addition, at an expert meeting to discuss the implementation and reformation of the 2001 EU *Framework Decision* held in Brussels in 2008, Victim Support Europe raised some real concerns about the present format of Article 10:

> VSE [the representative of Victim Support Europe] had a thorough debate on article 10, on restorative justice, and all agreed that it needs to be reformulated to say that victim–offender mediation may only take place when it does not damage the interests of the victim in any way. He said that the initiative for victim–offender mediation seemed to come more from the offender side than the victim side. VSE can accept the possibility of victim–offender mediation but only when it does not harm the interests of the victims. (European Commission 2008: 3)

Hence, even though restorative justice is usually conceived as focusing on the impacts of crime, there is still a concern among some victim advocates that these processes can be hijacked by the offender side of the equation.

Restorative justice is often traced back to traditional aboriginal methods of dispute resolution (Cornwell 2006) and, as such, four of the jurisdictions under review – New Zealand, Canada, Australia and South Africa – point to the practices of their own indigenous peoples as the inspiration for the development of modern restorative justice schemes. In New Zealand, which is often presented as the site of the earliest traditional restorative practices (see Erez 2004), the first statutory enshrinement of restorative justice principles came in the Families Act of 1989. This legislation set out a scheme of family group conferences for young offenders designed to:

> Make such decisions, recommendations and plans as are thought to be 'necessary or desirable in relation to the child or young person in respect of whom the conference was convened ...'. The 1989 legislation physically separated the youth justice system from the Family Court process by creating a specialist Youth Court. This was intended to keep 'care and protection' proceedings in the Family Court separate and to ensure that dispositions for offences were time-limited, commensurate with the offence, and just. While to some, it initially looked like a return to a culturally inappropriate adversarial system, it was hoped that Family Group Conferences would counter this by empowering the community. While the new youth justice system was an attempt to move away from the traditional welfare model, the system attempts to reconcile the dichotomies of 'justice' and 'welfare' by holding a young offender accountable while giving appropriate consideration to the needs of the young offender. It is the FGC process that largely facilitates this reconciliation. (Ferguson 2007: n.p.)

In more recent years, the key pieces of legislation in New Zealand pertaining to restorative justice (applying to adults as well as children) have been the Sentencing Act, the Parole Act and the Victims' Rights Act, all of 2002. In the Sentencing Act, s.10 requires a court to 'take into account any offer, agreement, response, or measure to make amends' made by the offender to the victim when passing sentence. Furthermore, s.9 of the Victims' Rights Act maintains:

> If a suitable person is available to arrange and facilitate a meeting between a victim and an offender to resolve issues relating to the offence, a judicial officer, lawyer for an offender, member of court staff, probation officer, or prosecutor should, if he or she is satisfied of the matters stated in subsection (2), encourage the holding of a meeting of that kind.

The New Zealand Ministry of Justice reports that the most common form of restorative justice in operation within its jurisdiction are pre-sentencing conferences in the District Court (in accordance with the Sentencing Act 2002). This is in addition to community-managed restorative justice programmes funded through the Crime Prevention Unit and a number of local community groups which receive referrals from the court but primarily rely on community sources for funding. In the latter case, interviews with victim support workers in New Zealand revealed that the availability of such schemes in local areas is very inconsistent: 'Restorative Justice is very supported by NGOs, but it's not universally available, it depends on the area and the providers' (interview with a representative of Victim Support New Zealand 2009).

As in other jurisdictions, the New Zealand Ministry of Justice is also presently engaged in a long-term series of evaluations of piloted court-referred restorative justice processes, presently in operation at the Waitakere, Auckland City, Hamilton and Dunedin District Courts (Victoria University of Wellington Crime and Justice Centre 2005). These have mainly taken the form of victim–offender mediation although they have faced some difficulties in appealing to victims themselves to become involved (Victoria University of Wellington Crime and Justice Centre 2005).

Cornwell (2006: xvii–xviii) notes that the New Zealand approach to restorative justice has been largely emulated in Canada, particularly with the Canadian adoption of the New Zealand model of family group conferencing:

> The Canadian perspective bears remarkable similarities to that from New Zealand in relation to the extent to which the particular needs and culture of Aboriginal peoples have been afforded evident recognition within considerations of criminal justice. This has, to some extent, opened the door to wider application of restorative principles within the mainstream debate and the determination of criminal justice policies and legislation.

As such, the Canadian criminal code was amended in 1996 to encourage restorative principles in sentencing. Paragraph 718(2)(e) of the code makes it a key objective of the sentencing exercise 'to promote a sense of responsibility in offenders, and acknowledgement of the harm done to victims and to the community', whereas paragraph 718.2(2) maintains: 'All available sanctions other than imprisonment that are reasonable in the circumstances should be considered for all offenders, with particular attention to the circumstances of Aboriginal offenders'.

In the Supreme Court case of *Gladue*[46] – which has since been labelled as 'a cornerstone for building Restorative Justice practices in Canada' (Achtenberg 2000: n.p.) – judges rejected the view that restorative justice was fundamentally a more lenient approach to crime, or that a sentence focusing on restorative justice is necessarily a lighter sentence. Policy makers and governments in all jurisdictions have been at pains to communicate the same message to the public, as illustrated by this example from Scotland: 'While such an approach can help steer first-time petty offenders away from the formal Children's Hearings system, I can reassure the public that this is not a soft option' (Scottish Executive 2004b). And in Ireland:

> Restorative justice approaches to crime can be perceived as being 'soft options' for offenders. However restorative justice does in fact place onerous demands on offenders to own up to their wrongdoing, apologize personally to their victim, and take active responsibility for putting things right, both in terms of helping their victims and reforming their own behaviour. (Martin and Haverty 2008: 101)

In Canada, having accepted this view in *Gladue*, the Court advocated the increased use and development of aboriginal practices in mainstream justice, which has had a long-term impact on the direction of Canadian penal policy (Turpel-Lafond 1999). Aside from a fairly standard model of victim–offender mediation, this has led to the application of a wide variety of restorative measures across Canada, including various forms of sentencing, healing and peacemaking circles, community hearings and 'healing lodges' (Canadian Resource Centre for Victims of Crime 2001). Victim participation in these processes varies from province to province, with British Columbia allowing for some of the most free and open interaction between offender and victims (Canadian Aboriginal Justice Directorate 2009). In contrast, victims in Ontario may be required to sit outside the circle as observers, or if they do enter the circle as participants they must read directly from their victim impact statement and cannot speak freely (Canadian Resource Centre for Victims of Crime 2001).

One area in which the moves towards restorative justice in Canada have been particularly emphasized is that of youth justice. Most of the countries under review have experimented with various forms of restorative-based diversion in youth cases, but Canada had faced particular difficulties prior to 2003 as the jurisdiction which imprisoned more youth than any other Western country (Statistics Canada 2005). The government's response came in the form of the Youth Criminal Justice Act 2003 which revolutionized the youth justice system and, once again, refocused it around restorative principles by promoting the use of extrajudicial resolutions.[47] Hence, s.38(2)(iii) of the Act mirrors the criminal code in proclaiming one of the goals of sentencing in such cases as 'promot[ing] a sense of responsibility in the young person, and an acknowledgement of the harm done to victims and the community'. Section 19 of the Act introduces a system of youth justice conferences 'to give advice on appropriate extrajudicial measures, conditions for judicial interim release, sentences, including the review of sentences, and reintegration plans'. The Canadian Department of Justice (2009: n.p.) notes that such conferences

> could be composed of a variety of people depending on the situation. It could include, for example, the parents of the young person, the victim, others who are familiar with the young person and his or her neighborhood, community agencies or professionals with a particular expertise that is needed for a decision.

It is important to note that, as with many restorative measures given legislative backing in Canada and the other jurisdictions under review, the informal use of conferencing in youth cases across Canada significantly predates the 2003 legislation and the accompanying guidelines from the attorney general (Canadian Resource Centre for Victims of Crime 2001). What is clear however is that youth imprisonment rates across Canada have dropped significantly since 2003, and currently stand at approximately half their pre-2003 levels (Statistics Canada 2009). Of course, as in other areas of victim reform, the reduction in prisoner numbers achieved by the more restorative approach adopted in the Youth Criminal Justice Act 2002 has brought a substantial cost benefit to the Canadian system. Cornwell (2006) notes how Canada has deliberately set out to reduce the use of imprisonment since the early 1990's, contrasting this with The Netherland's expansion of its prison population over the same period (see below). Nevertheless, the reasoning for this was not just philosophical, or based on traditional practices, but also 'social and fiscal' (p. xvii).

Nowhere has the advent of restorative justice been more grounded in the recent political context and history of a jurisdiction than in South Africa, where recent moves to embrace restorative practices have followed directly from the establishment of the Truth and Reconciliation Commission (TRC) set up to bear witness to the gross violations of human rights which took place during the apartheid era and, in some cases, to grant amnesty to the perpetrators. The TRC has itself been described as a 'shining beacon' of the restorative justice philosophy (De Lange 2006). Restorative justice is also seen as a direct reaction to the retributive justice strategies of the previous regime, as noted by one representative of the Department of Corrections:

> With Corrections Services ... the change that we have initiated is not to punish but to restore ... that's how we make the victim part of the process. That is why we have taken the approach of restorative justice: to ensure that the perpetrator owns up to the crime that he or she has committed and, in a way, shows the victim. (interview with a representative of the South African Department of Corrections 2009)

The TRC and wider restorative justice practices in modern South Africa have frequently been linked to traditional African and South African philosophies. These include *ubuntu*, which is usually understood as representing: 'A culture which places some emphasis on communality and on the interdependence of members of a community' (Kollapen 2006: 1). Certainly, unlike in most other jurisdictions, representatives of the South African Department of Justice and Constitutional Development reported no difficulties in persuading victims to become involved in restorative schemes once they were informed about them. Indeed, such representatives frequently referred to an extraordinary case where the offender and victim had got married following mediation.

In recent years, South Africa's commitment to the restorative justice movement has been affirmed both in legislation and in case law. The first legislation to specifically refer to restorative justice was the Probation Services Amendment Act of 2000, which defined the concept as 'the promotion of reconciliation, restitution and responsibility through the involvement of a child, the child's parents, family members, victims and communities' (s.1). This definition is set to be updated in the Child Justice Bill, where restorative justice is defined as 'an approach to justice that aims to involve the offender, the victim, the families concerned and community members to collectively identify and address harms, needs and obligations through accepting responsibility, making restitution, taking measures to prevent recurrence of the incident and promoting reconciliation' (Clause 1). Restorative justice is also presented as a central theme of South African criminal justice in the Traditional Courts Bill. This theme has been further cemented in a number of influential court judgments including *S v Makwanyane*;[48] *S v M*[49] and *Minister of Home Affairs v NICRO*.[50]

The South African Department of Justice and Constitutional Development points to a number of examples of restorative justice practices within its jurisdiction, emphasizing that such practices can be found within the work of formal justice and government agencies as well as in less formal modes of dispute resolution (South African Department of Justice and Constitutional Development 2009). These include the community courts where normal criminal procedure is followed but with a focus on the possibilities for restorative approaches. In keeping with the philosophies of the Truth and Reconciliation Commission, various state institutions set up after the end of apartheid to support democracy in South Africa also adopt restorative processes including the South African Human Rights Commission, the Commission for Gender Equality, and the Commission for Culture, Religion and Language. Mediation has also been part of family and divorce proceedings in South Africa since before the advent of democracy.[51] There is also a strong tradition of informal local courts, or *makgotla*, in South Africa where no distinction is made between civil and criminal disputes. The government has gradually formalized and integrated these institutions over a number of years (see Hund 1984; Mistry 2000).

The South African Victims' Charter strongly affirms the government's commitment to supporting and enhancing all restorative processes:

> Since 1994, and in keeping with the cultivation of a human rights culture, the focus has gradually moved from an adversarial and retributive criminal justice system to that of restorative justice. Central to the concept of restorative justice is the recognition of crime as more than an offence against the state, but also as an injury wrong done to another person. (South African Department of Justice and Constitutional Development (2008a: 3–4)

That said, despite restorative justice being more philosophically and historically grounded in the traditional cultures of South Africa than perhaps any other jurisdiction, representatives of the Department of Corrections were willing to admit that (as has been demonstrated in Canada and New Zealand) its revival also brought a practical benefit to the overstretched criminal justice system as a way out of overcrowding (interview with a representative of the South African Department of Corrections 2009) This once again demonstrates the presence of a *network* of policy considerations informing such developments, even where those reforms have such deep cultural and political routes within a jurisdiction.

The other jurisdiction under review in which restorative justice is often attributed to (domestic) traditional and aboriginal practices is that of Australia. Here, advocates and practitioners of restorative justice have once again tended to draw on the conferencing models of New Zealand, which have mostly been applied in youth cases. Strang (2001) compiled a detailed review of the development of restorative justice in all Australian territories. Her conclusion was that, while restorative conferencing in particular had become widespread and grounded in state/territorial legislation, proving the effectiveness of these measures was difficult both in Australia and in other jurisdictions:

> Before considering the means by which programs could be extended a prior question concerns the desirability of doing so. It is early days for restorative justice: it may be the oldest way of conflict and dispute resolution, but it is only a decade since such programs began to be mainstreamed, and a much shorter timeframe in which evaluation studies have been conducted. Even in relation to programs in the justice setting, where most of the evaluative research has taken place, we do not know yet very much about how effective the restorative approach may prove to be in reducing reoffending; this is especially difficult to estimate when programs are mostly directed at a population of offenders whose offences are minor and criminal careers brief. Large claims of 'success' among those who may never have reoffended anyway confuse and distract policymakers. (Strang 2001: 38)

Australian jurisdictions have drawn not only from the New Zealand experience of restorative justice but also from other jurisdictions under review in this volume. In Queensland, for example, government sources refer back to the movement towards restorative justice advocated by Quakers and Mennonites in Canada during the late 1970s and 1980s (Queensland Department of Communities 2009). More recently, in Australia the Victoria Courts Legislation (Neighbourhood Justice Centre) Act 2006 draws heavily on the example of community justice centres found in the UK and USA in the creation of the pilot Neighbourhood Justice Centre (NJC). The NJC is a three-year pilot project of the Victorian Department of Justice and the first of its kind in the city of Yara. The NJC aims to enhance community involvement in the justice system providing: a court, on-site support services for victims, witnesses, defendants and local residents, mediation and crime prevention programs, and community meeting facilities (Bassett 2007). As in the USA and UK centres, restorative justice principles heavily inform the work of the NJC:

> By seeking to involve those most affected by a crime in the process of resolving the crime, restorative approaches have the potential to build greater community ownership and understanding of the causes of crime and increase satisfaction with the justice system. Given the NJC's problem solving approach to breaking cycles of offending, restorative justice approaches are highly relevant. (Bassett 2007: 5)

In working to make justice a *local* resource for the community, the Victoria NJC experiment also has much in common with the South African community courts discussed earlier. Certainly the 2006 Act represents the first statutory acknowledgement of restorative justice in Victoria. As a whole, the Australian adoption of restorative justice demonstrates the transnational nature of the policy network influencing the development of these kinds of measures.

In other jurisdictions, while restorative justice arguably lacks the authority of the same local traditional roots, such practices have still constituted an important driver for reform. In England and Wales, as in other jurisdictions, these have had a particularly strong influence on the youth justice system. Here, the previous system of police cautions and final warning has been largely replaced in the Youth Justice and Criminal Evidence Act 1999 with a system of mandatory diversionary referral orders from the court for the majority of first-time young offenders who plead guilty. This differs from the approach taken in Scotland where, for minor crimes, the police remain the key actors in the issuing of 'restorative warnings' to young offenders and the police themselves facilitate a 20–30 minute meeting between themselves, those affected by the crime, and the offender's support person: 'To ensure that everyone can speak without interruption, in an open and honest manner, about the facts (what happened), the consequences (who has been affected) and the future (how future offending can be prevented)' (Restorative Justice in Scotland 2009: n.p.). Such a process has the effect of diverting the offender from the criminal justice system entirely, whereas in England and Wales young people still have to admit the offence to a court. English Youth Offending Panels are comprised of members of the local community and members of the local Youth Offending Team who meet with the offender to agree a contract in which the offender agrees to actions such as writing a letter of apology to the victim, removing graffiti or cleaning up estates and communities. In this respect the process bears some resemblance to the restorative practices implemented as part of Scotland's system of children's hearings found under the Children (Scotland) Act 1995. The victim is invited and encouraged to attend such meetings although, in practice, a key difficulty for the panels has been that they have thus far attracted very little victim involvement despite clear intentions to the contrary (Newburn *et al.* 2002; Crawford and Newburn 2003). The extent to which victims themselves wish to become involved in restorative processes is the subject of debate. Certainly, contrary to the English experience, the US Office for Victims of Crime (2000: n.p.) makes the following claim:

> Over the past 20 years and in thousands of cases throughout North America, experience has shown that the majority of victims presented with the option of mediation chose to participate in the process. A recent statewide public opinion poll in Minnesota found that 82 percent of a random sample of citizens from throughout the State would consider participating in a victim–offender mediation program if they were victims of property crime.

As noted by Miers (2001: 73), 'it is difficult to generalise the many restorative justice initiatives that have been introduced in the United States over the past 30 years, and impossible to summarise here even a small fraction of the massive quantity of research evidence'. It is however clear that most of the schemes that exist in the USA follow a basic model of victim–offender mediation or family group conferencing and:

> Take place within the context of the criminal justice system as an exercise in police, prosecutorial or judicial discretion. Mediation services are typically located in the police or prosecuting departments of a state's Attorney-General's office, or in non-profit making community or church-based organisations. (p. 73)

A 2000 survey of victim–offender mediation programmes in the USA carried out by the University of Minnesota Center for Restorative Justice and Peacemaking offered further insights into the nature of such schemes throughout the country:

Compensation, restitution and restorative justice

The vast majority of programs participating in the survey are nonpublic agencies. Of the 115 programs responding to this question, the largest single category (43 percent) of programs is private, community-based agencies. The second largest category (22 percent) is church-based programs. (Umbreit and Greenwood 1998, cited in Miers 2001: 74)

No right to restorative processes has yet developed at the national level in the USA, and the concept is not mentioned in the Justice for All Act.[52] That said, it is notable that most of these schemes were funded by either state or local government sources.

In England and Wales, in addition to the issue of victim involvement in Youth Offending Panels, at the time of its implementation some commentators (Haines 2000) argued that the system of Youth Offending Panels and referral orders under the Youth Justice and Criminal Evidence Act 1999 (the Act that introduced special measures) would exclude defendants from the process, affording them little to no bargaining power, and was therefore punitive. Similar criticisms, levied at other victim reforms across jurisdictions, were discussed in Chapter 4.[53]

That said, the evidence from England and Wales seems to confirm that when victims do become involved in restorative processes they draw benefits from doing so, as does the restorative enterprise itself (see Dignan 2005; Shapland *et al.* 2006). Indeed, evaluation of the three recent pilots of restorative justice schemes for adults in England and Wales seems to indicate that these processes are capable of seriously engaging with victims (Shapland *et al.* 2006). The transnational and international influences are once again clearly evident in these pilots, as the scheme organized by the Justice Research Consortium in three areas of England and Wales is very much based on a previous restorative justice project carried out by the directors in Canberra, Australia (see Strang 2001).

Two of the jurisdictions under review were markedly behind the others in the development of restorative justice practices; these being Ireland and The Netherlands. In Ireland, restorative justice is presently limited to diversion programmes and a conferencing system for young offenders under the Children Act of 2001. The prospect for further development of restorative justice in Ireland is presently being examined by a National Commission on Restorative Justice which was established in March 2007 and had not yet published its final report at the time of writing. In The Netherlands, despite the early adoption of the pioneering Dading mediation project in Amsterdam in 1990 (Tak 2003), Blad and Pemberton (2006: 1) have been critical of this jurisdiction's response to the growth in restorative justice seen elsewhere:

> In comparison with other neighbouring countries like Belgium, Germany and the United Kingdom the development of restorative justice practices in the Netherlands lags behind. Although mediation in the field of civil law is widely practiced and experiments with mediation in criminal cases have been undertaken since the 1980's the Netherlands still lacks a nationwide program for restorative justice.

Unlike most other jurisdictions, recent years have been characterized by an orchestrated expansion in the Dutch penal estate, which is clearly at odds with restorative ideals (see Wemmers 1996). That said, Daelemans (2006) has noted that The Netherlands has been at the head of the field in the development of what has been called 'restorative detention' applied to serving prisoners, which has also been seen in Scotland (Scottish Prisons Commission 2008). Article 77e of the Dutch criminal code does make provision for offenders' participation in a 'project' as a diversionary measure.[54] Blad (2009) argues that such participation would be very suitable for restorative processes. In 2007 a national scheme of victim–offender talks were rolled out in The Netherlands. Nevertheless, Blad argues that these do not constitute mediation as it is understood in the 2001 *EU Framework Decision*; they do not foresee any agreement made between victim and offender and they do not input into the criminal procedure. They are also one-sided, intended to address the therapeutic needs of victims with no impact on offenders. As such, Blad sees this scheme as potentially excluding the possibility of negotiating a restorative agreement and therefore disempowering both victims and offenders.

Restorative justice is clearly on the increase in all the jurisdictions under review and, as with other areas of reform impacting upon victims, we can appreciate from the above discussion that a wide variety of interrelated factors have influenced this development: from the increased focus on the harms caused by crime, to the growing costs of incarceration seen in all countries, to the increasing importance of international organizations and transnational policy networks for policy makers in all jurisdictions. As in other areas, these transnational influences have arguably led to a relatively globalized approach to restorative principles, influenced particularly by practices in New Zealand.

Of course, perhaps to a greater extent than the majority of reforms discussed in this volume, in practice restorative justice is often conceived principally as an offender-based development. This interpretation is supported by the difficulties faced in some jurisdictions in getting victims involved in the process at all. As such, restorative justice is rarely presented as a cure-all for the problems faced by victims in various criminal justice systems. This perspective has already been demonstrated in the views of policy makers at the European Commission and of Victim Support Europe in relation to Article 10 of the 2001 *EU Framework Decisions*.[55] Furthermore, even in New Zealand, the Law Commission has advocated caution in relation to the use of restorative justice to facilitate reparation from offenders to victims:

> This can, and does, occur through the restorative justice process. However, it would be entirely inappropriate to foist the services of an offender upon an unwilling victim where an offender is unable to pay reparation. In addition, many offenders simply lack the skills that would enable them to provide useful services. While greater use of restorative justice may assist in some cases, it cannot, in itself, resolve the problems with reparation. (New Zealand Law Commission 2008: para. 4.54)

It should be noted that, in most jurisdictions, restorative justice has so far had little influence beyond what are generally viewed as the most minor offences (in terms of seriousness if not numbers). For example, South Australia and New Zealand are the only jurisdictions in the world which routinely use conferencing to process youth accused of sexual assault. In all other jurisdictions sexual assault has deliberately been placed off the restorative justice agenda because it is widely considered either too sensitive or too risky to be handled by conference or to be diverted from court prosecution.[56] To arbitrarily rank the relative seriousness of different types of crime of course denies the subjective nature of the various impacts of crime (Shapland and Hall 2007). Nevertheless, this focus of restorative justice on what are generally considered less serious crimes represents a departure from the general observation that victims who have suffered most are generally receiving greater recognition in the reform agenda of most jurisdictions, which may further imply that restorative justice is not really 'about' victims at all. There is clearly much debate still to be had over the place, meaning, and expectations of restorative justice in all these jurisdictions, and the relevance of these developments to victims of crime. It is also worth pointing out that many advocates of restorative justice retain in their theorizing a place for more traditional forms of case disposal. This reflects the view of Bottoms (2003) who argues in terms of a separation between the criminal justice and restorative justice.

Shapland and Hall (2007) have observed that the demise of the victim in most criminal justice system, together with the concentration of courts centres in large towns and cities, represents the removal of justice as a *local* resource. Arguably the move towards restorative justice indicates the beginnings of a reversal in this trend. For present purposes however the key point is that, like other areas of reform discussed in this volume, the development of restorative justice and its impacts on victims exhibits the same transnational and international influences as other areas of victim reform. As such, this must be considered as part of the wider policy network driving such measures.

Compensating victims?

In sum, all the jurisdictions under review have witnessed a development from compensation to restitution to restorative justice in their reform agendas over the last 30 years. While victims of crime have figured prominently in the accompanying policy documents across all jurisdictions it is equally clear that these developments have been promoted by a wide variety of different pressures and considerations. These include financial considerations and concerns about low public confidence in the criminal justice system. This discussion has also demonstrated the difficulty of establishing to what extent these measures are focused primarily on the victim, as opposed to the offender. Even in relation to state-based compensation schemes, it is evident that the system in place in most jurisdictions is focused not on victims of crime as a whole but on a tiny subset of ideal victims, which is another theme emerging throughout this study. The other key observation to be drawn from the above discussion is the degree of overlap and replication of ideas and procedures seen in all these jurisdictions in relation to compensation, restitution, and restorative justice. Again this demonstrates the clear transnational and international scope of the policy networks informing and driving such reforms and adds weight to the contention that the support of victims is becoming globalized. The extent to which this has been demonstrated in the project as a whole will form much of the discussion in the final chapter.

Notes

1. The term 'restitution' is used in a number of ways in the relevant literature and in policy documents across the nine jurisdictions under review. For the purposes of this chapter the term is taken to mean the payment of financial compensation from offenders to victims, either directly as a result of court-imposed orders or indirectly through victim surcharges. This is an alternative to what will be called 'state-based' compensation, funded through taxation.
2. See Chapter 4.
3. The English and Welsh System extends to the entire UK and therefore covers Scotland.
4. Californian Government Code: para.139590(A).
5. Elias (1983: 27) refers to this justification as 'humanitarian theory'.
6. See p. 3.
7. See pp. 35–36.
8. See pp. 21–22.
9. Which is also one justification for the establishment of victims' funds, see below.
10. See p. 177.
11. The California Victim Compensation and Government Claim Board (2008) has stated an ambition for its state-based compensation scheme to become the standard model in use across the USA. The Californian system has indeed been replicated in several other states and, as such, will serve as the principal comparison system from the USA in this chapter.
12. Accident Compensation Act 2001, s.3.
13. Although such singling out has a very long history. Cavanagh (1984: 1) notes that 'the idea that a society should assist those of its citizens victimized by crime has been traced back to the ancient Babylonian Code of Hammurabi (c. 2038 B.C.), which provided that when a man was robbed or murdered the City in which the crime occurred should compensate the victim or his heirs for their losses'.
14. See Chapters 1 and 2.
15. Recalling that South Africa has no such scheme and that the UK has a unified scheme covering England and Wales and Scotland.
16. The UK and New Zealand systems being particularly detailed.
17. See below.
18. See Quebec Crime Victims Compensation Act 1971, s.1(b).
19. See for example the Californian Scheme and the Quebec Scheme.
20. Victims Support and Rehabilitation Act 1996.
21. Quebec Crime Victims Compensation Act 1971 s.3(c).
22. New South Wales Victims Support and Rehabilitation Act 1996, s.8.
23. Victims Support and Rehabilitation Act 1996, s.9.
24. Australian Northern Territory Victims of Crime Assistance Act 2006, s.14.

Victims and Policy Making

25 *A v The Roman Catholic Archdiocese of Wellington and Ors* [2007] 1 NZLR 536: para. 509.
26 The situation in which mental injury alone is compensable relates to the crime of trespass on the railways, see above.
27 Injury Prevention, Rehabilitation and Compensation Act 2001, s.23.
28 Recently published figures suggest that the Irish Criminal Injuries Compensation Tribunal provided compensation totalling €12.56m to individual victims of crime between 2005 and 2008. €4.46m was allocated to the Tribunal for this purpose in 2008 (Irish Department of Justice, Equality and Law Reform 2008).
29 Although other cases are assessed in a more individualized manner.
30 The Californian system also makes provision for 'rehabilitative services' (Californian Victim Compensation and Government Claims Board 2009: para. 649.7).
31 This may be partly attributable to the presence of the *partie civile* model in the Dutch criminal justice system as an alternative mechanism through which victims can receive compensation.
32 And, indeed, the ruling out of such a system in South Africa.
33 [1978] 2 S.C.R. 940.
34 (1974), 15 C.C.C. (2d) 296.
35 R.S., 1985, C-46.
36 Compensation orders in most jurisdictions can also be used to cover funeral expenses and to compensate for bereavement, with the notable exception of Scotland (Criminal Procedure (Scotland) Act 1995, as amended by the Criminal Proceedings etc. (Reform) (Scotland) Act 2007).
37 See Chapter 5 for discussion on the use of the term 'rights' in this context.
38 See, for example, *R v Munro* (24 July 2002) CA 132/02; *R v Sheehy* [2007] NZCA 519; *R v Brown* (26 November 1992) CA 267/92; *R v Price* (13 September 2006) HC ROT CRI -2006-063-2593, per Hansen J; *Devonshire v Police* (22 November 2003) HC HAM CRI -2003-419-51, per Chambers J.
39 S.130(1) states that a court 'may' impose such an order.
40 All the jurisdictions under review have victims' fund with the exception of South Africa, where there have been calls for the establishment of such a scheme. See http://www.saflii.org/za/other/zalc/dp/97/97-CHAPTER-9.html.
41 This goes beyond the requirements of federal legislation.
42 Although anecdotal evidence from discussions with sitting magistrates suggests that, in practice, benches often reduce fines not because of the offender's lack of means but to take account of the new victims' surcharge in reaching the overall desired figure for payment.
43 See p. 169–170.
44 Excellent overviews can be found in Graef (2000) and Dignan (2005).

Compensation, restitution and restorative justice

45 See Raye and Roberts (2007). For a more detailed review of restorative justice internationally see Miers (2001).
46 *R v Gladue (1999)* 23 C.C.R. (5th) 197.
47 The Act is presently in the process of being reviewed again.
48 1995 (2) SACR 1 (CC).
49 Case CCT 53/06.
50 2005 (3) SACR 280 (CC).
51 See *Townsend-Turner and another v Morrow* [2004] 1 All SA 235 (C).
52 This Act does nevertheless provide a right to restitution.
53 Although, subsequent evaluation seems to avert these fears (Crawford and Newburn 2003).
54 The so-called HALT sanctions.
55 See p. 189.
56 Although the 2000 report from the Minnesota Center for Restorative Justice and Peacemaking noted that victim–offender mediation schemes in the USA are being asked to mediate crimes of increasing severity and complexity (Coates and Umbreit 2000).

Chapter 7

Victims and policy making: a comparative perspective

In the first chapter, the research agenda for this volume was set out in terms of offering a comparative analysis between countries which would yield detailed explanations for the emergence of victims of crime as the objects of widespread policy rhetoric and reform at the level of individual jurisdictions and for international organizations. It was hypothesized that, as well as being relevant to the study of victimology, such an analysis would also cast light on how policy making in the wider sense operates at the transnational and international level.[1] To assist with these endeavours, a draft theoretical framework was presented which charted the emergence of societal changes at the transnational and international level through to the present position in which the victim reform agenda has arguably become globalized.[2] This draft framework will be drawn upon to provide a basic structure for the conclusions set out in this chapter and, as such, is worth replicating here (see Figure 7.1).[3]

The remainder of this final chapter will set out the evidence derived from all the preceding discussions concerning each of the four levels of this framework, drawing relevant conclusions in the process. The chapter will then discuss the possibility that the effective provision of support, care, rights, and the fulfilment of other victimogogic ideologies (van Dijk 1983) is becoming or has already become a principle of international law. Finally, the chapter will comment on the overall implications of this project and the questions it poses for the future research agenda in this area.

1	– The 'victimalization of morality' (Boutellier 2000) – Loss of faith in the efficiency of criminal justice systems – Concentration on harms suffered by (ideal) victims
	↓ ↓ ↓
2	Transnational and international policy networks (international organizations and influences between jurisdictions)
	↓ ↓ ↓
3	Domestic policy networks within individual jurisdictions
	↘ ↓ ↙
4	Globalization of victim policies

Figure 7.1 Draft conceptual framework of victim policy making internationally

Societal changes: the macro perspective

A consistent theme throughout the course of this volume has been the grounding of victim reform in wider social processes which has been witnessed to some extent in all the jurisdictions under review. The initial starting point for these discussions has been the work of Boutellier (2000) on the victimalization of morality, along with Garland's (2001) thesis concerning the reaction of government agencies to the perceived failure of criminal justice systems to control crime. As such, Chapter 1 set out an objective for this research to modify or refute the wider macro influences put forward by both commentators as an underlying foundation of victim policies internationally.

Expanding definitions: are we all victims now?

One clear conclusion to be drawn from across the nine jurisdictions under review is that official definitions of victims and victimization are indeed expanding. This was a consistent theme of Chapter 2, but is also reflected by developments in compensation provision to various kinds of (direct and indirect) victims, and through the identification of different categories of victims and/or witnesses as having rights (at least at the rhetorical level). Recent literature has attempted to analyse how cultural factors impact upon our ideas of victimhood and official constructions of victims (Cole 2007). This development of so-called 'cultural victimology' begs the question of whether we are to some extent 'all victims now'. This question has been the topic of recent discussion by Mythen (2007: 479). Here the author warns against the overuse of culture as a 'magic explanatory bullet through which the experiences of all victims can be deciphered'. As Mythen correctly points out, the nature of victimization is diverse to the point that any theory which purports to explain it in its entirety must be approached with a high degree of scepticism: 'Whilst macro theories are important tools in the development of Victimology, their generality affords them only partial utility across different contexts and situations' (p. 479). Nevertheless, Mythen remains confident that the cultural lens is an important tool in modern victimology, and her conclusion is one of cautious optimism as to the capacity of such cultural perspectives to explain the rise of the victim in recent decades. Mythen's conclusion also acknowledges that 'it is not beyond the politicians to noisily invite us to position ourselves as hypothetical victims' (p. 480). As such, Mythen responds to the question of whether we are all victim now with the succinct answer: 'No. But they're working on it' (p. 480).

Not all commentators are willing to accept an ever widening expansion of victimhood. Furedi (1998: 80) expresses concern regarding the victimalization of morality on a number of grounds, the most philosophical of which is that it denies individual responsibility and self-determination:

> Recent events in Britain indicate that the cult of vulnerability goes beyond the terms of the existing debate. This cult has emerged as a key element in a moralizing project that touches upon every aspect of social life. Critics of the culture of victimhood often direct their fire at its more mendacious and self-serving manifestations, such as the predictable demand for compensation or the evasion of responsibility for the outcome of individual action. There is, however a more profound issue at stake. The celebration of the victim identity represents an important statement about the human condition. It regards human action with suspicion. It presupposes that human beings can do very little to influence their destiny. They are the objects rather than the subjects of their destiny. Consequently the human experience is defined by not by what people do but has happened to them.

Regarding the first part of Furedi's argument, reports from England and Wales highlight the problem of false claims being made to the UK Criminal Injuries Compensation Authority (Verkaik 2001). The 'compensation factor' has also been the subject of discussions in the UK by the House of Commons Select Committee on Home Affairs, along with associated concerns of prompting false allegations (Select Committee on Home Affairs 2002). To give another example, the assertion of false or frivolous claims similarly marred the operation of the World Trade Center Victims Compensation Fund in the USA (Mullenix 2004). Aside from monetary compensation, the bulk of this volume has demonstrated that being attributed with victim status (or at least vulnerable witness status) certainly affords advantages within the criminal justice processes of most jurisdictions. Such advantages include separate waiting rooms at court; the use of specialist equipment to give evidence; respectful and sympathetic treatment from criminal justice personnel; and procedural protections from excessive questioning on matters such as sexual history. While this volume has assessed arguments to the effect that the application of victim and defendant rights is not a zero sum game,[4] those who contend that the victim agenda is skewing criminal justice systems too greatly in favour of the victim (at the expense of the defendant's right to due process) are certainly convinced of the beneficial nature of victim status in the criminal justice context (see Ashworth 2000).

More specifically for present purposes, Furedi (1998: 84) questions the authority now apparently being afforded to victims, as 'moral custodians', to influence policy debates:

> Other victims, notably Mrs. Frances Lawrence, whose teacher husband was murdered outside his school, were also elevated into 'expert' moral custodians for the rest of society. So far no leading politician has dared to ask the question of 'why should a tragic bereavement confer the right to dictate public policy?'

Importantly, Furedi's discussion goes beyond victimological or criminological issues to encompass wider societal developments. In the UK, the Institute for the Study of Civil Society (CIViTAS), a right-wing think tank, has drawn on similar themes to suggest that victim status[5] affords a degree of influence to such groups which is incompatible with liberal democracy (Green 2006). While this argument must be judged in the context of its specific political perspective, it does demonstrate the application of the victim label beyond crime. Indeed, perhaps one of the most telling observations made by Furedi (1998: 83) is that criminal victimization is an issue which is able to galvanize support from both sides of the political spectrum:

> Unlike traditional conservative contributors, who treated individuals as victims of evil, feminist and leftist writers portrayed them as victims of a system of patriarchy. But although there were differences in the interpretation of aspects of the problem, there was a shared assumption that people are victims. It was this unexpected ideological convergence between left and right around the celebration of the victim, which has given this cult so much influence in British society.

As such, it is perhaps this bridging of political divides which ultimately best explains the pervasiveness of the victim issue for policy makers in so many jurisdictions in recent years.

Restricting definitions: the role of suffering and 'idealness'

Notwithstanding the points made in the last section, to argue simply that cultural attitudes render us 'all victims now' is to ignore the crucial point that, in all the jurisdictions under review, the expansion of official notions of victimhood has been far from unrestricted. On the contrary, one general conclusion to be drawn from the preceding chapters is that bestowment of the victim title is usually based on specific (and exclusive) criteria. The most important of these are the degree of suffering experienced by the individual, coupled with the 'idealness' of that individual.

Suffering

On the first criterion, it has been noted that defining victims by the suffering they endure[6] in principle expands the concept of victimhood beyond the confines of distinct legalistic categories. In addition, such a conceptualization to some extent leaves victims to be self-defined. On the former point, the use of suffering or harm as the starting point for the identification of victims has been shown in all nine jurisdictions under review, and also in relevant documentation from the both the UN and the EU. As well as encompassing, in most cases, the wide range of physical, practical, psychological and emotional traumas suffered by primary victims, Chapter 2 has demonstrated that such definitions of victimhood now frequently include indirect victimization and secondary victimization at the hands of criminal justice systems. In addition, this volume has discussed the introduction of new crimes of witness intimidation; the recognition of *witnesses* as potential victims of crime;[7] and, in South Africa, the assertion that victimization can occur through suffering brought about by the 'loss or substantial impairment of [victims] fundamental rights' (South African Department of Justice and Constitutional Development 2008c: 1).

As noted previously, the identification of victims through their suffering is explained by Boutellier (2000) in terms of a common appreciation and sympathy retained post-secularization for the harm experienced by others in society. This is to some extent supported by victimological research, which suggests that victims place great value on the official *recognition* of their pain and suffering by courts (Miers 1980; Shapland 1990). Indeed, the procedural view of criminal justice advocated by Tyler (1990) implies that such recognition can be more important to victims than obtaining a favourable result (usually meaning a prosecution) in individual cases. The discussions in Chapter 6, concerning compensation and restitution to victims of crime, bear out this impression that the symbolic recognition of suffering is becoming increasingly important in many criminal justice systems (from the perspective of victim care) over and above the legally defined particulars of individual cases. As such, most state-based compensation schemes and offender-based restitution programmes from across these jurisdictions make it clear that monies paid to the victim are symbolic and do not reflect the actual hurt caused by crime in absolute financial terms. This is made explicit by the Dutch state compensation scheme.[8]

In addition, it has been noted that the state compensation systems in operation in New South Wales[9] and the UK provide lists of *injuries* (as opposed to *crimes*) which can be compensated. As such, it can be argued that improving the treatment of crime victims is becoming less centred on the prosecution of cases, or even the precise impact of crime on individuals. Rather, in many cases the specific nature of the suffering experienced by victims of crime, as defined in criminal statutes, matters less than the symbolic recognition that suffering *of some type* has occurred.[10] From the preceding data analysis, this conclusion appears to hold true in all the jurisdictions reviewed for this project.

The implication of the argument made in the last paragraph is that, in the present policy environment, the identification of victims of crime should be in the process of becoming less the exclusive preserve of criminal justice professionals, especially the police and prosecutors, and more that of victims. If indeed the label of victim is principally an indicator of some form of suffering, as opposed to compliance with complex legal criteria, then the victims themselves are surely in the best position to make such a determination. In other words, the victimalization of morality espoused by Boutellier (2000) might imply a reversal of the trends identified by Christie (1977) concerning the over-professionalization of criminal justice and the removal of conflicts from their rightful owners.

In reality however this has not been the case. Principally this is because, while all the jurisdictions under review have emphasized the suffering and harm caused to victims as the yardstick by which victim status is judged and applied, in practice it is specific *kinds* of suffering which are routinely emphasized and, more significantly, specific *kinds* of individuals. Hence, in Chapter 4 child victims, victims of human trafficking, and female victims of rape, domestic violence and sexual victimization were highlighted as receiving particular attention from policy makers in all nine countries. Conceptually, the fact that the types of victims receiving the most attention from policy makers seem to correspond with those whose suffering is most easily appreciable by society, as opposed to victims of white collar crime for example (see Nelken 2007b), is consistent with Boutellier's thought. In practice however, the difficulty raised by this state of affairs lies in the fact that, for the vast majority of victims, the impacts of crime appear to be both subjectively minor and short term (Shapland and Hall 2007). A system grounded on such principles is therefore likely to prioritize a selected few while excluding the vast majority of victims, a point reflected by the exclusive rules set down in most state-based compensation schemes.[11]

One key exception to the rule that greater service is generally afforded for greater suffering is the roll-out of restorative justice programmes across the nine countries under review, which at present tend to cater for objectively less serious crimes.[12] As argued in Chapters 4 and 6, this raises important questions concerning the diversion of *victims*, as well as *offenders*, from the formal criminal justice process and whether doing so reinforces the hierarchy of victimization spoken of by Carrabine *et al.* (2009). It also raises wider questions concerning the true nature of the international policy agenda on victims, given that most restorative justice programmes seem principally focused on *offenders*. It is also true that such diversionary processes, whether for offenders or victims, save money for criminal justice agencies. Such complexities, as demonstrated by the preceding chapters, reinforce Mythen's (2007) contention that macro or cultural factors alone are incapable of providing a truly nuanced understanding of the victim issue internationally.

The 'idealness' of victims

The focus on victims whose suffering is perceived to be greatest can be criticized on the grounds that the impacts of crime can be very specific to the individual (See Shapland and Hall 2007). As such, those tasked (whether officially or *de facto*) with ascribing victim status based on the perceived degree of harm endured[13] inevitably risk underestimating the effects of crime for some individuals and overestimating them for others. Indeed, from a sentencer's perspective, rectifying this difficulty is one of the clearer goals of victim impact statements.[14] On the other hand, the case could be made that it is precisely those victims of crime whose suffering is greatest who should naturally receive the greatest support, information, compensation and access to facilities like video-links, screens and witness protection programmes. After all, notwithstanding the highly subjective nature of the impacts of crime, few would dispute the contention that a victim of rape, or the family of a murder victim, will tend to suffer considerably more than the average victim of domestic burglary. Furthermore, while one may emphasize the fact that such policies have tended to focus on the minority of greatly suffering victims, in so doing they have also highlighted the needs of what Bottigliero (2004) calls the 'unordinary', invisible victims who were previously the most neglected by criminal justice actors in all jurisdictions. Under this construction such victims, far from being overemphasized, are simply receiving the levels of support and service they always required but have long been denied.

To some extent then, the link drawn between victim status and the harm principle[15] in all the jurisdictions under review can be justified conceptually. However, a key impression derived from the previous chapters is that victims are being identified and assisted in many instances not purely on the basis of their suffering, but on other personal characteristics. In other words, judgements are being made not only about the degree of harm suffered by victims, but about the victims themselves. This of course returns us to Christie's (1986) notion of the ideal victim as weak, respectable, and blameless.[16] The supremacy of such ideal victims in the policy agendas of most jurisdictions is another clear theme to emerge out of the previous chapters. This was particularly apparent in Chapter 6, where most state compensation systems were shown to follow a policy of compensating only innocent victims who follow a suitable 'way of life' (in the words of the Irish Criminal Injuries Compensation Tribunal (2009: para. 14)). Similarly, in New South Wales it was demonstrated that a when a court considers granting a compensation order[17] it must have regard to any behaviour, condition, attitude, or disposition of the victim in the case which may have contributed to the injury suffered.[18] The significance of this last example for present purposes lies in the fact that it effectively places the degree of suffering below the conduct of the victim in the hierarchy of factors relevant to decision making.

The focus on ideal victims in policy making across the nine jurisdictions under review can be demonstrated in many other contexts. These range from the dismissive attitudes taken by police and other service providers to rape complainants in rural areas of Victoria (Elding *et al.* 1999) and South Africa (Mistry 2000), to the denial of victim status for 'incarcerated individuals, persons accused of crimes, and some police officers' in a number of US states (Human Rights Watch 2008: 15). In New Zealand, Jordan (2009) has criticized the homogenization of victims in the eyes of policy makers and criminal justice practitioners, and argues that such bias is reflected by restrictive definitions in the Victims of Crime Act 2002 in that jurisdiction. Chapters 3 and 4 also highlighted the example of victims of human trafficking in Australia, who are viewed by many as deviant undesirables despite their high degree of suffering (Marmo and La Forgia 2008). As such, Chapter 3 of this volume has discussed arguments to the effect that Australian policy on trafficking tends to reward witnesses in such cases while ignoring victims (Burn and Simmons 2005). Indeed, the concentration on victims who are witnesses (as opposed to victims *per se*) is another consistent theme across all nine jurisdictions; witnesses being 'ideal' victims in the sense that they are cooperating with the authorities. Furthermore, it was argued in Chapter 4 that the specific focus in most of these jurisdictions on *vulnerable* witnesses serves to overemphasize the (often illusionary) contrast between strong, guilty offenders and weak, innocent victims.[19] This focus on vulnerable witnesses (with little to no mention of vulnerable *defendants*) was prevalent at the national level,[20] and is also appreciable at the International Criminal Court where special consideration is given to the needs of 'children, elderly persons, persons with disabilities and victims of sexual or gender violence' (International Criminal Court 2002: Rule 86).

As noted in Chapter 2, it is a fallacy to assume that ideal victims who assist the justice system necessarily suffer more than non-ideal victims who do not. Nevertheless, the evidence collected from the nine jurisdictions under review indicated a general tendency among policy makers and practitioners to prioritize the idealness of victims even above the harm they have suffered in the provision of services and support.[21] The assertion that such ideal victims cooperate with the criminal justice system (recalling that, across jurisdictions, most crime in fact goes unreported (van Dijk *et al.* 2008)) hints at the existence of more instrumental goals from the perspective of policy makers, specifically the boosting of system efficiency and raising confidence in the criminal justice process.

Victims as a yardstick for success in criminal justice?

Garland's (2001) analysis implies that, at a time of reduced public confidence in the efficiency of criminal justice systems and their ability to tackle crime, the treatment of victims has become the standard by which criminal processes are judged and legitimized (see Shapland and Hall 2010). Evidence in favour of this proposition has been forthcoming in the present volume in a number of contexts. In Chapter 4, for example, it was highlighted that policies which relate to victims of crime have been associated in all the jurisdictions under review with increasing public confidence in the criminal justice system. Indeed, this underlying goal had been acknowledged explicitly by a number of these governments when discussing victim reforms.[22] Chapter 2 linked this development to the expansion of official definitions of victimhood in support of the contention that the recognition of new types of victim and new types of suffering has become essential to bolstering the legitimacy of the justice process.

Approaching the point from a different angle (and drawing on the Dutch experience) Wemmers (1998) notes that the legitimacy of any criminal justice system is grounded on its ability to protect human rights. In this context, Chapter 5 demonstrated that victims are increasingly seen as the bearers of such rights in all the jurisdictions under review[23] and by international bodies.[24] The point is that the fulfilment of such rights has become a key indicator of the quality of any criminal justice system. This is judged by reference to national targets in individual jurisdictions,[25] but also by transnational and international standards set down by bodies like the UN and the EU.[26]

The real utility of Garland's (2001) thought for present purposes is that it conceptually links developments in vicitmogogic[27] reforms with the wider concerns of policy makers working in the criminal justice sphere. As such, the consideration of victims by policy makers in all jurisdictions is not just a matter of assessing the degree of harm suffered, or the personal idealness of a relevant group. In fact such policy makers are influenced by a wide range of other factors, including perceived confidence in the criminal justice process; system efficiency; crime control; and the pressures of populist punitiveness (Bottoms 1995).[28] As a consequence, and to varying degrees, the treatment of victims becomes a proxy indicator of success in all these areas.

A macro perspective?

In sum, the above section has demonstrated that wide, cultural influences can be identified in all the jurisdictions under review as a contributing factor to the development of victim policies internationally. Nevertheless, the limitations of this perspective must be acknowledged. It is important to emphasize in particular that while such arguments help explain the increased attention victims of crime are now receiving from policy makers in all jurisdictions, those policy makers are also influenced by pressures which are if anything more tangible, and certainly more measurable by public opinion samples and victim surveys. As such, while some groups of victims are consistently receiving more attention, support, and consideration in all the jurisdictions under review, others remain largely untouched by such developments. This latter group includes corporate victims, victims of environmental crime and victims of financial crime (Williams and Hall 2009). The harm principle and (perhaps more significantly) the tendency to prioritize ideal victims help explain such limitations, but by themselves leave the picture substantially incomplete. What we do know is that, as discussed by Garland (2001), the success of victim initiatives appears to have become entwined with the legitimacy and success of criminal justice systems as a whole in all nine jurisdictions under review. Achieving such success is however a multi-facetted challenge, and the question therefore becomes whether victims are now supported for their own sake, or as a means of reforming the justice systems in other ways.

The influence of policy networks

Having discussed wider societal influences, this section now concentrates attention on the more material elements of the transnational and international policy networks influencing victim reform in individual jurisdictions. This discussion will be split into two subsections. The first deals with the influence of specific 'victim-centred' international instruments from organizations like the UN and the EU. The second deals with the more diverse range of factors and concerns impacting upon and driving victim policies domestically within the nine jurisdictions under review.

The influence of international policy instruments on victims of crime

Assessing the influence of international policy instruments on victim reform agendas in individual jurisdictions is not straightforward; there is after all no internationally recognized treaty, agreement, or other instrument exercising significant *binding* force over individual states which compels their governments to pursue policies favourable to victims of crime. This last observation may seem to contradict much of the data presented in Chapter 3, but in fact the overriding conclusion to draw from that discussion is that few of the major international instruments setting down standards of victim care[29] have more than persuasive authority in individual jurisdictions. The most notable exception is the 2001 *EU Framework Decision of the Council of the European Union*, which is binding on all those to whom it is addressed. Nevertheless, in this case it has been noted that failure to conform with the standards set down in the document appears to have minimal implications for Member States.[30] As such, the preceding analysis supports an interpretation of international policy instruments on victim issues which is largely consistent with van Dijk's (1989) impression of the most important of these documents, the 1985 UN Declaration.[31] That is, rather than imposing requirements on national governments *per se*, such instruments provide a basis of comparison against which national-level reforms can be judged.

International instruments have stressed a number of key themes, which have been taken up in the victim reform agendas of the individual jurisdictions under review. In particular, Chapter 3 identified the provision of information; protection from intimidation; access to compensation and restitution schemes; and minimizing secondary victimization as consistent priorities in most of these documents. Chapter 4 has demonstrated that these same core themes have been carried through to the domestic reform agenda in all the jurisdictions under review. In addition, many of the international instruments discussed in this volume have concentrated attention on specific groups of victims including: victims of human trafficking,[32] terrorism,[33] domestic violence[34] and child victims.[35] This of course recalls the points made in the last section concerning the focus in individual jurisdictions on specific groups of previously 'invisible' (but relatively uncommon) victims of crime. As such, pressure on individual jurisdictions to address these specific groups has come from the international level as well as the domestic context.

One particularly relevant example is that of human trafficking. Given the transnational nature of this activity, it is unsurprising that this issue has been addressed so frequently at the international level.[36] This in turn helps explain why this particular group of victims have achieved prominence in domestic policy making, despite sometimes being perceived as less than ideal victims (Marmo and La Forgia 2008). While once again the measures taken at the international level concerning trafficking have had limited enforceability, it is an area in which countries have been specifically named and shamed for failure to live up to those standards in the US Department of State's *Annual Trafficking in Persons Report* (US Department of State 2009).

In Chapter 3, the bulk of international instruments which address the needs of victim were described as principled rather than practically orientated. As such, their influence on national jurisdictions may be less coercive and more persuasive. In other words, the utility of such instruments may lie in their encouragement of international acceptance that the needs of victims of crime should be addressed. In some ways this can be viewed as a natural progression from some of the earliest calls for victim reforms. As discussed in Chapter 1, this was always a distinctly international movement comprised of a wide range of interest groups from different jurisdictions. As such, international bodies,[37] while not compelling states to take action directly, can successfully foster an international environment in which jurisdictions feel obliged to assist victims of crime; just as in the decades after World War II, similar bodies created an environment favourable to the development of human rights (see Merrills and Robertson 2001).

The argument that international pressures create a context in which national jurisdictions (including all nine under review) feel obliged to assist victims can be taken a step further to encompass theories of policy making more generally. Here, the argument can be made that it is the nature of policy making that so-called new innovations must be presented in a way that grounds them in past developments. Rock (1986, 1990) refers to this principle in studying the development of victim policy in both Canada and the UK. In both jurisdictions his findings revealed that the 'latest' innovation on victim reform would be packaged by government departments as the *continuation* of work that had already been done, and therefore already met with political acceptance: 'You don't say you're launching a new initiative. You say you are simply escalating, strengthening, responding in some way to public pressure, regarding something that's already been going on and has a long and solid history' (Rock 1986: 282) and 'Policy innovations would have been made to seem not only the inevitable result of all that had gone before, but the natural precursor of what was to come' (Rock 1990: 253). As such, international developments have given national jurisdictions the required background of policy measures and rhetoric to initiate their own reform agendas. This also reflects what Rein and Rabinovitz (1978, cited in Burnham and Weinberg 1978), termed the 'principle of circularity', whereby policy formation feeds into implementations, which feeds into policy evaluation and contributes to the formation of new or developed policies (Nakamura and Smallwood 1980).

In sum, pressures from international bodies can still exercise real influence over the reform agendas of individual jurisdictions both through the naming and shaming of those who fall below specified standards, and through the creation of an international policy environment which is conducive to introducing relevant reform. Under this construction, the criticisms made at the end of Chapter 3 that international instruments relating to victim care tend to be both idealistic and vague matters less than the overall message they send out to individual jurisdictions. As such, Chapters 4, 5, and 6 all demonstrate similar reforms being implemented in different jurisdictions, aimed at similar groups of victims. Furthermore, in the longer term, there is the possibility that such non-binding common practice among and between states can come to be regarded as a principle of international law (see Boyle 2006). This last point will be discussed in more detail towards the end of this chapter.

Wider transnational and international elements to the policy network

International instruments[38] putting pressure on individual jurisdictions to achieve victimogogic ends within and beyond their criminal justice systems have given significant impetus to the roll-out of relevant reform agendas in all the countries under review. However, it is important to appreciate that documents like the 1985 *UN Declaration* and the 2001 *EU Framework Decision* are only one component of the broader policy network behind such reforms. Indeed, Chapter 4 has demonstrated that the desire or need to support victims of crime is just one of a number of diverse influences driving reforms which have impacted on crime victims in all nine jurisdictions. Such influences were seen to include: the lobbying of victim support organizations and other NGOs; the development of crime prevention techniques; populist punitiveness; the human rights agenda; the 'discovery' of several groups of particularly vulnerable victims; drives to improve efficiency in criminal justice; and a new consumer focus exhibited by many criminal justice systems. The conclusion to be drawn from this list is that the policies under review in this volume are to some extent derived from factors which, at best, are only tangentially related to victims of crime themselves. Indeed, this conclusion may constitute a feature of modern policy making in a general sense, as indicated to me by one policy maker in the UK Office for Criminal Justice reform when interviewed for an earlier project: 'There's so many ways you can cut things, always so much work that overlaps, in any policy job that I've ever had' (representative of the UK Office for Criminal Justice Reform, quoted in Hall 2009c: 69).

The conclusion then is that the widespread roll-out of victim reform agendas in the nine countries under review can be explained by reference to transnational and international policy networks comprised of a diverse assortment of interrelated policy pressures. Significantly, such pressures have come not only from government actors or international organizations, but from NGOS and victim organizations, with examples including Victims Support Europe, Victim Support Australasia, and Human Rights Watch. The significant contribution of Victim Support Europe to the rekindling of interest in victims at the European Commission is a significant case in point.[39] As such, it is important to acknowledge that such policy networks include non-governmental bodies, and therefore reflect the development of governance (Crawford 1997). This is notwithstanding the evidence put forward in Chapter 4 that governments have in fact retained significant influence over the composition of policy networks in this area,[40] accepting victim support organizations to the table only when those organizations accede to certain conditions, including the abandonment of political activism.

Nevertheless, this understanding is not immune to criticism. Petek (2008: 72) has pointed out some of the weaknesses inherent in the use of policy networks (linking them to notions of governance) in the study of public policy in the following terms:

> The basic assumption of the approach is that contemporary policy-making is characterized by sharing of responsibilities for policy-making among state and the non-state actors. The approach is faced with a critical charge that it doesn't make a

clear distinction between dependent and independent variables, and that it does not contain an implicit causal logic that could be falsified.

As such, the criticism can be made that attributing such reforms to a wide range of factors effectively fails to take forward our understanding; victim reform agendas are merely placed in the context of an interconnected set of influences with no way of establishing causal directions. Put another way, the network approach may successfully *describe* the policy environment in which such reforms occur, but it cannot *explain* why the policy exists in different jurisdictions. Petek's (2008: 72) response to such criticism is to point out that policy networks constitute a *model* rather than a *theory* of policy making. As such, policy networks provide 'an analytical tool-box for organizing empirical material' which, the author argues, is particularly suited to the specific forms of governance that have emerged in recent times. As a model, policy networks lack the explanative power of a theory but this does not render them valueless. For example, the discussions above and in Chapter 4 clearly expands understating of this complex issue beyond the four vicitmogogic ideologies put forward by van Dijk (1983). They also expand the list of influences on victim policy put forward by Rock (1986) in Canada and the UK (Rock 1990, 2004).

Are these policies 'about victims'?

If policies which impact upon, and indeed benefit, victims of crime across the nine jurisdictions under review are in fact partly based on an entirely different (or loosely connected) set of policy concerns and pressures, what implications does this have for victims themselves and for the wider criminal justice systems under review? Throughout this volume the discussion has referred to warnings from Elias (1983 1986), Fattah (1992) and Ashworth (2000) that victims are effectively being recruited to the cause of political vote-catching and populist punitiveness. This perspective was also reflected in the above discussion of Furedi's (1998) argument that victimization now forms the basis of what amounts to a rather callous attempt to harness public sympathy (itself nurtured by politicians) for the fulfilment of political objectives. As such, this subsection will concentrate specific attention on the question of whether the reforms under review in this volume are effectively intended to achieve punitive aims in the context of the wider social changes discussed earlier.

Chapter 4 highlighted the association between certain victim reforms and punitive outcomes, emphasizing crime control over due process in the jurisdictions under review. For example, it has been demonstrated how the increased focus on victimization through non-criminal behaviour, so-called anti-social behaviour, widens the category of deviant acts attracting the attention of the criminal justice system. This has been a particular theme in England and Wales (UK Home Office 2010), the USA (US Department of Health and Human Services 2000), and Canada (Collin 2006). In line with this discussion, victims of anti-social behaviour are often portrayed as entirely blameless, despite the findings of Hunter and Nixon (2006) that the victims and perpetrators of such behaviour frequently overlap. In terms of expanding the scope of the criminal justice system to new individuals through reforms ostensibly presented as victimogogic, we might also include pro-arrest policies in cases of domestic violence. Other examples include the enactment of rape shield laws. While protecting victims from uncomfortable cross-examination when they appear in court as witnesses in rape trials, such laws have been seen as restricting the arguments of the defendants. In addition, this chapter has already referred to the focus of much of the policy literature in all the jurisdictions under review on so-called vulnerable witnesses, with almost no mention made of vulnerable *defendants*.

Indeed, it is the focus of the reform agenda not just on victims, but on victims *as witnesses* which has prompted much of the argument against such reforms on the grounds that they restrict defendants' rights, and are therefore punitive. On this point the words of Bruce and Isserow (2005: 45) in their report of a survey of witness satisfaction carried out in Gauteng, South Africa, are worth repeating here:

> Underpinning this concern is a belief that witnesses (including victims who are witnesses) should be supported in participating in the criminal justice system, not only because they have needs and concerns, but because this will serve the cause of improving the effectiveness and efficiency of the criminal justice system in its task of bringing offenders to justice.

Again, crime control is here presented as the ultimate goal of such measures. Other examples concerning court proceedings include the relaxing of hearsay rules in most jurisdictions and the increasing acceptability of evidence of a defendant's bad character. In addition, Chapter 5 has discussed the growing acceptance of anonymizing witnesses giving evidence in court in the USA (Parker 1981), the UK

(Ward 2009) and Canada (Ferguson 2007). Following the trial proper, discussions in Chapter 5 raised the issue of victim impact statements, and in particular Ashworth's (1993, 2000) concerns that such schemes result in inconsistent sentencing for offenders.

For victim activists, the real concern here is that the goals of victim care are not always compatible with this more punitive ethos. As such, this volume has discussed Temkin's (2002) argument that despite recent policy changes in the UK, USA, Ireland, Australia, Canada and New Zealand which are apparently aimed at making the justice process less hostile to rape victims, these states still essentially use rape victims as a prosecutorial tool to achieve convictions, often with little regard to their personal circumstances or feelings about the justice process. Cretney and Davis (1997) have demonstrated similar trends regarding victims in domestic violence cases in England and Wales. While some jurisdictions, notably the USA (Ellison 2002), have attempted to address such problems through victimless prosecutions, the tension between crime control and victim empowerment is a permanent dilemma for the victims' movement.[41]

In sum, despite the recent development of a form of middle-ground 'second-order consensus' on law and order issues (Downes and Morgan 2002) in most of the countries under review, Young (2003) argues that punitive impetus remains behind many reforms purporting to assist victims. For Garland (2001) victims are used to justify punitive measures by governments appealing to victims' 'need' to be protected and have their voices heard. For McBarnet (1983), vicitmologists have themselves facilitated this process by concentrating on the same stereotypical definitions of victimhood which are employed by most states. For Williams (1999b) the confusion between crime control and victim policies is most advanced in the USA, with the UK and Canada judged as achieving a better balance, and restorative justice experiments giving cause for further optimism. Nevertheless, while certainly many of these reforms have improved the situation for victim immensely (especially those few victims giving evidence as witnesses), it is equally clear that they have alternative, less paternalistic goals which are not always conducive to victims' needs. The conclusion is therefore that in any given jurisdiction, certainly in the sample under review by this volume, 'victims' is not so much a 'policy' as an area of overlap between a diverse range of 'policies', some of which have essentially punitive goals. Chapter 4 has demonstrated how such goals are themselves intertwined with financial, political, and legitimacy concerns regarding the criminal justice system.

A globalization of victim policies?

Throughout this volume mention has been made of globalization and the contention that, owing to the clear repetition of themes and policies relating to victim of crime in all nine countries under review, such policies may be described as having become globalized. Globalization is a term often used loosely to convey a sense of transnational interconnectedness between processes previously isolated within individual states.[42] As such, Beerkens (2004: 13) defines globalization in the following broad terms:

> The world-wide interconnectedness between nation-states becomes supplemented by globalization as a process in which basic social arrangements (like power, culture, markets, politics, rights, values, norms, ideology, identity, citizenship, solidarity) become disembedded from their spatial context (mainly the nation-state) due to the acceleration, massification, flexibilization, diffusion and expansion of transnational flows of people, products, finance, images and information.

For Giddens (1990: 64) the key characteristic of globalization is the decoupling of time and space, hence:

> Globalization can thus be defined as the intensification of worldwide social relations which link to distant localities in such a way that local happenings are shaped by events occurring miles away and vice versa.

Similarly, Scholte (2000: 46) prefers to think of globalization as deterritorialization. Nevertheless, as noted in Chapter 4, Scholte is also keen to emphasize the further point that 'the only consensus about globalization is that it is contested' (p. 41). The definition of globalization employed also seems to depend on the specific issues being studied.[43] Indeed, such is the conceptual confusion surrounding globalization that Wallerstein (2000: 28) expresses doubts as to the overall utility of the term: 'Personally I think it [globalization] is meaningless as an analytical concept and serves primarily as a term of political exhortation'. As such, it can be convincingly argued that to label the processes that have been exemplified in the present volume as aspects of globalization takes us no further forward in the analysis and understanding of such measures. Nevertheless, the link between globalization and the policies under discussion in this volume is pursued in this section for two key reasons. First, it is argued that globalization plays a similar role in these debates as the concept of policy networks given above. That is to say, while globalization is not an explanative theory, it does provide a framework in which to conceptualize such developments which itself expands our understanding of the dimensions of these reforms. This contention is supported by the second point, that a number of the concerns expressed in the wider criminological literature about globalization in general have particular resonance with several of the themes identified in this volume.

One such example is that of crime prevention, which Loader and Sparks (2007) identify as an 'anxiety' encountered in the criminological literature on globalization, specifically the advent of crime prevention networks at the transnational level. As the authors note: 'The concern here is that, far from rebuilding the capacity of states to deal in effective *and* accountable ways with transnational organised crime, the fears of such crimes are, instead, being 'exploited with a view to cutting normative corners and eroding civil rights' (Ruggiero 2000: 30)' (Loader and Sparks 2007: 90).

The most obvious correlation between this observation and the policies under review in this volume is the particular concentration on victims of human trafficking witnessed in all the countries under review. That this might reflect still broader developments in the globalization of public policy in criminal justice complements the above discussions on the singling-out of this non-ideal set of victims across and between jurisdictions. In a wider sense, however, it has been shown that crime prevention can be consistently identified as an underlying influence on the victim reform agendas of many countries in general. Again, this adds weight to the notion that 'victim policies' (if that is what they are to be called) in fact reflect much wider societal changes being experienced across jurisdictions. One such change is described by Goodey (2005) as 'a continuum of insecurities' in which people conflate fear of crime at the local, neighbourhood level with much wider fears about the supposed global criminal threat of 'outsiders':[44]

> In sum, people's sense of risk and insecurity is experienced at the level of the local but reflects global shifts concerning change and threats to the established social order (Girling *et al.* 2000) ... Here concerns about crime/victimization, fear of crime, and globalization merge. (p. 20)

This again reflects how globalization creates an environment in which governments feel obliged to restore falling confidence in the ability of their criminal justice systems to reduce risk.

Walklate (2007b) has drawn links between the economic aspects of globalization and the development of victim policies. In particular, Walklate's argument is that this development opened criminal justice systems in many countries to economic demands like efficiency, effectiveness, and value for money, all of which are reflected as elements of the policy network discussed above and in Chapter 4. Drawing once again on Garland's (2001) discussion, Walklate argues that in response the UK Government looked towards the USA for guidance, which has led to the proliferation of populist punitiveness. The data presented in this volume extend this argument to encompass jurisdictions beyond the UK.

The argument that globalization has to some extent facilitated the creation of new types of crime is a familiar one in the criminological literature (Nelken 1997b). The fact that globalization also creates new victims has only very recently come to the attention of commentators in the field (van Dijk and Letschert 2010). The significance of the discussion in this section, and indeed in this volume as a whole, is that this process of victim creation operates not just as a result of new, transnational crimes being facilitated through the cross-jurisdictional integration that come about as a result of globalization, but through the associated advent of transnational and international policy networks emphasizing the themes discussed above and in Chapter 4.

Victim support as a principle of international law?

Before making some concluding comments regarding the impact and scope of this research as a whole, this penultimate section will pause to reflect on the implications of the transnational and international reform agendas set out in this volume from the perspective of international law. This is useful because discussions surrounding international law are frequently required to address issues such as the sources of legal rules (or purported legal rules) in the international order. Most academic discussions surrounding domestic legal issues are able to take for granted facts like the binding nature of legislation and other forms of domestic law in any given jurisdiction, and the related imposition of legal obligations. By contrast, Thirlway (2006) describes how international lawyers deal much more regularly with so-called secondary rules which determine the sources and authority of international law. Such secondary rules have particular relevance for the present research, which has recurrently dealt with non-binding declarations and codes of practice issued by national governments and international organizations. As such, analyzing such developments from the perspective of international law will furnish us with a ready-made vocabulary in which to conceptualize such measures as well as presenting another dimension of the transnational and international policy networks connecting such reforms in all nine jurisdictions under review, and beyond.

It has been demonstrated through the course of this volume that measures which impact upon victims of crime in each of the nine jurisdictions under review have frequently been influenced by factors beyond the level of the state. In particular, this volume has noted the importance of the 1985 *UN Declaration* and its implementation in the form of legislation and codes of practice in most of the jurisdictions under review. Different examples of such domestic measures refer back to the 1985 *Declaration* to greater and lesser extents,[45] but it has been demonstrated that this instrument has been highly influential on the domestic policy agenda in all the jurisdictions under review. This is despite the fact that, as a Declaration of the United Nations General Assembly, the 1985 document is entirely non-binding from the traditional perspective of international law (Brownlie 2008).

In Chapter 3 it was argued that, from the perspective of victim activists, the non-binding nature of the 1985 *Declaration* matters less than its status as a statement of ideals, relatively unmarred by political concerns, against which national policies across jurisdictions can be measured and compared (van Dijk 1989). According to a policy analysis, the importance of the *Declaration* as a key component of the international policy network surrounding victims is therefore clear. From a *legal* perspective, however, the question becomes whether the 1985 *Declaration* has acquired (or could acquire) the status of binding international law, or could at least contribute to the development of such binding international legal rules in the future.

A conventional account holds that the sources of international law are classified into two groups: material sources and formal sources. Material sources normally take the form of documents or judicial decisions which set out the specific content of legal rules. However, such rules do not become law unless they can be said to derive authority from one of the 'formal sources' of international law. These are listed in Article 38 of the Statute of the International Court of Justice as treaties or conventions (Art.38(1)(a)); international custom as evidence of a general practice accepted as law (Art.38(1)(b)); and the general principles of law recognised by civilized nations (Art.38(1)(c)).[46] The first of these can be dismissed relatively quickly for present purposes; the 1985 instrument is a Declaration of the UN General Assembly rather than a treaty or convention entered into between states. It is well established that the General Assembly is not a law-making body in the conventional sense. Resolutions and declarations made by the Assembly may form material sources of international law, but never constitute formal sources of law in themselves (Klabbers 1996).

As noted earlier, Article 38 of the Statute of the International Court of Justice holds that custom is also a formal source of international law. A binding rule of international law is said to derive from custom through the demonstration of common practices by states[47] carried out in a manner which demonstrates a subjective belief that such practices are made obligatory by international law. The classic pronouncement of this is found in the judgment of the International Court of Justice in the *North Sea Continental Shelf* case: 'Not only must the acts concerned amount to a settled practice, but they must also be such, or be carried out in such a way, as to be evidence of a belief that this practice is rendered obligatory by the existence of a rule of law requiring it'.[48] In light of this understanding, the key question for international lawyers is the degree to which governments[49] introducing similar (perhaps globalized) practices related to victims of crime are doing so based on the subjective impression that such practices are now *de facto* obligatory. If this psychological element, which international lawyers call *opinio juris*, were established in relation to practices consistent with the 1985 *Declaration*, or any other such document, then such practices may be recognized as *lex lata* (law which has become binding). The material source of such law becomes the *Declaration*, or other such statement of victims' rights, with the formal source or authority deriving from custom. The implications of such a finding would be significant indeed from the perspective of the victims' movement, given that customary international law is usually thought to be binding on *all* states, not just those who took part in the establishment of such custom (Shaw 2007). In making such a determination, international lawyers would look at the language of the *Declaration* and the pronouncements of various states on its implementation. On the former point, the predominant use of non-obligatory language in the *Declaration* itself[50] might detract from its (potential) legal status. On the other hand, statements made in official documents relating to victims in some of the countries under review seem to affirm the belief that these states now feel *obliged* to introduce such reforms. Take, for example, the preamble from the South African Service Charter for Victims of Crime:

> Government's commitment to implement measures aimed at continuous reform of the criminal justice system to protect and promote the rights of victims in compliance with international obligations under international human rights instruments, such as the UN Declaration of Basic Principles of Justice for Victims of Crime and Abuse of Power (1985) and the Prevention and Eradication of Violence Against Women and Children Addendum to the 1997 SADC Declaration on Gender and Development. (South African Department of Justice and Constitutional Affairs 2008a: 2)

This clearly presents the 1985 *Declaration*, and other ostensibly non-binding instruments, as creating obligations. In Ireland, the Commission for the Support of Victims of Crime recommended that the newly established Office for Victims of Crime in that jurisdiction should 'advise the Minister on Ireland's compliance with international obligations to assist victims of crime and their support groups' (2008: para. 7.5). Again, the language of 'obligations' is evident.

There is the remaining hurdle that, conventionally, international law is conceived as applying only to states' relations with other states. As such, Thirlway (2006) contends that purely internal customs, such as those relating to domestic criminal justice systems, cannot amount to the requisite practices to be recognized as international law, as they do not impact upon other states. Nevertheless, this ignores the reality that a great deal of international law now relates to matters which previously would have been considered internal to specific states, including criminal justice matters (Brownlie 2008). Even if this were not the case, states are increasingly being called upon to address the needs of transnational victims as well as tackling transnational crime, with particular emphasis on victims of human trafficking.[51] Finally, Thirlway (2006) acknowledges that human rights matters might be an exception to the general principle he puts forward. As noted in Chapter 5, the distinction between 'human rights' and 'victims' rights' is increasingly difficult to draw.

As intriguing as the prospect may be, it is not the purpose of the preset section to judge the degree to which the process described in the last paragraph is underway, let alone concluded.[52] The goal here is more modest, being simply to demonstrate the *legal* relevance[53] (or at least potential relevance) of the non-binding instruments introduced both nationally and internationally which purport to address the needs of victims of crime. At the international level, some legal scholars have chosen to endow instruments like the 1985 *UN Declaration* with the label of 'soft law', which has the capacity to form the material basis of customary law[54] and can be converted into 'hard law' though its enshrinement in treaties (Boyle 2006).[55] The concept of soft law is greatly contested in the relevant literature (see Klabbers 1996). To some extent, whether or not one chooses to call the 1985 *UN Declaration* 'soft law' has little bearing on the arguments concerning its potential either to become hard law or constitute an important step in the process towards the establishment of internationally binding legal principles relating to victims of crime. Indeed, d'Aspremont (2008: 1088) has reflected on the argument that, given the operation of policy networks, legally binding instruments are not always needed to achieve significant ends:

> Many recent developments, like networks among governmental officials or transnational law, have shown that non-legal instruments may prove more adapted to the speed and complexity of modern international relations and are more and more resorted to in practice. Non-legal instruments can be at least as integrative for a community as legal ones.

This section has to some extent presented an alternative, legalistic perspective on the international victim reform agenda. It has done so principally in support of contentions made earlier in this volume that the lack of enforceability of most national and international instruments related to victims of crime does not detract from their significance as part of the international policy network surrounding such reforms. More specifically, this section has demonstrated the importance of these conceptual legal debates as yet another component of this overriding policy network. Indeed, no jurisdiction can afford to ignore such legal implications of their reforms relating to victims, given that all jurisdictions have the potential to find themselves bound by such principles sometime in the future.

Conclusion

The international progression of the victims' movement has continued to gather pace in recent years, fostering legislative and administrative reforms in most jurisdictions within and beyond the sample of nine countries under review in this volume. The analysis presented here demonstrates the complexity of this process, along with the interaction of national, transnational and international factors which have led to such policy reforms at the domestic level in individual states and at the level of international organizations. As such, it is wrong to think of such developments as a chronological list of breakthroughs in individual jurisdictions. It may even be wrong to think of these as 'victim policies' *per se* given the divergent pressures at work behind them. The concept of policy networks helps us conceptualize these developments, although in reality it may serve as only a starting point for a more detailed analysis which encompasses political, social and legal elements.

The wider point is that the observations made in this volume concerning the driving forces behind victim reform can be applied to modern public policy making in general, certainly within criminal justice, if not beyond it. As such, it can be seen how such policy is driven to a large extent by broad societal changes witnessed across jurisdictions, which are continuing to develop. While the present study takes 'victims of crime' as a principal example of such processes in action, future research could apply the same critical perspective to other areas of public policy reform, and to other jurisdictions. From a socio-legal perspective, further examination of how such political and societal factors interact with legal principles to create internationally binding obligations on states regarding victims of crime (and, indeed, other areas) is an obvious starting point for future research. Nevertheless, the inherent danger in all this is that the victims of crime themselves get lost in the confusion; the very problem these policies are ostensibly intended to correct.

Notes

1 A list of more specific objectives was set out on pp. 13–14.
2 The wider implications of this development are discussed on pp. 224–226 below.
3 See pp. 11–13 for full discussion of the components of this framework along with possible criticisms.
4 See pp. 142–143.
5 Defined in this case in terms of falling within the six (now seven) protected groups overseen by the UK Equality and Human Rights Commission.

6 Which traces back to the 1985 UN Declaration (Art.1).
7 Australian Capital Territory Victims of Crime Act 1994, s.3.
8 'The amount of this one-off payment may therefore differ from the actual amount of damage you suffer' (Schadefonds Geweldsmisdrijven 2008: 6). See p. 173.
9 In the Victims Support and Rehabilitation Act 1996.
10 There are of course exceptions, including the system of restitution in place in New York, which specifically points out that 'Restitution is *not* for payment of damages for future losses, mental anguish or 'pain and suffering" (New York State Crime Victims Board 2008: 1) but is instead intended to genuinely compensate for practical losses.
11 See pp. 175–182.
12 Although this differs markedly by country, see pp. 187–202.
13 Whether this be the police in deciding to press charges, the prosecution in deciding to run a trial, or the relevant authority in deciding to award state-based compensation.
14 Although evidence from a number of jurisdictions indicates that victim impact statements are thought by judges not to contain much unexpected information concerning the impacts of crime (see pp. 140 and 142).
15 See pp. 30–34.
16 See pp. 47–52.
17 That is, ordering the offender to compensate the victim, see p. 48.
18 Victim Support and Rehabilitation Act 1996, s.30(a).
19 See p. 105.
20 A particularly good example being the Youth Justice and Criminal Evidence Act 1999 of England and Wales.
21 South Africa is one possible exception to this rule, although here much of the victim policy agenda is focused on battered wives in rural areas.
22 New Zealand, England and Wales, and Ireland. See UK Home Office (2003d) for a discussion of the conflict in policy aims inherent in prioritizing confidence in the criminal justice system *and* efficiency.
23 Particularly in South Africa, where less explicit distinctions are being drawn by policy makers between 'victims' rights' and 'human rights'.
24 See also Chapter 3.
25 Set down in documents like the victims' charters.
26 See for example the annual *Trafficking in Persons* report which names and shames those jurisdictions not doing enough to tackle people trafficking (see p.127). This bears some resemblance to the naming-and-shaming exercise conducted in the EU against countries not fulfilling the requirements of the 2001 *Framework Directive* (European Union 2009a).
27 See p. 3.
28 Conclusions regarding the policy networks created by such issues will be explored in greater detail in the following section.
29 At least, relating to victims as a whole.
30 See p. 74.

31 See p. 64.
32 For example, the *United Nations Convention against Transnational Organized Crime*, see p. 66–67.
33 For example, the Council of Europe's 2005 Convention on the Prevention of Terrorism, see p. 70.
34 See Council of Europe Recommendation R (06) 8.
35 For example, the *United Nations Convention against Transnational Organized Crime*, and its supplementary *Protocol to Prevent, Suppress and Punish Trafficking in Persons, Especially Women and Children*, see p. 66–67.
36 See pp. 117–121.
37 Which includes non-government organizations such as Victim Support Europe, see p. 80.
38 Whether through binding instruments or (more often) persuasive authorities.
39 See p. 219.
40 See Richardson (2000).
41 Another good example is the ultimately unsuccessful attempt to revise Witness Orders in the UK, see p. 128.
42 Reinicke (1997) criticizes the fact that the term 'globalization' is often used interchangeably with 'interdependence'.
43 For example, an *economic* definition of the concept reads, 'The increasing integration of national markets that were previously segmented from one another' (Begg *et al.* 2003: 92).
44 Again reflecting Gidden's (2000) point concerning the decoupling of time and space.
45 For example, the *South African Code of Practice for Victims of Crime* follows the structure of the *Declaration* very closely.
46 The last of these will not be discussed in this section owing to its general lack of development both by the International Court of Justice and in the literature (see Thirlway 2006). For completeness, the Statute also lists a fourth 'subsidiary' (material) source of international law as 'judicial decisions and legal teachings'.
47 Enough to constitute a generality of practice, with particular regard to those sates most affected by a given practice (Brownlie 2008).
48 *North Sea Continental Shelf, Judgment, ICJ Reports 1969*: p. 3, para. 77.
49 See Brownlie (2008) for discussion of the problem of 'states' holding subjective beliefs. For simplicity this complex debate is bypassed here in favour of interpreting this as vesting such belief in domestic governments.
50 'Judicial and administrative mechanisms *should* be established and strengthened where necessary to enable victims to obtain redress' (Annex A(5), emphasis added).
51 Indeed, it was noted in Chapter 3 that several of the international instruments concerning human trafficking are, unlike the 1985 UN Declaration, already binding.

52 Although the potential for further research as part of a dedicated legal analysis is clear.
53 As opposed to political relevance.
54 Cheng (1965) has gone so far as to suggest that an appropriately worded UN resolution can create *instant* customary law.
55 A significant case in point being the *UN Universal Declaration of Human Rights* of 1948, enshrined in 1966 in the International Covenant on Civil and Political Rights.

References

Achtenberg, M. (2000) 'Understanding restorative justice practice within the Aboriginal context', *FORUM on Corrections Research*, 12: 1–6.

Advocates for Victims of Homicide (Ireland) (2010) *Information* [online]. Available at: http://www.advic.ie/information/information1.asp

African Union (2001) *Principles and Guidelines on the Rights to a Fair Trial and Legal Assistance in Africa*. Pretoria: African Union.

Alexander, R. (2002) *Domestic Violence in Australia: The Legal Response*. Annandale, IL: Federation Press.

Altheide, D. (1987) 'Ethnographic Content Analysis', *Qualitative Sociology*, 10: 65–77.

Amir, M. (1971) *Patterns in Forcible Rape*. Chicago, IL: University of Chicago Press.

Angle, H., Malam, S. and Carey, C. (2003) *Witness Satisfaction: Findings from the Witness Satisfaction Survey 2002*, Home Office Online Report 19/03. London: Home Office.

Argentina Ministry of Justice (2009) *Attorney General* [online]. Available at: http://www.jus.gov.ar/ministerio/sec_justicia.shtml

Arts, K. (2006) 'General introduction: a child rights-based approach to international criminal accountability', in K. Arts and V. Popovski (eds), *International Criminal Accountability and the Rights of Children*. Cambridge: Cambridge University Press, 3–16.

Arts, K. and Popovski, V. (eds) (2006) *International Criminal Accountability and the Rights of Children*. Cambridge: Cambridge University Press.

Ashworth, A. (1986) 'Punishment and compensation: victims, offenders and the state', *Oxford Journal of Legal Studies*, 6: 86–122.

Ashworth, A. (1993) 'Victim impact statements and sentencing', *Criminal Law Review*, 40: 498–509.

Ashworth, A. (1998) *The Criminal Process: An Evaluative Study*. Oxford: Oxford University Press.
Ashworth, A. (2000) 'Victims' rights, defendants' rights and criminal procedure', in A. Crawford and J. Goodey (eds), *Integrating a Victim Perspective Within Criminal Justice: International Debates*. Aldershot: Ashgate Dartmouth, 185–204.
Associated Press (2006) 'Six get heavy sentences in Dutch human trafficking trial', *USA Today*, 7 November, 12.
Atkinson, M. and Coleman, W. (1992) 'Policy networks, policy communities and the problems of governance', *Governance*, 5: 154–180.
Audit Office of New South Wales (1998) *Management of Court Waiting Times*. Sydney: Audit Office of New South Wales.
Auditor General of Tasmania (2008) *Timeliness in the Magistrates' Court*, Special Report No. 73. Hobart: Government Printer.
Auld, Lord Justice (2001) *Review of the Criminal Courts of England and Wales*. London: HMSO.
Australian Broadcasting Corporation (2009) *Child Safety Failed Rape Victim* [online]. Available at: http://www.abc.net.au/7.30/content/2007/s2115957.htm

Bache, I. (2003) 'Governing through governance: education policy control under new labour', *Political Studies*, 51: 300–314.
Bacik, I. (2002) 'Women and the criminal justice system', in P. O'Mahony (ed.), *Criminal Justice in Ireland*. Dublin: Institute of Public Administration, 134–154.
Bassett, L. (2007) *Restorative Justice: Background and Discussion Paper*. Melbourne: Victoria Department of Justice.
Bazemore, G. (1998) 'The juvenile court and the future response to youth crime: a vision for community juvenile justice', *Juvenile & Family Court Journal*, 49: 55–87.
BBC (2006) *Extra £2.5 Million for July Bomb Victims* [online]. Available at: http://news.bbc.co.uk/1/hi/uk/5001734.stm
Beerkens, E. (2004) *Global Opportunities and Institutional Embeddedness; Higher Education Consortia in Europe and Southeast Asia*. Enschede: CHEPS.
Begg, D., Fischer, S. and Dornbusch, R. (2003) *Economics*. Maidenhead: McGraw-Hill.
Benhabib, S. (2005) 'Beyond interventionism and indifference: culture, deliberatio and pluralism', *Philosophy and Social Criticism*, 31: 753–772.
Bernstein, S. and Cashore, B. (2000) 'Globalization, four paths of internationalization and domestic policy change: the case of EcoForestry in British Columbia, Canada', *Canadian Journal of Political Science*, 33: 67–99.
Blad, J. (2009) 'Restorative justice in The Netherlands: blockades and opportunities'. Paper presented at the Hungarian Crime Prevention Board *Best Practices of Restorative Justice in the Criminal Procedure* conference, Budapest: 27–29 April 2009.

References

Blad, J. and Pemberton, A. (2006) 'Implementing restorative justice in The Netherlands'. Paper presented at the *4th Conference of the European Forum for Restorative Justice – Restorative justice: An agenda for Europe*, Barcelona: 15–17 June 2006.

Booth, T. and Carrington, K. (2007) 'Setting the scene: a question of history', in S. Walklate (ed.), *Handbook of Victims and Victimology*. Cullompton: Willan, 380–416.

Bottigliero, I. (2004) *Redress for Victims of Crimes Under International Law*. Leiden: Martinus Nijhoff.

Bottoms, A. (1995) 'The philosophy and politics of punishment and sentencing', in C. Clark and R. Morgan (eds), *The Politics of Sentencing Reform*. Oxford: Clarendon Press, 17–50.

Bottoms, A. (2003) 'Some sociological reflections on restorative justice', in A. von Hirsh, J. Roberts, A. Bottoms, K. Roach and M. Schiff (eds), *Restorative Justice and Criminal Justice: Competing or Reconcilable Paradigms?* Oxford: Hart, 79–114.

Boutellier, H. (2000) *Crime and Morality: The Significance of Criminal Justice in Post-modern Culture*. Dordrecht: Kluwer.

Boyle, A. (2006) 'Soft law in international law-making', in M. Evans (ed.), *International Law*. Oxford: Oxford University Press, 141–158.

Braithwaite, J. and Parker, C. (1999) 'Restorative justice is republican justice', in L. Walgrave and G. Bazemore (eds), *Restoring Juvenile Justice: An Exploration of the Restorative Justice Paradigm for Reforming Juvenile Justice*. Monsey: Criminal Justice Press, 103–126.

Brienen, M. and Hoegen, H. (2000) *Victims of Crime in 22 European Criminal Justice Systems: The Implementation of Recommendation (85) 11 of the Council of Europe on the Position of the Victim in the Framework of Criminal Law and Procedure*. Niemegen: Wolf Legal Productions.

Brownlie, I. (2008) *Principles of Public International Law*. Oxford: Oxford University Press.

Bruce, D. and Isserow, M. (2005) *Putting People First? A Survey of Witness Satisfaction in Three Gauteng Magistrates' Courts*. Johannesburg: Centre for the Study of Violence and Reconciliation.

Burn, J. and Simmons, F. (2005) 'Rewarding witnesses, ignoring victims: an evaluation of the New Trafficking Visa Framework', *Immigration Review*, 24: 6–13.

Burnham, W. and Weinberg, M. (1978) *American politics and public policy*, Cambridge: MIT Press.

Cabinet Office (1999) *Modernising Government*, Cm 4310. London: The Stationery Office.

Californian Department of Corrections and Rehabilitation (2009) *Restitution Responsibilities, Information for Adult Offenders* [online]. Available at: http://www.cdcr.ca.gov/Victim_Services/restitution_responsibilities.html

Californian Victim Compensation and Government Claims Board (2008) *Strategic Plan 2008–2012*. Sacramento, CA: Californian Victim Compensation and Government Claims Board.

Californian Victim Compensation and Government Claims Board (2009) *Victim Compensation Program (VCP) Regulations*. Sacramento, CA: Californian Victim Compensation and Government Claims Board.

Camerer, L., Louw, A., Shaw, M., Artz, L. and Scharf, W. (1988) *Crime in Cape Town: Results of a City Victim Survey*, ISS monograph series. Cape Town: Institute for Security Studies.

Campbell, S. (2002) *A Review of Anti-social Behaviour Orders*. Home Office Research Study 236. London: UK Home Office.

Canadian Aboriginal Justice Directorate (2009) *The Aboriginal Justice Strategy* [online]. Available at: http://www.justice.gc.ca/eng/pi/ajs-sja/index.html

Canadian Department of Justice (2000) *Charging and Prosecution Policies in Cases of Spousal Assault: A Synthesis of Research, Academic, and Judicial Responses*. Ottawa: Canadian Department of Justice.

Canadian Department of Justice (2003) *Canadian Statement of Basic Principles of Justice for Victims of Crime*. Ottawa: Canadian Department of Justice.

Canadian Department of Justice (2008) *The Evolution of Federal Initiatives to Support victims of Crime* [online]. Available at: http://www.victimsweek.gc.ca/home-acceil.html

Canadian Department of Justice (2009) *Federal Victims Strategy, Mid-term Evaluation* [online]. Available at: http://www.justice.gc.ca/eng/pi/eval/rep-rap/08/fvs-vic/p2.html

Canadian Department of Justice (2009) *The Youth Criminal Justice Act: Summary and Background* [online]. Available at: http://www.justice.gc.ca/eng/pi/yj-jj/ycja-lsjpa/back-hist.html

Canadian Resource Centre for Victims of Crime (2001) *Restorative Justice in Canada*. Ottawa: Canadian Renounce Centre for Victims of Crime.

Canadian Resource Centre for Victims of Crime (2006) *Victims' Rights in Canada*. Ottawa: Canadian Resource Centre for Victims of Crime.

Canadian Resource Centre for Victims of Crime (2010) *About Us* [online]. Available at: http://crcvc.ca/en/about/

Cape, E. (ed.) (2004) *Reconcilable Rights? Analysing the Tension between Victims and Defendants*. London: Legal Action Group.

Carrabine, E., Cox. P., Lee, M., Plummer, K. and South, N. (2009) *Criminology: A sociological introduction*. New York: Routledge.

Cavanagh, M. (1984) *Compensation for Crime Victims*. Issue Brief Number IB74014. Washington, DC: The Library of Congress Congressional Research Service.

Cavadino, M. and Dignan, J. (2007) *The Penal System: An Introduction*. London: Sage Publications.

Chankova, D. (1998) *Recent Developments in Victim-related Policies in Bulgaria* [online]. Available at: http://www.restorativejustice.org/10fulltext/chankova/view

References

Cheng, B. (1965) 'United Nations resolutions on outer space: "instant" customary law?', *Indian Journal of International Law*, 5: 23–48.

Christie, N. (1977) 'Conflicts as property', *British Journal of Criminology*, 17: 1–15.

Christie, N. (1986) 'The ideal victim', in E. Fattah (ed.), *From Crime Policy to Victim Policy*. Basingstoke: Macmillan, 17–30.

Coates, R. and Umbreit, M. (2000) *Restorative Justice Circles in South Saint Paul*. Minneapolis, MN: Centre for Restorative Justice and Peacemaking.

Coffey, A. and Atkinson, P. (1996) *Making Sense of Qualitative Data*. London: Sage.

Cole, A. (2007) *The Cult of True Victimhood*. Stanford, CA: Stanford University Press.

Coleman, W. and Perl, A. (1999) 'Internationalized policy environments and policy network analysis', *Political Studies*, 47: 691–709.

Collin, C. (2006) *Substance Abuse and Public Policy in Canada: V. Alcohol and Related Harms*. Ottawa: Parliamentary Information and Research Service.

Collins, S. and Cattermole, R. (2003) *Anti-social Behaviour: Power and Remedies*. London: Sweet and Maxwell.

Commission of the European Union (2009) *Report Pursuant to Article 18 of the Council Framework Decision of 15 March 2001 on the Standing of Victims in Criminal Proceedings*. Brussels: Commission of the European Union.

Commonwealth of Nations (2002) *Commonwealth Statement of Basic Principles of Justice for Victims of Crime*. London: Commonwealth of Nations.

Commonwealth Secretariat (2002) *Commonwealth Guidelines for the Treatment of Victims of Crime*. London: Commonwealth Secretariat.

Commonwealth Secretariat (2008) *An Action Plan to End Human Trafficking*. London: Commonwealth Secretariat.

Commonwealth Secretariat (2009) *Guidelines for Police Training on Violence Against Women and Child Sexual Abuse*. London: Commonwealth Secretariat.

Cornwell, D. (2006) *Criminal Punishment and Restorative Justice: Past, Present and Future Perspectives*. Winchester: Waterside Press.

Council of Europe (2005a) *Convention on the Prevention of Terrorism*. Warsaw: Council of Europe.

Council of Europe (2005b) *Convention on Action against Trafficking in Human Beings*. Warsaw: Council of Europe.

Council of the European Union (2001) *Council Framework Decision of 15 March 2001 on the Standing of Victims in Criminal Proceedings*. Brussels: Council of the European Union.

Council of the European Union (2009) *The Stockholm Programme: An Open and Secure Europe Serving the Citizen*. Brussels: Council of the European Union.

Coy, M., Kelly, L. and Foord, J. (2008) *The Postcode Lottery of Violence Against Women Support Services in Britain*. London: Fawcett Society.

Crawford, A. (1997) *The Local Governance of Crime: Appeals to Partnerships and Community*. Oxford: Clarendon Press.

Crawford, A. and Newburn, T. (2003) *Youth Offending and Restorative Justice: Implementing Reform in Youth Justice*. Cullompton: Willan.

Crawford, K. (1990) 'Due obedience and the rights of victims: Argentina's transition to democracy', *Human Rights Quarterly*, 12: 17–52.

Cressey, D. (1986) 'Research implications of conflicting conceptions of victimology', in E. Fattah (ed.), *Towards a Critical Victimology*. London: Macmillan, 43–54.

Cretney, A. and Davis, G. (1997) 'Prosecuting domestic assault: victims failing courts or courts failing victims?', *Howard Journal of Criminal Justice*, 36: 146–157.

Criminal Justice Joint Inspection (2009) *Executive Summary of the Report of a Joint Thematic Review of Victim and Witness Experiences in the Criminal Justice System*. London: HM Crown Prosecution Service Inspectorate.

Criminal Justice Transition Coalition (2009) *Improving Likelihood of Victim Restitution* [online]. Available at: http://2009transition.org/criminaljustice/index.php?option=com_content&view=article&id=63&Itemid=62

Croall, H. (2007) 'Victims of white-collar and corporate crime', in P. Davies, P. Francis and C. Greer (eds), *Victims, Crime and Society*. London: Sage, 78–108.

Daalder, A. (2007) *Prostitution in the Netherlands Since the Lifting of the Brothel Ban*. The Hague: Netherlands Ministry of Justice.

Daelemans, A. (2006) 'Guiding the change process in Belgian prisons: towards a restorative prison policy'. Paper presented at the *4th Conference of the European Forum for Restorative Justice – Restorative Justice: An Agenda for Europe*, Barcelona: 15–17 June 2006.

Dandurand, Y. (2009) *Addressing Inefficiencies in the Criminal Justice Process*. Vancouver: International Centre for Criminal Law Reform and Criminal Justice Policy.

d'Aspremont, J. (2008) 'Softness in international law: a self-serving quest for new legal materials', *The European Journal of International Law*, 19: 1057–1093.

David, J., Stubbs, J. and Pegrum, F. (1990) *Services for Victims of Crime in Australia*, Griffith: Criminological Research Council.

Davies, G. (1999) 'The impact of television on the presentation and reception of children's testimony', *International Journal of Law and Psychiatry*, 22: 241–256.

Davis, R. (2007) *Domestic Violence: Intervention, Prevention, Policies, and Solutions*. Boca Raton: CRC Press.

Davis, R. and Smith, B. (1994) 'The effect of victim impact statements on sentencing decisions: a test in an urban setting', *Justice Quarterly*, 11: 453.

Delport, E., Koen, K. and Songololo, M. (2007) *Human Trafficking in South Africa: Root Causes and Recommendations*. Paris: United Nations Educational, Scientific and Cultural Organisation.

References

De Lange. J. (2006) 'The politics of restorative justice in post conflict South Africa and beyond'. Paper presented at the *International Conference on the Politics of Restorative Justice in Post Conflict South Africa and Beyond*, University of Cape Town: 21 September 2006.

Department of Justice and Attorney General of New South Wales (2009) *Helping Victims of Crime* [online]. Available at http://www.lawlink.nsw.gov.au/lawlink/Corporate/ll_corporate.nsf/pages/attorney_generals_department_helping_victims

De Smith, S. and Brazier, R. (1998) *Constitutional and Administrative Law*. London: Penguin.

Dignan, J. (1992) 'Repairing the damage: can reparation be made to work in the service of diversion?', *British Journal of Criminology*, 32: 453–472.

Dignan, J. (2002a) 'Restorative justice and the law: the case for an integrated, systemic approach', in L. Walgrave (ed.), *Restorative Justice and the Law*. Cullompton: Willan, 168–190.

Dignan, J. (2002b) 'Towards a systematic model of restorative justice', in A. von Hirsh, J. Roberts, A. Bottoms, K. Roach and M. Schiff (eds), *Restorative Justice and Criminal Justice*. Oxford: Hart, 135–156.

Dignan, J. (2005) *Understanding Victims and Restorative Justice*. Maidenhead: Open University Press.

Dignan, J. and Cavadino, M. (1996) 'Towards a framework for conceptualising and evaluating models of criminal justice from a victim's perspective', *International Review of Victimology*, 4: 153–182.

Doak, J. (2003) 'The victim and the criminal process: an analysis of recent trends in regional and international tribunals', *Legal Studies*, 23: 1–32.

Doak, J. (2005) 'Victims' rights in criminal trials: prospects for participation', *Journal of Law and Society*, 32: 2924–2316.

Doak, J. and O'Mahony, D. (2006) 'The vengeful victim? Assessing the attitudes of victims participating in restorative youth conferencing', *British Journal of Criminology*, 13: 1–21.

Dorey, P. (2004) 'Attention to detail: the conservative policy agenda', *The Political Quarterly*, 75: 373–377.

Douglas, R. and Laster, K., (1994) *Victim Information and the Criminal Justice System: Adversarial or Technocratic Reform?* Griffith: Australian Criminology Research Council.

Downes, D. and Morgan, R. (2002) '"The skeletons in the cupboard": the politics of law and order at the turn of the millennium', in M. Maguire, R. Morgan and R. Reiner (eds), *The Oxford Handbook of Criminology*. Oxford: Oxford University Press, 286–321.

Doyle, C. (2008) *Crime Victims' Rights Act*. New York: Nova.

Easteal, P. (ed.) (1998) *Balancing the Scales: Rape, Law Reform, and Australian Culture*. Sydney: Federation Press.

ECPAT The Netherlands (2009) *Offenders Beware: Child Sex Tourism Case Studies*. Amsterdam: ECPAT.

Edwards, I. (2002) 'The place of victims' preferences in the sentencing of "their" offenders', *Criminal Law Review*, Sep: 689–702.

Edwards, I. (2004) 'An ambiguous participant: the crime victim and criminal justice decision-making', *British Journal of Criminology*, 44: 967–982.

Edelhertz, H. and Geis, G. (1974) *Public Compensation to Victims of Crime*. New York: Praeger.

Egeberg, M. (1999) 'The impact of bureaucratic structure on policy making', *Public Administration*, 77: 155–170.

Elding, M., Donnelly, J. and Sanderson, K. (1999) 'The challenge of delivering services which provide for restoration to rurally isolated communities: the Victorian example'. Paper presented at the *Restoration for Victims of Crime*, Melbourne: September 1999.

Eley, S. (2005) 'Changing practices: the specialised domestic violence court process', *Howard Journal of Criminal Justice*, 44: 113–124.

Elias, R. (1983) *Victims of the System: Crime Victims and Compensation in American Politics and Criminal Justice*. New Brunswick, NJ: Transaction.

Elias, R. (1986) *The Politics of Victimization: Victims, Victimology and Human Rights*. New York: Oxford University Press.

Ellison, L. (2001) *The Adversarial Process and the Vulnerable Witness*. Oxford: Oxford University Press.

Ellison, L. (2002) 'Cross-examination and the intermediary: bridging the language divide', *Criminal Law Review*, Feb: 114–127.

Ellison, L. (2003) 'Case note: the right of challenge in sexual offence cases: *Sn v Sweden*', *International Journal of Evidence and Proof*, 7: 1–2.

Epstein, J. and Langenbahn, S. (1994) *The Criminal Justice and Community Response to Rape*. Washington, DC: US Department of Justice, National Institute of Justice.

Erez, E. (1994) 'Victim participation in sentencing: and the debate goes on', *International Review of Victimology*, 3: 17–32.

Erez, E. (1999) 'Who's afraid of the big bad victim? Victim impact statements as victim empowerment and enforcement of justice', *Criminal Law Review*, Jul: 545–556.

Erez, E. (2000) 'Integrating a victim perspective in criminal justice through victim impact statements', in A. Crawford and J. Goodey (eds), *Integrating a Victim Perspective Within Criminal Justice: International Debates*. Aldershot: Ashgate Dartmouth, 165–184.

Erez, E. (2004) 'Integrating restorative justice principles in adversarial proceedings through victim impact statements', in E. Cape (ed.), *Reconcilable Rights? Analysing the Tension between Victims and Defendants*. London: Legal Action Group, 81–96.

Erez, E. and Rogers, L. (1999) 'Victim impact statements and sentencing outcomes and processes: the perspective of legal professions', *British Journal of Criminology*, 39: 216–239.

Erez, E., Leigh, R. and O'Connell, M. (1996) *Victim Impact Statements in South Australia*. Canberra: Australian Institute of Criminology.

Erez, E., Roeger, L. and Morgan, F. (1997) 'Victim harm, impact statements and victim satisfaction with justice: an Australian experience', *International Review of Victimology*, 5: 37–60.

European Commission (2008) *Meeting Report: Experts' Meeting on Victims of Crime Brussels – 17 November 2008*. Brussels: Commission of the European Communities.

European Commission (2009) *Report from the Commission Pursuant to Article 18 of the Council Framework Decision of 15 March 2001 on the Standing of Victims in Criminal Proceedings*, 2001/220/JHA. Brussels: Commission of the European Communities.

European Union (2009a) *Proposal for a Council Framework Decision on Combating the Sexual Abuse, Sexual Exploitation of Children and Child Pornography, Repealing Framework Decision 2004/68/JHA*, MEMO/09/130 [online]. Available at: http://europa.eu/rapid/pressReleasesAction.do? reference= nMEMO/09/130&format= HTML&aged=0&language=EN&guiLanguage=en

European Union (2009b) *Report on the Implementation of the Directive on Compensation to Crime Victims*, MEMO/09/159 [online]. Available at: http://europa.eu/rapid/pressReleasesAction.do?reference= nMEMO/09/159&format= HTML&aged=0&language=EN&guiLanguage=en

Everts, D. (2003) 'Human trafficking: the ruthless trade in human misery', *Brown Journal of World Affairs*, 10: 149–158.

Fattah, E. (ed.) (1992) *Towards a Critical Victimology*. New York: Macmillan.

Ferguson, K. (2007) *Practical Information About Family Group Conferences for Young People and Their Families* [online]. Available at: http://www2.justice.govt.nz/youth/about-youth/family-group-conference.asp

Ferrero-Waldner, B. (2006) 'Combating trafficking in human beings: the EU's response'. Paper presented at the *Organization for Security and Co-operation in Europe High-level Conference on Combating Trafficking in Human Beings, Especially Women and Children*, Vienna: 17 March 2006.

Fife-Yeomans, J. (2009) 'Victims to get veto over plea bargains', *The Daily Telegraph*, 12 August [online]. Available at: http://www.dailytelegraph.com.au/news/victims-to-get-veto-over-plea-bargains/story-e6freuy9-1225760414552

Fiselier, J. (1978) *Slachtoffers van Delicten: Een Onderzoek naar Verborgen Criminaliteit* [*Victims of Crime: A Study of the Dark Figure of Crime*]. Utrecht: Ars Aequi.

Fitzgerald, C. (1984) 'Note: evidence – sexual assault victim's prior sexual conduct admissible if three conditions met', *Marquette Law Review*, 67: 398–399.

Fleming, J. (2008) *Rules of Engagement: Policing Anti-social Behaviour and Alcohol-related Violence in and Around Licensed Premises*. Sydney: New South Wales Bureau of Crime Statistics and Research.

Fletcher, M., Loof, R. and Gilmore, B. (2008) *EU Criminal Law and Justice*. Camberley: Edward Elgar.

Freckleton, I. (1998) 'Compensating the sexually assaulted', in P. Easteal (ed.), *Balancing the Scales: Rape, Law Reform and Australian Culture*. Sydney: Federation Press, 191–202.

Fritzler, R. and Simon, L. (2000a) 'Creating a domestic violence court', *Court Review*, Spring: 28–39.

Frizler, R. and Simon, L. (2000b) 'The development of a specialized domestic violence court in Vancouver, Washington utilizing innovative judicial paradigms', *University of Missouri-Kansas City Law Review*, 69: 139–145.

Furedi, F. (1998) 'A new Britain: a nation of victims', *Society*, 35: 80–84.

Garkawe, S. (2004) 'Revisiting the scope of victimology: how broad a discipline should it be?', *International Review of Victimology*, 11: 275–294.

Garland, D. (2001) *The Culture of Control: Crime and Social Order in Contemporary Society*. Oxford: Oxford University Press.

Gerguson, G. (2007) 'Protection and treatment of witnesses and informants under the United Nations Convention against corruption and under Canadian law'. Paper presented at the International Centre for Criminal Law Reform and Criminal Justice Policy *Symposium on Canada–China Cooperation in Promoting Criminal Justice Reform*, Vancouver, 19–21 June 2007.

Giddens, A. (1990) *The Consequences of Modernity*. Cambridge: Polity.

Giliberti, C. (1991) 'Evaluation of victim impact statement projects in Canada: a summary of the findings', in G. Kaiser, H. Kury and H. Albrecht (eds), *Victims and Criminal Justice*. Eigenverlag: Max-Planck Institut, 703–718.

Girling, E., Loader, I. and Sparks, R. (2000) *Crime and Social Change in Middle England: Questions of Order in an English Town*. London: Routledge.

Glaser, B. and Strauss, A. (1967) *The Discovery of Grounded Theory: Strategies for Qualitative Research*. Chicago, IL: Aldine.

Goddard, J. (1997) 'Methodological issues in researching criminal justice policy: belief systems and the "causes of crime"', *International Journal of Sociology and Law*, 25: 411–430.

Goodey, J. (2005) *Victims and Victimology: Research, Policy and Practice*. Edinburgh: Pearson.

Gorard, S., Selwyn, N. and Rees, G. (2002) '"Privileging the visible": a critique of the National Learning Targets', *British Educational Research Journal*, 28: 309–325.

Gotell, L. (2002) 'The ideal victim, the hysterical complainant, and the disclosure of confidential records: the implications of the Charter for sexual assault law', *Osgoode Hall Law Journal*, 40: 251–295.

Goyer, K. (2001) 'A price worth paying? The cost of South Africa's private prisons', *Nedbank ISS Crime Index*, 5: 1–2.

Graef, R. (2000) *Why Restorative Justice? Repairing the Harm Caused by Crime*. London: Calouste Gulbenkian Foundation.

Greater London Authority (2005) *The Second London Domestic Violence Strategy*. London: Greater London Authority.

Green, D. (2006) *We're (Nearly) All Victims Now!* London: CIViTAS.

Greener, I. (2004) 'The three moments of New Labour's health discourse', *Policy & Politics*, 32: 303–316.

Groenhuijsen, M. (2006) *Implementing and Complying with the UN Basic Principles of Justice for Victims of Crime and Abuse of Power* [online]. Available at: http://www.narcis.info/research/RecordID/OND1314809/Language/en/

Guo-An, M. (2001) 'Victims in the criminal justice system in China', *The Victimologist*, 5: 1–9.

Haaglanden Police (2005) *Police Action in Cases of Domestic Violence.* The Hague: Haaglanden Police.

Hagemann-White, C., Katenbrink, J. and Rabe, H. (2006) *Combating Violence Against Women: Stocktaking Study on Measures and Actions Taken in Council of Europe Member States.* Strasbourg: Directorate General of Human Rights.

Haines, K. (2000) 'Referral orders and youth offender panels: restorative approaches and the new youth justice', in B. Goldson (ed.), *The New Youth Justice.* Lyme Regis: Russell House, 58–80.

Hall, M. (2009a) 'Children giving evidence through special measures in the criminal courts: progress and problems', *Child and Family Law Quarterly*, 21: 65–86.

Hall, M. (2009b) 'Giving evidence at four: just means to just ends?', *Family Law*, 39: 608–611.

Hall, M. (2009c) *Victims of Crime: Policy and Practice in Criminal Justice.* Cullompton: Willan.

Hamlyn, B., Phelps, A. and Sattar, G. (2004) *Key Findings from the Surveys of Vulnerable and Intimidated Witnesses 2000/01 and 2003.* Home Office Research Findings 240. London: UK Home Office.

Hamlyn, B., Phelps, A., Turtle, J. and Sattar, G. (2004) *Are Special Measures Working? Evidence from Surveys of Vulnerable and Intimidated Witnesses.* Home Office Research Study 283. London: UK Home Office.

Hanly, C. (2003) *Finding Space for Victims' Human Rights in Criminal Justice.* Dublin: Irish Law Society.

Hanna, C. (1996) 'No right to choose: mandated victim participation in domestic violence prosecutions', *Harvard Law Review*, 109: 1849–1910.

Hannah-Moffat, K. (1995) 'To charge or not to charge: front line officers' perceptions of mandatory charge policies', in M. Valverde, L. Macleod and K. Johnson (eds), *Wife Assault and the Canadian Criminal Justice System.* Toronto: University of Toronto, 35–46.

Hannum, H. (1997) 'Human rights', in C. Joyner (ed.), *The United Nations and International Law.* Cambridge: Press Syndicate of the University of Cambridge, 131–154.

Harland, A. (1978) 'Compensating the victim of crime', *Criminal Law Bulletin*, 14: 203–224.

Harris, G. (2009) 'Scottish courts still betray rape victims', *The Sunday Times*, 26 April [online]. Available at: http://women.timesonline.co.uk/tol/life_and_style/women/article6168307.ece

Hart, T. (1994) *Openbaar Ministerie en Rechtshandhaving: Een Varkenning*. Arnhem: Gouda Quint.

Harvey, W. (2002) *The Use Of Technology with the Vulnerable Witness: Some Legal and Practice Issues for the Prosecution*. Toronto: Office of the Attorney General of Ontario.

Hayward, K. (2004) *City Limits: Crime, Consumer Culture and the Urban Experience*. London: Routledge-Cavendish.

Healey, D. (1995) *Victim and Witness Intimidation: New Developments and Emerging Responses*. Washington: US Department of Justice.

Heidensohn, F. (1991) 'Women and crime in Europe', in F. Heidensohn and M. Farrell (eds), *Crime in Europe*. London: Routledge, 3–13.

Heinz, J., Laumann, E., Salisbury, R. and Nelson, R. (1990) 'Inner circles or hollow cores? Elite networks in national policy systems', *Journal of Politics*, 52: 356–390.

Henning, T. and Bronitt, S. (1998) 'Rape victims on trial: regulating the use and abuse of sexual history evidence', in P. Easteal (ed.), *Balancing the Scales: Rape, Law Reform and Australian Culture*. Sydney: Federation Press, 76–93.

Herlin-Karnell, E. (2008) 'In the Wake of Pupino: Advocaten voor der Wereld and Dell'Orto', *German Law Journal*, 8: 1147–1160.

Hickman, J. (2004) 'Playing games and cheating: fairness in the criminal justice system', in E. Cape (ed.), *Reconcilable Rights? Analysing the Tension between Victims and Defendants*. London: Legal Action Group, 50–64.

Hillyard, P. (2006) 'Crime obsessions: crime isn't the only harm', *Criminal Justice Matters*, 62: 46.

Hindelang, M. (1982) 'Victimization surveying: theory and research', in H. Schneider (ed.), *The Victim in International Perspective*. Berlin: de Gruyter, 151–165.

Ho, H. (2008) *A Philosophy of Evidence Law: Justice in the Search for Truth*. Oxford: Oxford University Press.

Hodgson, J. and Kelley, D. (eds) (2004) *Sexual Violence: Policies, Practices and Challenges in the United States and Canada*. New York: Criminal Justice Press.

Holder, R. (2007) 'Through the looking glass: Victims of crime and confidence in the courts'. Paper presented at the Australian Institute of Criminology *Confidence in the Courts* conference, Canberra: 9–11 February 2007.

Hough, M. (1986) 'Victims of violent crime: findings from the first British crime survey', in E. Fattah (ed.), *From Crime Policy to Victim Policy*. Basingstoke: Macmillan, 117–132.

Hoyano, L. and Keenan, C. (2007) *Child Abuse, Law and Policy Across Boundaries*. Oxford: Oxford University Press.

Hoyle, C., Cape, E., Morgan, R. and Sanders, A. (1999) *Evaluation of the 'One Stop Shop' and Victim Statement Pilot Projects*. London: UK Home Office.

References

Human Rights Watch (2008) *Mixed Results: US Policy and International Standards on the Rights and Interests of Victims of Crime*. New York: Human Rights Watch.

Hund, J. (1984) 'Formal justice and township justice', *Philosophical Papers*, 13: 50–58.

Ijeoma, E. (2008) 'Globalisation and reflective policy-making in South Africa', *Journal of Public Administration*, 43: 99–112.

Institute of Law Research and Reform (1968) *Compensation for Victims of Crime*, Report No.1. Edmonton: University of Alberta.

Inter-American Development Bank (1997) *The Cost of Domestic Violence: A Persuasive Drain on the Region's Economies* [online]. Available at: http://www.iadb.org/exr/IDB/stories/1997/eng/XV2e.htm

International Criminal Court (ICC) (2002) *Rules of Procedure and Evidence*. The Hague: International Criminal Court.

International Criminal Court (ICC) (2005) *Code of Judicial Ethics*. The Hague: ICC.

International Criminal Court (ICC) (2006) *Rights of the Defences* [online]. Available at: http://www.icc-cpi.int/Menus/ICC/Structure+of+the+Court/Defence/

International Organization for Migration (2008) *The IOM Handbook on Direct Assistance for Victims of Trafficking*. Geneva: International Organization for Migration.

Irish Commission for the Support of Victims of Crime (2008) *Recommendations for Future Structures and Services for Victims of Crime*. Dublin: Irish Department of Justice, Equality and Law Reform.

Irish Criminal Injuries Compensation Tribunal (2009) *Scheme of Compensation for Personal Injuries Criminally Inflicted – As Amended from 1 April 1986*. Dublin: Irish Criminal Injuries Compensation Tribunal.

Irish Department of Justice, Equality and Law Reform (1999) *Victims' Charter and Guide to the Criminal Justice System*. Dublin: Irish Department of Justice, Equality and Law Reform.

Irish Department of Justice, Equality and Law Reform (2008) *Minister Urges Victims of Crime Support Organisations to Apply for Grant Funding* [online]. Available at: http://www.inis.gov.ie/en/JELR/Pages/Minister%20urges%20Victims%20of%20Crime%20Support%20Organisations%20to%20apply%20for%20grant%20funding

Irish National Commission on Restorative Justice (2008) *National Commission on Restorative Justice*. Dublin: Irish National Commission on Restorative Justice.

Irish Office of the Minister for Children and Youth Affairs (2009) *Report of the Commission to Inquire into Child Abuse Implementation Plan*. Dublin: Irish Office of the Minister for Children and Youth Affairs.

Irish Youth Justice Alliance (2005) 'Anti Social Behaviour Orders (ASBOs): A briefing paper prepared by the Irish Youth Justice Alliance'. Paper presented at the *Oireachtas Joint Committee on Justice, Equality, Defence and Women's Rights*, Dublin: 23 February 2005.

Irvin, R. and Stansbury, J. (2004) 'Citizen participation in decision making: is it worth the effort?', *Public Administration Review*, 64: 55–65.

Jackson, J. (1990) 'Getting criminal justice out of balance', in S. Livingstone and J. Morison (eds), *Law, Society and Change*. Aldershot: Dartmouth, 114–133.

Jackson, J. (2003) 'Justice for all: putting victims at the heart of criminal justice?', *Journal of Law and Society*, 30: 309–26.

Jackson, J. (2004) 'Putting victims at the heart of criminal justice: the gap between rhetoric and reality', in E. Cape (ed.), *Reconcilable Rights? Analysing the Tension between Victims and Defendants*. London: Legal Action Group, 65–80.

Jacobson, J., Millie, A. and Hough, M. (2008) 'Why tackle anti-social behavior?', in P. Squires (ed.), *ASBO Nation: The Criminalization of Nuisance*. Bristol: The Policy Press, 37–56.

Jamaican Ministry of Justice (2006) *Towards a Victims' Charter*. Kingston: Jamaican Ministry of Justice.

Johnson, S. and Bowers, K. (2003) *Reducing Burglary Initiative: The Role of Publicity in Crime Prevention*. Home Office Research Findings 213. London: HMSO.

Joint Committee on Justice, Equality, Defence and Women's Right (2004) *Report on a Review of the Criminal Justice System*. Dublin: Joint Committee on Justice, Equality, Defence and Women's Rights.

Jordan, A., Rüdiger, K. and Zito, A. (2005) 'The rise of "new policy" instruments in comparative perspective: has governance eclipsed government?', *Political Studies*, 53: 477–496.

Jordan, J. (2001) 'Worlds apart? Women, rape and the police reporting process', *British Journal of Criminology*, 41: 679–706.

Jordan, J. (2009) 'Lest we forget: recognising and validating victims' needs'. Paper presented at the *Addressing the Underlying Causes of Offending: What Is the Evidence?* conference, University of Wellington: 27 February 2009.

Joutsen, M. (1989) 'Foreword', in HEUNI (ed.), *The Role of the Victim of Crime in European Criminal Justice System*. Helsinki: HEUNI.

Joutsen, M. and Shapland, J. (1989) 'Changing victims policy: the United Nations Victim Declaration and recent developments in Europe', in HEUNI (ed.), *The Role of the Victim of Crime in European Criminal Justice System*. Helsinki: HEUNI, 1–31.

JUSTICE Committee (1998) *Victims in Criminal Justice: Report of the JUSTICE Committee on the Role of Victims in Criminal Justice*. London: JUSTICE.

Justice Department of Quebec (2010) *Witnesses: Your Role in Criminal Court* [online]. Available at: http://www.justice.gouv.qc.ca/english/publications/generale/temoins-a.htm

References

Kearon, T. and Godfrey, B. (2007) 'Setting the scene: a question of history', in S. Walklate (ed.), *Handbook of Victims and Victimology*. Cullompton: Willan, 17–36.

Kenney, J. (2003) 'Gender roles and grief cycles: observations of models of grief and coping in homicide survivors', *International Review of Victimology*, 10: 19–49.

Kenney, J. (2004) 'Human agency revisited: the paradoxical experiences of victims of crime', *International Review of Victimology*, 11: 225–257.

Kickert, W., Klijn, E.-H. and Koppenjan, J. (eds) (1997). *Managing Complex Networks: Strategies for the Public Sector*. London: Sage, 166–191.

Kilpatrick, D. (2004) 'What is violence against women?', *Journal of Interpersonal Violence*, 19: 1209–1234.

Kirchhoff, G. (1994) 'Victimology: History and basic concepts', in G. Kirchhoff, E. Kosovski and H. Schneider (eds), *International Debates of Victimology*. Monchengladbach: WSV Publishing, 1–81.

Klabbers, J. (1996) 'The redundancy of soft law', *Nordic Journal of International Law*, 65: 167–180.

Knaggs, T., Leahy, F., Soboleva, N. and Ong, S. (2008) *The Waitakere and Manukau Family Violence Courts: An Evaluation Summary*. Wellington: New Zealand Ministry of Justice.

Kollapen, J. (2006) 'Affirming a culture of values in the human rights framework', *Pambazuka News*, 281: 6–12.

Koloto, A. (2003) *The Needs of Pacific Peoples When They Are Victims of Crime*. Wellington: New Zealand Ministry of Justice.

Laing, L. (2002) *Responding to Men who Perpetrate Domestic Violence: Controversies, Interventions and Challenges, Issues Paper 7*. Sydney: Australian Domestic and Family Violence Clearinghouse.

Laumann E, and Knoke, D. (1987) *The Organizational State: Social Choice in National Policy Domains*. Madison, WI: University of Wisconsin Press.

Laville, S. (2001) 'Degraded victim abandons anonymity', *The Daily Telegraph*, 18 May [online]. Available at: http://www.telegraph.co.uk/news/uknews/1330709/Degraded-victim-abandons-anonymity.html

Lawrence, R. (2006) 'Research dissemination: activity bringing the research and policy worlds together', *Evidence & Policy*, 2: 373–384.

Laycock, G. (1984) *Reducing Burglary: A Study of Chemists' Shops*. Home Office Crime Prevention Unit Paper 1. London: UK Home Office.

Leblanc, L. (1995) *The Convention on the Rights of the Child: United Nations Lawmaking on Human Rights*. Lincoln, NE: University of Nebraska Press.

Lee, M. (2007) *Human Trafficking*. Cullompton: Willan.

Lees, S. (2002) *Carnal Knowledge: Rape on Trial*. London: Women's Press.

Levi, M. and Pithouse, A. (1992) 'The victims of fraud', in D. Downes (ed.), *Unravelling Criminal Justice*. London: Macmillan.

Lilly, J. and Knepper, P. (1993) 'The corrections-commercial complex', *Crime & Delinquency*, 39: 150–166.

Lindblom, C. (1968) *The Policy-Making Process*. Englewood Cliffs, NJ: Prentice Hall.

Ljungwald, C. and Svensson, K. (2007) 'Crime victims and the social services: social workers' viewpoint', *Journal of Scandinavian Studies in Criminology and Crime Prevention*, 8: 138–156.

Loader, I. and Sparks, R. (2007) 'Contemporary landscapes of crime, order and control: governance, risk and globalization', in M. Maguire, R. Morgan and R. Reiner (eds), *The Oxford Handbook of Criminology*. Oxford: Oxford University Press, 78–101.

Lord, V. and Rassel, G. (2004) 'Law enforcement's response to sexual assault: a comparative study of nine counties in North Carolina', in J. Hodgson and D. Kelley (eds), *Sexual Violence: Policies, Practices and Challenges in the United States and Canada*. New York: Criminal Justice Press, 1–14.

Louw, A. (1998) *Crime in Pretoria: Results of a City Victim Survey*. ISS monograph series. Cape Town: Institute for Security Studies.

Louw, A., Shaw, M., Camerer, L. and Robertshaw, R. (1988) *Crime in Johannesburg: Results of a City Victim Survey*. ISS monograph series. Cape Town: Institute for Security Studies.

Lowman, J. (1986) 'You can do it, but don't do it here: some comments on proposals for the reform of Canadian prostitution law', in J. Lowman, M. Jackson, T. Palys and S. Gavigan (eds), *Regulating Sex: An Anthology of Commentaries on the Findings and Recommendations of the Badgley and Fraser Reports*. Burnaby: Simon Fraser University, 25–76.

Lynch, T. (2006) *The Rights of Defendants in the ICTY* [online]. Available at: http://www.wcl.american.edu/hrbrief/fall98/icty.html

McBarnet, D. (1983) 'Victim in the witness box: confronting victimology's stereotype', *Crime, Law and Social Change*, 7: 293–303.

McDermott, Y. (2009) *The Lubanga Trial at the International Criminal Court* [online]. Available at: http://www.lubangatrial.org/contributors/

McLeay, E. (1998) 'Policing policy and policy networks in Britain and New Zealand', in D. Marsh (ed.), *Comparing Policy Networks*. Buckingham: Open University Press, 110–131.

McMahon, W. (2005) 'Concern over ASBOS', *Criminal Justice Matters*, 59: 43.

Maginnis, J. (2002) *The 9/11 Victim Compensation Fund: Overview and Comment*, Washington, DC: The Federalist Society for Law and Public Policy Studies.

Maguire, M. (1991) 'The needs and rights of victims of crime', in M. Tonry (ed.), *Crime and Justice: A Review of Research*. Chicago, IL: Chicago University Press, 363–433.

Maguire, M. (2007) 'Crime data and statistics', in M. Maguire, R. Morgan and R. Reiner (eds), *The Oxford Handbook of Criminology*. Oxford: Oxford University Press, 241–301.

Maguire, M. and Shapland, J. (1997) 'Provision for victims in an international context', in R. Davis, A. Lurigio and W. Skogan (eds), *Victims of Crime*. Thousand Oaks, CA: Sage, 211–230.

Maloney, W., Jordan, G. and McLaughlin, A. (1994) 'Interest groups and public policy: the insider/outsider model revisited', *Journal of Public Policy*, 14: 17–38.

Malsch, M. (1999) 'Victims' wishes for compensation: the immaterial aspect', *Journal of Criminal Justice*, 27: 239–247.

Marcus, J. (1989) 'Prisoner of discourse: The dingo, the dog and the baby', *Anthropology Today*, 5: 15–19.

Marmo, M. and La Forgia, R. (2008) 'Inclusive national governance and trafficked women in Australia: otherness and local demand', *Asian Criminology*, 3: 173–191.

Marshall, T. (1999) *Restorative Justice: An Overview*. London: UK Home Office Research Development and Statistics Directorate.

Martin, M. and Haverty, M. (2008) 'The work of the National Commission on restorative justice: promoting cooperation amongst society'. Paper presented at the *5th Conference of the European Forum for Restorative Justice, Building Restorative Justice in Europe: Cooperation between the Public, Policy Makers, Practitioners and Researchers*, Verona: 17–19 April 2008.

Mattinson, J. and Mirrlees-Black, C. (2000) *Attitudes to Crime and Criminal Justice: Findings from the 1998 British Crime Survey*. Home Office Research Study 200. London: UK Home Office.

Mawby, R. (2000) 'The impact of repeat victimisation on burglary victims in East and West Europe', in G. Farrell and K. Pease (eds), *Repeat Victimization*. Monsey: Criminal Justice Press.

Mawby, R. and Walklate, S. (1994) *Critical Victimology*. Thousand Oaks, CA: Sage.

Maxwell, G. and Carroll-Lind, J. (1998) 'Distorted childhoods: the meaning of violence for children', *Social Policy Journal of New Zealand*, 10: 1–17.

Mayer, I., Edelenbos, J. and Monnikhof, R. (2005) 'Interactive policy development: undermining or sustaining democracy?', *Public Administration*, 83: 179–199.

Meek, S. (1999) *Protecting Our Future: Children as Victim of Crime in South Africa*. Nedbank ISS Crime Index 3(2). Cape Town: Institute for Security Studies.

Mendelsohn, B. (1956) 'A new branch of bio-psychological science: la victimology', *Revue Internationale de Criminologie et de Police Technique*, 2.

Merrills, J. and Robertson, A. (2001) *Human Rights in Europe*. Manchester: Manchester University Press.

Miers, D. (1980) 'Victim compensation as a labelling process', *Victimology*, 5: 3–16.

Miers, D. (1991) *Compensation for Criminal Injuries*. London: Butterworths.

Miers, D. (1997) *State Compensation for Criminal Injuries*. London: Blackstone.

Miers, D. (2001) *An International Review of Restorative Justice*. Crime Reduction Research Series Paper 10. London: UK Home Office.

Miller, G. and Fontes, N. (1979) *Videotape on Trial*. Thousand Oaks, CA: Sage.

Minnesota Judicial Branch (2004) *Performance Measures Fourth Judicial District Criminal Division*. St. Paul, MN: Minnesota Judicial Branch.

Mistry, D. (2000) 'The Dilemma of Case Withdrawal: Policing in the "New" South Africa'. Paper presented at the British Society of Criminology *British Criminology Conference*, Liverpool: July 1999.

Morgan, J. and Zedner, L. (1992) *Child Victims: Crime, Impact, and Criminal Justice*. Oxford: Oxford University Press.

Morgan, R. and Sanders, A. (1999) *The Use of Victim Statements*. London: UK Home Office.

Mothers Against Drunk Driving (2004) *Press Release – Federal Victim Rights Law: Crime Victim Advocates Applaud Enactment of "Ground-Breaking" Federal Victim Rights Law* [online]. Available at: http://www.madd.org/chapter/5300_9035.

Moxon, D., Martin, J. and Hedderman, C. (1992) *Developments in the Use of Compensation Orders in Magistrates' Courts since October 1988*. Home Office Research Study 126. London: UK Home Office.

Mullenix, L. (2004) 'The future of tort reform: possible lessons from the World Trade center victim compensation fund', *Emory Law Journal*, 53: 1315–1347.

Murphy, G. (2005) 'Interest groups in the policy-making process', in J. Coakley and M. Gallagher (eds), *Politics in the Republic of Ireland*. New York: Routledge, 211–241.

Mythen, G. (2007) 'Cultural victimology: are we all victims now?', in S. Walklate (ed.), *Handbook of Victims and Victimology*. Cullompton: Willan, 464–483.

Nagin, D., Farrington, D. and Moffitt, T. (1995) 'Life-course trajectories of different types of offenders', *Criminology*, 33: 111–139.

Nakamura, R. and Smallwood, F. (1980) *The Politics of Implementation*. New York: St. Martin's Press.

National Center for Victims of Crime (2010) *Legislative Agenda*. Washington, DC: National Centre for Victims of Crime.

National Council for Childhood and Motherhood (2005) *The MENA Regional Consultation on Violence Against Children Outcome Document of the Regional Consultation*. NCCM: Cairo.

National Victims Constitutional Amendment Project (2003) *Recent News/Chronology* [online]. Available at: http://www.nvcap.org/

Needham, C. (2009) 'Policing with a smile: narratives of consumerism in New Labour's Justice Policy', *Public Administration*, 87: 91–116.

Nelken, D. (1997) 'The globalization of crime and criminal justice: prospects and problems', *Current Legal Problems*, 50: 251–277.

References

Nelken, D. (2007a) 'Comparing criminal justice', in M. Maguire, R. Morgan and R. Reiner (eds), *The Oxford Handbook of Criminology*. Oxford: Oxford University Press, 139–158.

Nelken, D. (2007b) 'White-collar and corporate crime', in M. Maguire, R. Morgan and R. Reiner (eds), *The Oxford Handbook of Criminology*. Oxford: Oxford University Press, 733–770.

Netherlands Ministry of Justice (1997) *Domestic Violence in the Netherlands: Summary*. The Hague: Netherlands Ministry of Justice.

Netherlands Ministry of Justice (2002) *Private Violence: Public Issue*, Memorandum 05/02. The Hague: Netherlands Ministry of Justice.

Newburn, T. (1988) *The Use and Enforcement of Compensation Orders in Magistrates' Courts*. Home Office Research Study 102. London: UK Home Office.

Newburn, T. and Reiner, R. (2007) 'Policing and the police', in M. Maguire, R. Morgan and R. Reiner (eds), *The Oxford Handbook of Criminology*. Oxford: Oxford University Press, 910–952.

Newburn, T., Crawford, A., Earle, R., Goldie, S., Hale, C., Masters, G. et al. (2002) *The Introduction of Referral Orders into the Youth Justice System*. Home Office Research Study 242. London: UK Home Office.

New York State Crime Victims Board (2008) *A Guide To Crime Victims Compensation in New York State*. New York: New York State Crime Victims Board.

New Zealand Crown Law Office (2010) *Prosecution Guidelines*. Wellington: New Zealand Crown Law Office.

New Zealand Law Commission (2008) *Compensating Crime Victims*, Issues Paper 11. Wellington: New Zealand Law Commission.

New Zealand Ministry of Justice (2004) *Report of the Ministry of Justice: Baseline Review Document*. Wellington: New Zealand Ministry of Justice.

Newfoundland and Labrador Department of Justice (2002) *Annual Report of Victims Services For the Period April 1, 2001–March 31, 2002*. St John's: Newfoundland Department of Justice.

Nixon, J., Hunter, C. and Parr, S. (2004) *What Works for Victims and Witnesses of Anti-social Behaviour?* London: UK Home Office.

Nixon, J., Hunter, C., Parr, S., Myers, S., Whittle, S. and Sanderson, D. (2006) *Anti-Social Behaviour Intensive Family Support Projects: An Evaluation of Six Pioneering Projects*. London: Office of the Deputy Prime Minister.

Noseweek (2009) *Should the State Pay Victims of Crime?* [online]. Available at http://www.noseweek.co.za/article.php?current_article=2122

Office of the Attorney General of Arizona (2009) *Victims' Rights Enforcement Officer* [online]. Available at: http://www.azag.gov/victims_rights/enforcement.html

Office of the Attorney General of California (2010) *Serving Victims* [online]. Available at: http://ag.ca.gov/victims.php

Office of the Attorney General of Ontario (2008) *Justice on Target*. Toronto: Office of the Attorney General of Ontario.

Office of the Attorney General of Texas (2009) *Crime Victims' Compensation* [online]. Available at: http://www.oag.state.tx.us/victims/about_comp.shtml

Organization for Security and Co-operation in Europe (2002) *Victim Advocacy Manual*. Vienna: Organization for Security and Co-operation in Europe.

Ostrom, B. and Hanson, A. (2000) *Efficiency, Timeliness, and Quality: A New Perspective From Nine State Criminal Trial Courts*. Washington, DC: US Department of Justice.

Paes-Machado, E. and Nascimento, A. (2006) 'Bank money shields: work-related victimisation, moral dilemmas and crisis in the bank profession', *International Review of Victimology*, 13: 1–25.

Parker, J. (1981) 'Rights of child witnesses: is the court a protector or perpetrator?, *New England Law Review*, 17: 643–662.

Pearce, G. and Mawson, J. (2003) 'Delivering developed approaches to local governance', *Policy & Politics*, 31: 51–67.

Pease, K. (1997) 'Crime prevention', in M. Maguire, R. Morgan and R. Reiner (eds), *The Oxford Handbook of Criminology*. Oxford: Oxford University Press, 963–95.

Pemberton, A. (2010) 'Needs of victims of terrorism', in R. Letschert, I. Staiger and A. Pemberton (eds), *Assisting Victims of Terrorism*. London: Springer.

People's Daily (2007) *China's Supreme Court Calls for State Relief for Victims of Violent Crime*, 14 September [online]. Available at: http://www.gov.cn/english/2007-09/14/content_749872.htm

Petek, A. (2008) 'Policy networks and public policy research: advantages and disadvantages', *Politička misao*, 45: 55–72.

Peterson, J. (1992) *Policy Networks*, Political Science Series 90. Vienna: Institute for Advanced Studies.

Peterson, J. and Bomberg, E. (1999) *Decision-making in the European Union*. New York: Palgrave.

Pointing, J. and Maguire, M. (1988) 'Introduction: the rediscovery of the crime victim', in M. Maguire and J. Pointing (eds), *Victims of Crime: A New Deal?* Milton Keynes: Open University Press, 1–13.

Priestley, M. (2002) 'Whose voices? Representing the claims of older disabled people under New Labour', *Policy & Politics*, 30: 361–372.

Prison Reform Trust (1997) 'Privatisation under way in South Africa', *Prison Privatisation Report International*, 10: 1.

Queensland Department of Communities (2009) *Youth Justice Conferencing in Queensland: Restorative Justice in Practice*. Brisbane: Queensland Department of Communities.

Queensland Department of Justice and Attorney General (2006) *Vulnerable Person Policy: Statement to Improve Services*. Brisbane: Queensland Department of Justice.

Queensland Department of Justice and Attorney General (2009) *Victims of Crime Review Report*. Brisbane: Queensland Department of Justice and Attorney General.

Raaflaub, T. (2006) *Human Trafficking*/Ottawa: Parliamentary Information and Research Service.

Ramcharan, B. (2008) *Contemporary Human Rights Ideas*. New York: Routledge.

Raunch, J. (2001) *The 1996 National Crime Prevention Strategy*. Johannesburg: Centre for the Study of Violence and Reconciliation.

Raye, B. and Roberts, A. (2007) 'Restorative processes', in G. Johnstone and D. van Ness (eds), *Handbook of Restorative Justice*. Cullompton: Willan, 211–229.

Reese, C. (2000) 'The implementation of the UN Declaration of Basic Principles of Justice for Victims of Crime and abuse of power in France', *The Victimologist*, 4: 1–2.

Reeves, H. (2003) *The Relevance Today of Recommendation N° R (87) 21 on Assistance to Victims and Prevention of Victimisation*. PC-CSC (2003) 1. Strasbourg: Council of Europe.

Reid Howie Associates (2005) *Information on Victims and Witnesses in the Scottish Justice System*. Research Findings No. 82/2005. Edinburgh: Scottish Executive.

Reier, R. (2000) *The Politics of the Police*. Oxford: Oxford University Press.

Rein, M. and Rabinowitz, F. (1978) 'Implementation: a theoretical perspective', in W. Burnham and M. Weinberg (eds), *American Politics and Public Policy*, Cambridge: MIT Press, 125–169.

Reiner, R. (2000) *The Politics of the Police*. Oxford: Oxford University Press.

Restorative Justice in Scotland (2009) *Police Restorative Warnings* [online]. Available at: http://www.restorativejusticescotland.org.uk/html/police_warnings.html

Rijken, C. (2003) *Trafficking in Persons: Prosecution from a European Perspective*. The Hague: Asser Press.

Reinicke, W. (1997) 'Global public policy', *Foreign Affairs*, 76: 127–151.

Richards, K. (2009) *Child Complainants and the Court Process in Australia*. Trends and Issues in Crime and Criminal Justice No. 380. Canberra: Australian Institute of Criminology.

Richardson, J. (2000) 'Government, interest groups and policy change', *Political Studies*, 48: 1006–1025.

Riley, D. and Mayhew, P. (1980) *Crime Prevention Publicity: An Assessment*. Home Office Research Study 63. London: HMSO.

Rock, P. (1986) *A View from the Shadows: The Ministry of the Solicitor General of Canada and the Making of the Justice for Victims of Crime Initiative*. Oxford: Clarendon Press.

Rock, P. (1990) *Helping Victims of Crime: The Home Office and the Rise of Victim Support in England and Wales*. Oxford: Oxford University Press.

Rock, P. (1993) *The Social World of an English Crown Court: Witnesses and Professionals in the Crown Court Centre at Wood Green*. Oxford: Clarendon Press.

Rock, P. (1998) *After Homicide: Practical and Political Responses to Bereavement*. Oxford: Clarendon Press.

Rock, P. (2002) 'On becoming a victim', in C. Hoyle and R. Young (eds), *New Visions of Crime Victims*, Oxford: Hart Publishing, 1–22.

Rock, P. (2004) *Constructing Victims' Rights: The Home Office, New Labour and Victims*. Oxford: Clarendon Press.

Rock, P. (2007) 'Theoretical perspectives on victimisation', in S. Walklate (ed.), *Handbook of Victims and Victimology*. Cullompton: Willan, 37–61.

Rodger, J. (2008) *Criminalising Social Policy*. Cullompton: Willan.

Rollings, K. and Taylor, N. (2008) *Measuring Police Performance in Domestic and Family Violence*. Trends and Issues in Crime and Criminal Justice No. 367. Canberra: Australian Institute of Criminology.

Roth, M. (2002) 'Hammurabi's Wronged Man', *Journal of the American Oriental Society*: 122, 38–45.

Roux, N. (2002) 'Public policy-making and policy analysis in South Africa amidst transformation, change and globalisation: views on participants and role players in the policy analytic procedure', *Journal of Public Administration*, 37: 418–437.

Ruggiero, V. (2000) 'Transnational crime: official and alternative fears', *International Journal of the Sociology of Law*, 28: 187–199.

Rydeberg, A. (2004) 'Victims and the International Criminal Tribunal for the former Yugoslavia', in H. Kaptein and M. Malsch (eds), *Crime, Victims and Justice*. London: Ashgate, 122–134.

Sanders, A. (2002) 'Victim participation in an exclusionary criminal justice system', in C. Hoyle and R. Young (eds), *New Visions of Crime Victims*. Portland, OR: Hart, 197–222.

Sanders, A. and Young, R. (2000) *Criminal Justice*. London: Butterworths.

Sanders, A., Hoyle, C., Morgan, R. and Cape, E. (2001) 'Victim impact statements: don't work, can't work', *Criminal Law Review*, Jun: 437–458.

Sanderson, I. (2003) 'Is it "what works" that matters? Evaluation and evidence-based policy-making', *Research Papers in Education*, 18: 331–345.

Sankoff, P. and Wansbrough, L. (2006) 'Is Three Really a Crowd? Thoughts About Victim Impact Statements and New Zealand's Revamped Sentencing Regime'. Paper presented at the *21st International Conference of the International Society for the Reform of Criminal Law*, Brisbane: July 2006.

References

Schadefonds Geweldsmisdrijven (2008) *Have You Been the Victim of Violence?* Rijswijk: Schadefonds Geweldsmisdrijven.

Schafer, S. (1968) *The Victims and His Criminal: A Study in Functional Responsibility.* New York: Random House.

Schneider, H. (1991) 'Restitution instead of punishment: reorientation of crime prevention and criminal justice in the context of development', in G. Kaiser, H. Kury and H. Albrecht (eds), *Victims and Criminal Justice.* Eigenverlag: Max-Planck Institut, 363–380.

Scholte, J. (2000) *Globalization: A Critical Introduction.* London: Macmillan.

Schurink, W., Snyman, I. and Krugel, W. with Slabbert, L. (1993) *Victimization: Nature and Trends.* Pretoria: South African Human Sciences Research Council.

Scottish Executive (2001) *Scottish Strategy for Victims.* Edinburgh: Scottish Executive.

Scottish Executive (2004a) *Coping with Grief When Someone Close to You Has Been Killed.* Edinburgh: Scottish Executive.

Scottish Executive (2004b) *Restorative Justice Approach Goes National* [online]. Available at http://www.scotland.gov.uk/News/Releases/2004/06/5692

Scottish Executive (2005) *National Standards for Victims of Crime.* Edinburgh: Scottish Executive.

Scottish Government (2007) *Information on Victims and Witnesses in the Scottish Justice System.* Edinburgh: Scottish Government.

Scottish Government (2008) *Restorative Justice Services for Children and Young People and Those Harmed by Their Behaviour.* Edinburgh: Scottish Government.

Scottish Prisons Commission (2008) *Scotland's Choice Report of the Scottish Prisons Commission.* Edinburgh: Scottish Prison Commission.

Segrave, M., Milivojevic, S. and Pickering, S. (2009) *Sex Trafficking: International Context and Response.* Cullompton: Willan.

Select Committee on Home Affairs (2002) *The Conduct of Investigations into Past Cases of Abuse in Children's Homes*, Fourth Report of session 2001–02. London: The Stationery Office.

Shapland, J. (1990) 'Bringing victims in from the cold: victims' role in criminal justice', in J. Jackson and K. Quinn (eds), *Criminal Justice Reform: Looking to the Future.* Belfast: Queens University Belfast, 1–10.

Shapland, J. (2002) 'Sentencing: an art or a science?'. Paper presented at the *SLS/Criminal Bar Association of Northern Ireland Conference*, Belfast: 19 October 2002.

Shapland, J. and Hall, M. (2007) 'What do we know about the effect of crime on victims?', *International Review of Victimology*, 14: 175–217.

Shapland, J. and Hall, M. (2010) 'Victims at court: necessary accessories or principal players at centre stage?', in A. Bottoms and J. Roberts (eds), *Hearing the Victim: Adversarial Justice, Crime Victims and the State.* Cullompton: Willan, 163–199.

Shapland, J., Atkinson, A., Atkinson, H., Chapman, B., Colledge, E., Dignan, J. et al. (2006) *Restorative Justice in Practice: Findings from the Second*

Phase of the Evaluation of Three Schemes. Home Office Research Findings 274. London: UK Home Office.

Shapland, J., Willmore, J. and Duff, P. (1985) *Victims and the Criminal Justice System*. Aldershot: Gower.

Shaw, M. (1997) *South Africa: Crime in Transition*, Occasional Paper No. 17. Cape Town: South African Institute for Security Studies.

Shaw, M. (2007) *International Law*. Cambridge: Cambridge University Press.

Shaxson, L. (2005) 'Is your evidence robust enough? Questions for policy makers and practitioners', *Evidence & Policy*, 1: 101–111.

Sieber, J. (1998) 'Planning ethically responsible research', in L. Bickman and D. Rog (eds), *Handbook of Applied Social Research Methods*. Thousand Oaks, CA: Sage, 127–156.

Simpson, G. (1996) *Crime and Violence: The Need for Victim Support in South Africa*. Johannesburg: Centre for the Study of Violence and Reconciliation.

Slatter, M. (2007) 'The accidental leader: South Australia and the creeping control of tenants' behaviour'. Paper presented at the University of Tasmania Australia Housing and Community Research Unit *Anti-social Behaviour, Housing and the Law* conference, Hobart: 31 August 2007.

Smith, J. (2005) *Sixth Report – Shipman: The Final Report*. Norwich: HMSO.

Smith, M. (2004) 'Toward a theory of EU foreign policy-making: multi-level governance, domestic politics, and national adaptation to Europe's common foreign and security policy', *Journal of European Public Policy*, 11: 740–758.

South African Department of Justice and Constitutional Development (2007) *Africa and Victims Rights*. Pretoria: DoJCD.

South African Department of Justice and Constitutional Development (2008a) *Service Charter for Victims of Crime in South Africa*. Pretoria: DoJCD.

South African Department of Justice and Constitutional Development (2008b) *Understanding the South African Victims' Charter: A Conceptual Framework*. Pretoria: DoJCD.

South African Department of Justice and Constitutional Development (2008c) *What the Victims' Charter Can Do for You*. Pretoria: DoJCD.

South African Department of Justice and Constitutional Development (2009) *Examples of Restorative Justice in South Africa*. Pretoria: DoJCD.

Spalek, B. (1999) 'Exploring the impact of financial crime: a study looking into the effects of the Maxwell scandal upon Maxwell prisoners', *International Review of Victimology*, 6: 166–179.

Spalek. B. (2001) 'White collar crime and secondary victimisation, an analysis of the effects of the closure of BCCI', *Howard Journal of Criminal Justice*, 40: 166–179.

Spalek, B. (2006) *Crime Victims: Theory, Policy and Practice*. New York: Palgrave Macmillan.

Spencer, J. and Flin, R. (1993) *The Evidence of Children: The Law and the Psychology*. London: Blackstone.

References

State of California (2008) *Text of Proposed Laws: Proposition 9*. Sacramento, CA: State of California.

Statistics Canada (2005) *Youth Correctional Services: Key Indicators 2003/04*. Ottawa: Statistics Canada.

Statistics Canada (2009) *Youth Correctional Services, Average Counts of Young Persons in Provincial and Territorial Correctional Services*. Ottawa: Statistics Canada.

Steiner, H. and Alston, P. (2000) *International Human Rights in Context*. Oxford: Oxford University Press.

Stewart, J. (2006) *Specialist Domestic/Family Violence Courts within the Australian Context*, Issues Paper 10. Wellington: Australian Domestic & Family Violence Clearing House.

Strang, H. (2001) *Restorative Justice Programs in Australia*. Griffith: Australian Criminology Research Council.

Strauss, A. and Corbin, J. (1994) 'Grounded theory methodology: an overview', in N. Denzin and Y. Lincoln (eds), *Handbook of Qualitative Research*. Thousand Oaks, CA: Sage, 262–272.

Swart, A. (1993) 'The Netherlands', in C. van den Wyngaert (ed.), *Criminal Procedure Systems in the European Community*. London: Butterworths, 279–316.

Tak, P. (2003) *The Dutch Criminal Justice System: Organization and Operation*. The Hague: Netherlands Ministry of Justice.

Tapley, J. (2002) *From Good Citizen to Deserving Client: Relationships between Victims and the State Using Citizenship as the Conceptualizing Tool*. Southampton: University of Southampton.

Temkin J. (1999) 'Reporting rape in London: a qualitative study', *Howard Journal of Criminal Justice*, 38: 17–41.

Temkin, J. (2002) *Rape and the Legal Process*. Oxford: Oxford University Press.

Tennessee Economic Council on Women (2002) *Economic Impact on the Legal Systems* [online]. Available at: http://www.state.tn.us/sos/ecw/initiatives/impact_legal.htm

Thirlway, H. (2006) 'The sources of international law', in M. Evans (ed.), *International Law*. Oxford: Oxford University Press, 115–140.

Thomas, S. (2005) 'Taking teachers out of the equation: constructions of teachers in education policy documents over a ten-year period', *The Australian Educational Researcher*, 32: 45–62.

Tisdall, E. and Davis, M. (2004) 'Making a difference? Bringing children's and young people's views into policy-making', *Children & Society*, 18: 131–142.

Toombs, S. (2005) 'Corporate crime', in C. Hale, K. Hayward, A. Wahidin and E. Wincup (eds), *Criminology*, Oxford: Oxford University Press, 267–287.

Trocmé, N., Fallon, B., MacLaurin, B., Daciuk, J., Felstiner, C., Black, L.T. *et al*. (2003) *Canadian Incidence Study of Reported Child Abuse and Neglect –*

2003: Major Findings. Gatineau: Ministry of Public Works and Government Services.

Turpel-Lafond, M. (1999) 'Sentencing within a restorative justice paradigm: procedural implications of R. v. Gladue', *Criminal Law Quarterly*, 4: 34–56.

Tyler, T. (1990) *Why People Obey the Law*. New Haven, CT: Yale University Press.

Tyler, T. and Huo, Y. (2002) *Trust in the Law: Encouraging Public Cooperation with the Police and Courts*. New York: Russell-Sage Foundation.

UK Criminal Injuries Compensation Authority (2008) *The Criminal Injuries Compensation Scheme*. London: CICA.

UK Crown Prosecution Service (CPS) (2004) *The Code for Crown Prosecutors*. London: CPS.

UK Crown Prosecution Service (2005) *The Prosecutors' Pledge* [online]. Available at: http://www.cps.gov.uk/publications/prosecution/prosecutor_pledge.html

UK Crown Prosecution Service (CPS) (2007) *Victim Focus Scheme Guidance on Enhanced CPS Service of Bereaved Families*. London: CPS.

UK Department of Transport (2004) *Graffiti and Vandalism On and Around Public Transport: Briefing Paper*. London: UK Department of Transport.

UK Home Office (1990) *Victims' Charter: A Statement of the Rights of Victims*. London: UK Home Office.

UK Home Office (2000) *Setting the Boundaries: Reforming the Law on Sex Offences*. London: UK Home Office.

UK Home Office (2001a) *Criminal Justice: The Way Ahead*, Cm 5074. London: Stationery Office.

UK Home Office (2001b) *The Review of the Victim's Charter*. London: UK Home Office.

UK Home Office (2002) *Justice for all*, Cm 5563. London: The Stationery Office.

UK Home Office (2003a) *A New Deal for Victims and Witnesses: National Strategy to Deliver Improved Services*. London: UK Home Office.

UK Home Office (2003b) *Securing the Attendance of Victims in Court: A Consultation Paper*. London: HMSO.

UK Home Office (2004a) *Compensation and Support for Victims of Crime: A Consultation Paper on Proposals to Amend the Criminal Injuries Compensation Scheme and Provide a Wide Range of Support for Victims*. London: UK Home Office.

UK Home Office (2004b) *Criminal Case Management Framework*. London: UK Home Office.

UK Home Office (2005a) *Rebuilding Lives: Supporting Victims of Crime*. London: The Stationery Office.

UK Home Office (2005b) *The Code of Practice for Victims of Crime*. London: UK Home Office.

UK Home Office (2005c) *Hearing the Relatives of Murder and Manslaughter Victims: The Government's Plans to Give the Bereaved Relatives of Murder and Manslaughter Victims a Say in Criminal Proceedings: Consultation*. London: UK Home Office.

UK Home Office (2006a) *Rebalancing the Criminal Justice System in Favour of the Law Abiding Majority: Cutting Crime, Reducing Reoffending and Protecting the Public*. London: UK Home Office.

UK Home Office (2006b) *Specialist Domestic Violence Court Programme Resource Manual*. London: UK Home Office.

UK Home Office (2010) *Anti-social Behaviour* [online]. Available at:http://www.homeoffice.gov.uk/anti-social-behaviour/

UK Home Office and Scottish Executive (2006) *Tackling Human Trafficking: Consultation on Proposals for a UK Action Plan*. London: HMSO.

UK Home Office and Scottish Government (2009) *Update to the UK Action Plan on Tackling Human Trafficking*. London: UK Home Office.

UK Ministry of Justice (2009) *The Departmental Annual Report 2008/09*. London: UK Ministry of Justice.

Umbreit, M. and Greenwood, J. (1998) *National Survey of Victim Offender Mediation Programs in the US*. Minneapolis, MS: University of Minnesota Center for Restorative Justice and Peacemaking.

United Nations (1999) *Handbook on Justice for Victims*. New York: United Nations Office for Drug Control and Crime Prevention.

United Nations Office on Drugs and Crime (2006) *Handbook on Restorative Justice Programmes*. New York: United Nations.

United Nations Office on Drugs and Crime (2008) *Good Practices on the Protection of Witnesses in Criminal Proceedings Involving Organised Crime*. New York: United Nations.

US Department of Health and Human Services (2000) *National Household Study on Drug Abuse: Main Findings 1998*. Rockville: National Clearinghouse for Alcohol and Drug Information.

US Department of Justice (2002) *Claimant Award Summaries*. Washington, DC: US Department of Justice.

US Department of State (2008) *Trafficking in Persons Report 2008*. Washington, DC: Department of State.

US Department of State (2009) *Trafficking in Persons Report 2009*. Washington, DC: Department of State.

US National Center for Victims of Crime (2010) *Legislative Agenda* [online]. Available at: http://www.ncvc.org/ncvc/main.aspx?dbID=DB_Agenda774

US Office for Victims of Crime (1998) *'Restitution' New Directions from the Field: Victims' Rights and Services for the 21st Century*. Washington, DC: U.S. Department of Justice.

US Office for Victims of Crime (2000) 'A description of victim–offender mediation', *OVC Bulletin*, July: 1–5.

Valler, D. and Betteley, D. (2001) 'The politics of "integrated" local policy in England', *Urban Studies*, 38: 2393–2413.

van Dijk, J. (1983) 'Victimologie in theorie en praktijk: een kritische reflectie op de bestaande en nog te ceëren voorzieningen voor slachtoffers van delicten', *Justitiële verkenningen*, 6: 5–35.

van Dijk, J. (1988) 'Introduction: the rediscovery of the crime victim', in M. Maguire and J. Pointing (eds), *Victims of Crime: A New Deal?* Milton Keynes: Open University Press, 1–13.

van Dijk, J. (1989) 'Benchmarking legislation on crime victims: the UN Victims Declaration of 1985', in M. Joutsen and J. Shapland (eds), *Changing Victim Policy: The United Nations Victim Declaration and Recent Developments in Europe.* Helsinki: HEUNI, 202–225.

van Dijk, J. (1998) 'A new society of victimology? A letter from the president', *The Victimologist*, 1: 2–3.

van Dijk, J. and Groenhuijsen, M. (2007) 'Benchmarking victim policies in the framework of European Union Law', in S. Walklate (ed.), *Handbook of Victims and Victimology*. Cullompton: Willan, 363–379.

van Dijk, J. and Letschert, R. (2010) *Globalisation and Victims Rights*. London: Springer.

van Dijk, J., van Kesteren, J. and Smit, P. (2008) *Criminal Victimisation in International Perspective, Key Findings from the 2004–2005 ICVS and EU ICS*. The Hague: Boom Legal Publishers.

van Waaredn, F. (2006) 'Dimensions and types of policy networks', *European Journal of Political Research*, 21: 29–52.

Verkaik, R. (2001) 'Britain now the world's compensation capital, with payouts set to keep rising', *The Independent*, 26 March [online]. Available at: http://www.independent.co.uk/news/uk/crime/britain-now-the-worlds-compensation-capital-with-payouts-set-to-keep-rising-689105.html

Vetten, L. (2005) 'Violence against women: good practices in combating and eliminating violence against women'. Paper presented at the *Expert Group Meeting Organized by: UN Division for the Advancement of Women in Collaboration with: UN Office on Drugs and Crime*, Vienna: 17–20 May 2005.

Victim Support Australasia (2008) *Services and Rights for Crime Victims in Australia: A Brief Profile*. Sydney: Victim Support Australasia.

Victim Support Australasia (2009) *A Human Rights Charter for Australia: Submission from Victim support Australasia Inc*. Sydney: Victim Support Australasia.

Victim Support England and Wales (2001) *Manifesto 2001*. London: Victim Support England and Wales.

Victim Support England and Wales (2002a) *After Shipman*. London: Victim Support England and Wales.

Victim Support England and Wales (2002b) *Criminal Neglect: No Justice Beyond Criminal Justice*. London: Victim Support England and Wales.

Victim Support England and Wales (2002c) *New Rights for Victims of Crime in Europe: Council Framework Decision on the Standing of*

Victims in Criminal Proceedings. London: Victim Support England and Wales.

Victim Support England and Wales (2007) *Annual Reports & Accounts 2007.* London: Victim Support England and Wales.

Victim Support England and Wales (2008) *Annual Reports & Accounts 2008.* London: Victim Support England and Wales.

Victim Support England and Wales (2009) *Trustees' Annual Report and Financial Statements for the Year Ended 31 March 2009.* London: Victim Support England and Wales.

Victim Support Europe (2009) *A Manifesto for Europe.* Utrecht: Victim Support Europe.

Victim Support New Zealand (2008) *Briefing to Incoming Minister.* Wellington: Victim Support New Zealand.

Victim Support Scotland (2006) *Supporting Young Victims of Crime.* Edinburgh: Victim Support Scotland.

Victim Support Scotland (2009) *Victims' Fund Launched* [online]. Available at: http://www.victimsupportsco.org.uk/page/news/article.cfm?articleId=46

Victoria Department of Justice (2009) Melbourne: Victoria Department of Justice.

Victoria University of Wellington Crime and Justice Centre (2005) *Evaluation of Court-Referred Restorative Justice Pilot.* Wellington: Victoria University of Wellington Crime and Justice Centre.

Voelker, J. and Kritzer, H. (1997) *Court User Opinions: Incorporating Consumer Research Into Strategic Planning.* Madison, WI: Supreme Court, Office of Court Operations.

von Hentig, H. (1948) *The Criminal and His Victim.* New Haven, CT: Yale University Press.

Walklate, S. (1989) *Victimology: The Victim and the Criminal Justice Process.* London: Unwin Hyman.

Walklate, S. (1994) 'Can there be a progressive victimology?', *International Review of Victimology*, 3: 1–15.

Walklate, S. (ed.) (2007a) *Handbook of Victims and Victimology.* Cullompton: Willan, 484–494.

Walklate, S. (2007b) *Imagining the Victim of Crime.* Maidenhead: Open University Press.

Waller, I. (2001) 'The United Nations and victims', *The Victimologist*, 5: 1–2.

Wallerstein, I. (2000) 'From sociology to historical social science: prospects and obstacles', *British Journal of Sociology*, 51: 25–35.

Ward, A. (2009) 'The evidence of anonymous witnesses in criminal courts: Now and into the future', *Denning Law Journal*, 26: 67–92.

Webster, N. (2008a) 'Reflections on victim empowerment'. Paper presented at the *10 Year Anniversary of the Victim Empowerment Programme* conference, Durban: 18–20 August 2008.

Webster, N. (2008b) *Rights and Responsibilities in Our Democracy: A Case Study of the Victims' Charter*. Pretoria: DoJCD.

Wemmers, J.-A. (1996) *Victims in the Criminal Justice System*. Amsterdam: Kugler Publications.

Wemmers, J.-A. (1998) 'Procedural justice and Dutch victim policy', *Law & Policy*, 20: 57–76.

Wemmers, J.-A., van der Leeden, R. and Steensa, H. (1995) 'What is procedural justice: criteria used by Dutch victims to assess the fairness of criminal justice procedures', *Social Justice Research*, 8: 329–350.

Wemmers, J.-A. (2008) 'Where do they belong? Giving victims a place in the criminal justice process?'. Paper presented at the *National Victims of Crime Conference*, Adelaide: 23–24 September 2008.

Widom, C. (1994) 'The cycle of violence', in B. Finkelman (ed.), *Child Abuse: Short- and Long-term Effects*. New York: Garland.

Williams, B. (1999) 'The Victims' Charter: citizens as consumers of criminal justice services', *Howard Journal of Criminal Justice*, 38: 384–396.

Williams, B. (1999) *Working with Victims of Crime: Policies, Politics and Practice*. London: Jessica Kingsley.

Williams, B. and Goodman, H. (2007) 'The role of the voluntary sector', in S. Walklate (ed.), *Handbook of Victims and Victimology*. Cullompton: Willan, 240–254.

Williams, B. and Hall, M. (2009) 'Victims in the criminal justice process', in A. Hucklesby and A. Wahidin (eds), *Criminal Justice*. Oxford: Oxford University Press, 279–294

Wilson, J. (2000) *Children as Victims*. Washington, DC: US Department of Justice.

Winford, S. (2006) *A New (Legal) Threat to Public Space: The Rise and Rise of the ASBO*. Fitzroy: Fitzroy Legal Service.

Winkel, F. (1991) 'Police, victims, and crime prevention', *British Journal of Criminology*, 31: 250–265.

Wolfgang, M. (1958) *Patterns in Criminal Homicide*. New York: New York University Press.

World Society of Victimology (2006) *The Challenge* [online]. Available at: http://www.worldsocietyofvictimology.org/

Wright, P. (1998) '"Victims' rights" as a stalkinghorse for state repression', *Journal of Prisoners on Prisons*, 9: 1–4.

Wurtzburg, S. (2003) 'The Pacific Island community in New Zealand: Domestic violence and access to justice', *Criminal Justice Policy Review*, 14: 423–446.

Wykes, M. and Welsh, K. (2008) *Violence, Gender and Justice*. London: Sage.

Young, J. (2003) '"Winning the fight against crime?" New Labour, populism and lost opportunities', in J. Young, and R. Matthews (eds), *The New Politics of Crime and Punishment*. Cullompton: Willan, 23–47.

Young, J. and Matthews, R. (eds) (2003) *The New Politics of Crime and Punishment*. Cullompton: Willan, 1–32.

Young, M. (1997a) 'Ideological trends within the victims' movement: an international perspective', in R. Davis, A. Lurigio and W. Skogan (eds), *Victims of Crime*. Thousand Oaks, CA: Sage Publications, 115–126.

Young, M. (1997b) 'Victim rights and services: a modern saga', in R. Davis, A. Lurigio and W. Skogan (eds), *Victims of Crime*. Thousand Oaks, CA: Sage, 194–210.

Young, M. and Stein, J. (2004) *The History of the Crime Victims' Movement in the United States* [online]. Available at: http://www.ojp.usdoj.gov/ovc/ncvrw/2005/pg4c.html

Young, R. (2000) 'Integrating a multi-victim perspective into criminal justice through restorative justice conferences', in A. Crawford and J. Goodey (eds), *Integrating a Victim Perspective Within Criminal Justice: International Debates*. Aldershot: Ashgate Dartmouth, 227–252.

Zauberman, R. (2002) 'Victims as consumers of the criminal justice system?', in A. Crawford and J. Goodey (eds), *Integrating a Victim Perspective within Criminal Justice: International Debates*. Aldershot: Ashgate Dartmouth, 37–54.

Zebr, H. and Mika, H. (2003) 'Fundamental concepts of restorative justice', in E. McLaughlin, R. Fergusson, G. Hughes and L. Westmarland (eds), *Restorative Justice: Critical Issues*. London: Sage.

Zedner, L. (2002) 'Victims', in M. Maguire, R. Morgan and R. Reiner (eds), *The Oxford Handbook of Criminology*. Oxford: Oxford University Press, 419–456.

Zedner, L. (2003) 'Useful knowledge? Debating the role of criminology in post-war Britain?', in L. Zedner and A. Ashworth (eds), *The Criminological Foundations of Penal Policy: Essays in Honour of Roger Hood*. Oxford: Oxford University Press, 197–237.

Zehr, H. (1991) *Changing Lenses: New Focus for Crime and Justice*. Scottdale: Herald Press.

Index

Added to the page number 'f' denotes a figure and 'n' denotes a footnote.

A v New Zealand Parole Board and Peter Mana McNamara 158
9/11, state compensation 35–6, 171, 209
1985 UN Declaration 22–3, 38, 42, 62–6, 108, 161, 217, 219
   and crime prevention advice 102
   defining victims 30, 33
   ensuring support and services 43
   and ideal victims 48, 49
   implementation 64–6
   principles 63–4, 65
   status in international law 227, 228–9, 230
   and victims of non-criminal acts 54
2001 EU Framework Decision 2, 24, 32, 45, 51, 73–8, 87, 159, 161, 217, 219
   criticism 163
   defining victims 30–1, 77
   impact 73–4
   implementation 73, 74–6, 78
   and indirect victimization 38
   and restorative justice 188, 201
   rights language 108
   updating and development 76–7, 78
   and Victim Support England and Wales 73, 96, 98–9
abused children 45, 46
   Council of Europe Convention 70–1
   EU measures 79
academic study of victimology 15–18
adversarial justice systems
   comparisons between inquisitorial and 5
   difficulties for witnesses 41
   and meeting victims' needs 2
   and sexual and familial violence 112
Advocates for Victims of Homicide (AdVIC) 96
African Union 86
America *see* US
Angus Sinclair v Her Majesty's Advocate 158
Annual Trafficking in Persons Report 218
'anti-criminal or radical justice' ideology 3

Index

anti-social behaviour 222
Anti-social Behaviour Act (2003) (England and Wales) 52
'anti-social behaviour orders' (ASBOS) 52–3, 58–9
Argentina 2
Asia 2
Australia
  anti-social behaviour 53–4
  child victims 116
  crime prevention initiatives 104–5
  defining victims 32, 36–7, 39
  domestic violence 111, 113, 123
  efficiency savings in the criminal justice system 124, 126, 128
  ideal victims 56
  inclusion in research project 7
  interactive governance 94
  model of vulnerability 46, 122
  people trafficking 50–1, 118, 119, 120–1, 214
  questioning about sexual history 46
  rape complainants 214
  restitution 183, 184
    victims' fund 185
  restorative justice 2, 7, 196–7, 201
  state compensation 21–2, 172–3, 175, 176, 177, 179, 181, 211, 214
  victim impact statements 128, 141, 154, 156
  victim notification schemes 145
  victim rights 156
    enforcement 151
  victims' charters 42, 143, 144, 145
  victims' movement 12, 19–20, 23, 24
  VSOs 7, 19, 99–100
  witnesses
    victims as 42
    waiting times 129–30

'baby-dingo' case (1980) 115
Badgley Committee (1988) 115
Baegen v Netherlands 160
balance and victim rights 139–40, 142, 158, 161

Basic Act on Crime Victims (2004) (Japan) 2
Basic Principles and Guidelines on the Rights to a Remedy and Reparation for Victims of Gross Violations of International Human Rights Law and Serious Violations of International Humanitarian Law (IHRIHL) 67–8
Basic Principles on the Use of Restorative Justice Programmes in Criminal Matters 188
Blue Blindfold campaign 117
Brazil 2
Britain *see* UK
British Commonwealth *see* Commonwealth of Nations
British Crime Survey (1998) 141
British Witness Satisfaction Surveys 145
Bulger, James 115

California Victim Compensation and Government Claim Board (2008) 176, 178, 180, 203n
Californian Victims Compensation Program 185
Canada
  anti-social behaviour 54
  child victims 115, 116
  crime prevention 103–4
  defining victims 31–2
  development of governance and policy networks 94
  domestic violence 111, 113, 123
  efficiency savings in the criminal justice system 124, 125, 126, 128
  ideal victims 48
  inclusion in research project 7
  indirect victims 60n
  people trafficking 118
  populist punitiveness 107
  questioning about sexual history 46, 47
  restitution 182, 183
    victims' fund 185

267

restorative justice 7, 128, 191–3, 196
rights discourse 108, 155–6, 158–9
state compensation 21, 168, 172, 175, 176–7, 181
use of imprisonment 193
victim reform agenda 1–2, 4
  and the criminal justice system 44
victim surveys 16
victims' movement 21, 23
VSOs 19, 100, 102
vulnerable witnesses 46
witnesses
  anonymizing 222–3
  waiting times 129
Canadian Statement of Basic Principles of Justice for Victims of Crime 146, 148
'care ideology' 3
Carol X 112
Catholic Church and child victimization 116
CEDAW (*Convention on the Elimination of Discrimination against Women*) (1979) 24–5, 66
Central America, victim reform agenda 2
CEPJ (European Commission for the Efficiency of Justice) 124
Chamberlain, Lindy 115
Child Justice Bill (South Africa) 194
child victims 2, 114–17, 121
  abused *see* abused children
  lasting impact on 116–17
  United Nations (UN) measures 68
child witnesses 46, 153
Children Act (1997) (Ireland) 46
Children Act (2001) (Ireland) 199
Children (Scotland) Act (1995) 198
children's hearings 198
China
  definition of victims 30
  indirect victims 39
  state compensation 2

CICA 179, 186
  false claims 209
Civil Liabilities Act (1961) (Ireland) 179
Code for Crown Prosecutors (England and Wales) 147
Code of Practice for Victims of Crime in England and Wales 31, 38, 99, 129, 143, 145, 146, 149, 150
Commonwealth Guidelines for the Treatment of Victims of Crime 23
Commonwealth of Nations 82–4, 105
  identification of victims 55
  victims' movement 23
community courts 195, 197
community-managed restorative justice programmes 190–1
compensation 34, 207, 211
  benefits 140
  cross-border 78
  false claims 209
  through the state *see* state compensation
  in victims' charters 146
  see also restitution
compensation orders 183, 184, 186, 204n, 214
conferencing models 190, 191, 196, 198
consultative participation 138, 139, 147–8, 154, 157, 158, 161
consumers of criminal justice, victims as 30, 128–32
'a continuum of insecurities' 225
Convention on Action Against Trafficking in Human Beings (2005) 51, 70, 79
Convention against Transnational Organized Crime (2000) 66–7
Convention on the Compensation of Victims of Violent Crime (1983) 63, 69
Convention on the Elimination of Discrimination against Women (1979) (CEDAW) 24–5, 66

Index

Convention on the Prevention of Terrorism (2005) 70
Convention on the Protection of Children Against Sexual Exploitation and Sexual Abuse (2007) 70–1
Convention on the Rights of the Child (CRC) (1989) 25, 66, 116
Convention on the Rights of the Child, on the Sale of Children, Child Prostitution and Child Pornography (2000) 117
conviction, effect on state compensation 177–8
corporate crime, victims of 51, 216
Council of Europe 22, 24, 63, 69–72
   conventions and recommendations 23, 69–72
counselling 179
courtesy to victims 144–5
courts
   official recognition of suffering 211
   see also community courts; domestic courts; domestic violence courts; Family Courts; informal local courts; international courts; Youth Courts
Courts Legislation (Neighbourhood Justice Centre) Act (2006) (Australia) 196, 197
CRC (*Convention on the Rights of the Child*) (1989) 25, 66, 116
crime
   assisting the police in prevention 175–6
   fear of 225
   impact 212, 213
   politicization 106, 107
   see also corporate crime; environmental crime; financial crime; transnational crime; violent crime
crime control 5, 10, 102–3, 139, 222
   victim empowerment and 106, 223
   see also 'culture of control'; 'due process verses crime control' dichotomy
Crime and Disorder Act (1998) (England and Wales) 52
crime prevention 102–6, 225
   and people trafficking 120
   state compensation for injuries arising from assisting police 175–6
Crime Victims' Bill of Rights Act (2008) (US) 151
Crime Victims Compensation Act (1996) (Canada) 176–7
Crimes Act (1961) (New Zealand) 60n
Criminal Case Management Framework in England and Wales 125–6
The Criminal and His Victim 16
Criminal Injuries Compensation Authority *see* CICA
Criminal Injuries Compensation Scheme 35–6
Criminal Justice Act (1991) (England and Wales) 46
Criminal Justice Act (1993) (Ireland) 154, 184
Criminal Justice Act (1999) (Ireland) 39
criminal justice agencies
   and 'evidence-based' policy making 131
   performance *see* performance of criminal justice agencies
   putting obligations on 142
Criminal Justice and Public Order Act (1994) (UK) 39
'criminal justice or retributive' model 3
criminal justice systems
   approach to children 116–17
   effectiveness and legitimacy 5, 10, 11, 58, 106, 108, 132–3, 174–5, 215–16, 226
   efficiency and monetary concerns 122–8, 212, 215, 226
   expanding the scope 222

269

and female victims of sexual and familial violence 112, 113–14
historical perspective on victim involvement 1
and homicide survivors 35
over professionalization 17, 212
procedural rights *see* procedural rights
and protection of human rights 108, 215
restorative justice and 40, 188, 202, 212
symbolic recognition of suffering 211
and the victim reform agenda 42–7, 58
and victim status 31–2
advantages 209
victims as consumers 30, 128–32
victims suited for redress by 40
see also adversarial justice systems; courts; inquisitorial justice systems; youth justice systems
Criminal Law (Human Trafficking) Act (2008) (Ireland) 118
Criminal Neglect: No Justice Beyond Criminal Justice 43
Criminal Procedure Act (1977) (South Africa) 22, 183
criminal victimization 28
cross-examination, and secondary victimization 46–7, 113, 153–4, 222
'cultural victimology' 208
'culture of control' 106
customer-orientated criminal justice 128–32

Dading mediation project 199–200
decision makers in criminal justice, victims as 138–9, 140, 161
Declaration of Basic Principles of Justice for Victims of Crime and Abuse of Power (1985) *see* 1985 UN Declaration
Declaration on the Elimination of Violence Against Women (1993) 66
defendant rights 162–3, 222
balancing victim rights with 139–40, 142, 158
zero sum game between victim rights and 7, 142, 161, 209
defendants, vulnerable 122, 214, 222
definitions of victims 23, 28–59
expanding 207–10
and the harm principle 1, 11, 28, 30–4, 57, 187, 210, 211, 213, 216
official verses unofficial 55–7
restricting criteria 210–15
Denmark, victim support groups 26n
'derivative victims' 176
domestic courts, victim rights 155–9
domestic policy making 91–133
domestic violence 2, 45, 84, 106, 113–14, 120, 131, 223
and efficiency concerns within criminal justice systems 123–4
domestic violence courts 113–14
Domestic Violence, Crime and Victims Act (2004) (England and Wales) 99, 150, 185, 186
Doorson v Netherlands 160
Douglas Oliver Kelly v California 157
due process 138, 161
'due process versus crime control' dichotomy 139, 222

ECtHR (European Court of Human Rights) 159–60
Effective Trial Management Programme 125
El Salvador 2
emotional crisis 114
'emotional suffering' 31
enforcement
of international policy instruments 217, 218, 219
of national legislation 150–3, 155
and victims' charters 148–9, 151, 155

Index

England
- child victims 116
- crime prevention 103
- criminal justice system 17
  - efficiency savings 124, 125–6, 127
- defining victims 56
- domestic violence 123–4, 223
- inclusion in research project 7
- indirect victims 34, 37–8
- politicization of victim policies 13
- rape and sexual assault 111
  - definitions 33
- restitution 184, 186
  - victims' funds 185
- restorative justice 197–8, 199
- rights discourse 108, 109, 153, 157, 161
- use of recorded video evidence 45–6
- victim impact statements 141, 156, 157
- victim notification schemes 145
- victim reform agenda 4, 104
- victim and witness surveys 130
- Victims Code of Practice 31, 38, 99, 129, 143, 145, 146, 148–9, 150
- victims' movement 19–20, 22, 23, 24
- victims of non-criminal acts 52–3, 222
- VSOs *see* Victim Support England and Wales
- vulnerable victims 110, 153
- witness waiting times 129, 130

English Criminal Case Management Framework 125–6

environmental crime, victims of 216

EU 72–81, 88
- crime victims as a priority 80–1
- and restorative justice 188–9
- vagueness of legislation 87

EU *Directive on Compensation to Crime Victims* (2004) 78, 82

EU *Directive on People Trafficking* (2004) 78–9

EU *Framework Decision on Combating Child Pornography and the Sexual Abuse and Sexual Exploitation of Children* (2004) 79

EU *Framework Decision on Preventing and Combating Trafficking in Human Beings, and Protecting Victims* 79

EU *Framework Decision on the Standing of Victims in Criminal Proceedings* (2001) *see* 2001 EU Framework Decision

EU *Framework Decision on Trafficking in Human Beings* (2002) 79

EU *Framework Decision on Victim Support Organizations* 76

EU *Proposal for a Council Directive on Short-term Residence Permit Issues in Relation to Victims of Action to Facilitate Illegal Immigration or Trafficking in Human Beings* (2002) 118

Europe
- comparison of victims' movements in US and 12, 20–1, 25
- efficiency savings in criminal justice systems 124
- rights discourse 20, 108–9, 159–60
- victim reform agenda 2
- VSOs *see* Victim Support Europe
- *see also individual countries* e.g. Netherlands

European Commission for the Efficiency of Justice (CEPJ) 124

European Convention on Human Rights 24, 53, 109

European Court of Human Rights (ECtHR) 159–60

European Court of Justice 24

European Forum for Victim Services 26n, 80
- *see also* Victim Support Europe

European Institute for Crime Prevention and Control (HEUNI) 23

271

European Union *see* EU
evidence
    tape recorded 45–6, 116
    video-linked 45–6, 71, 113, 116, 121
'evidence-based' policy making 131
expressive participation 138

Families Act (1989) (New Zealand) 190
families of direct victims 36
    state compensation for 176–7
families of murder victims *see* homicide survivors
Family Courts 190
family group conferencing 190, 191, 198
Family Violence Prevention and Service Act (1984) (US) 104
fear of crime 225
Federal Evidence Act (2005) (Canada) 116
Federal Victims Strategy (2009) (Canada) 44
female victimization 111–14
feminism, impact on the victims' movement 18, 112
financial crime, victims of 216
formal rights of victims 143–60
    in domestic courts 155–60
    in international courts 159–60
    in national legislation *see* national legislation
    victims' charters *see* victims' charters
formal sources of international law 227–8
France
    victims' movement 23
    VSOs 18
freedom perspective 139–40, 142
Fry, Margaret 21, 169

'general victimology' 16–17
generalizations, issues of 93–5
Germany, VSOs 18–19

globalization
    and the creation of new types of crime 226
    defining 224
    economic aspects 226
    and policy making 93, 224–6
    and restorative principles 200
    and South Africa 94–5
    and state compensation 175
    and victim rights 161
    of victim support 12
Good Practices for the Protection of Witnesses in Criminal Proceedings Involving Organized Crime 67
governance
    defining 11, 92–3
    extent to which government has ceded to 102
    interactive 94
    policy networks and development of 220
    see also 'multi level governance'
Great Britain *see* UK
grounded theory 8–9
Guatemala 2
Guidelines on Justice in Matters involving Child Victims and Witnesses of Crime (2005) 68
Guidelines for the Treatment of Victims of Crime in Commonwealth Countries (2002) 83–4

Hague Convention (2004) 80
harm principle 1, 11, 28, 30–4, 57, 187, 210, 211, 213, 216
HEUNI (European Institute for Crime Prevention and Control) 22
'hierarchy of victimization' 48
homicide survivors 34–6, 48
    in an international context 38
    representation 37–8
homogenization of victim policies 12
'hospitality', doctrine 121
human rights
    breaches 54

Index

criminal law and 53
development 107–10
distinction between victim rights and 163, 229
protection by criminal justice systems 108, 215
and victimology 16
see also European Convention on Human Rights
Human Rights Act (1998) (UK) 24
human trafficking *see* people trafficking

ICC 25, 84–6
defining victims 32–3
ideal victims 49–50
victim participation rights 160
and vulnerable witnesses 214
ICC *Code of Judicial Ethics* (2005) 84
ICC *Rules of Procedure and Evidence* (2002) 84–5
ICCPR (International Covenant on Civil and Political Rights) 24
ICVS (International Crime Victimization Survey) 16, 44, 145
ideal victims 23–4, 29, 47–52, 56–7, 58, 59, 110, 122, 213–15, 216
characteristics 29, 47
suffering 214–15
witnesses as 214
IHRIHL (*Basic Principles and Guidelines on the Rights to a Remedy and Reparation for Victims of Gross Violations of International Human Rights Law and Serious Violations of International Humanitarian Law*) 67–8
Immigration and Refugee Protection Act (2002) (Canada) 118
Immigration, Residence and Protection Bill (Ireland) 118
imprisonment, use of 193, 195
inclusive victims' approach, combining inquisitorial justice systems with 139
indirect victims 30, 34–40, 58, 210
compensation 35–6

representation 37
right to speak in court 37
victim impact statements from 157
individual responsibility, denial 208
informal local courts 195
information provision
by victims 138
to victims 139, 145, 159
Injury Prevention, Rehabilitation and Compensation Act (2001) (New Zealand) 177
inquisitorial justice systems
combining an inclusive victim rights approach with 139
comparisons between adversarial and 5
difficulties for witnesses 41
domestic violence cases 123
interactive governance 94
'interactive policy making' 93
international courts
victim rights 159–60
see also European Court of Justice; ICC
International Covenant on Civil and Political Rights (ICCPR) 25
International Crime Victimization Survey (ICVS) 16, 44, 145
International Criminal Court *see* ICC
International Criminal Tribunals for the former Yugoslavia 85–6
international law
sources 227–8
victim support as a principle 226–30
international organisations 62–88
Commonwealth of Nations *see* Commonwealth of Nations
Council of Europe *see* Council of Europe
EU *see* EU
ICC *see* ICC
instruments, guidelines and conventions 87–8
interest in victims of crime 22, 86–7

and restorative justice 188
United Nations (UN) *see* United Nations (UN)
victim assistance 81–2
International Organization for Migration 86
International Organization for Victim Assistance (IOVA) 82
international policy instruments
 influence 217–19
 see also individual instruments e.g. 1985 UN Declaration
international policy networks, transnational and *see* transnational and international policy networks
'invisible' victims 213, 218
Ireland
 ASBO framework 53
 child victims 115–16
 compliance with international obligations 229
 consultative participation 154, 157
 crime prevention 105
 criminal justice system 132
 efficiency savings 125
 defining victims 32
 discussion of policies 94
 homicide survivors 35
 inclusion in research project 6, 7
 people trafficking 117–18, 120
 restitution 184
 restorative justice 187, 192, 199
 sexual and familial violence 111, 112, 113, 146, 154
 state compensation 22, 172, 175, 176, 178, 179, 180, 214
 victim rights 153, 159, 163
 victims' charter 24, 32, 35, 112, 144, 145–6, 147, 148, 149, 154
 VSOs 18, 96, 97, 99
'issue networks' *see* policy networks

Japan 2
'just desserts' 3

Justice for All Act (2004) (US) 31, 100, 152–3, 157, 199
Justice on Target strategy (2008) (Canada) 125
Justice for Victims of Crime initiative (1982) (Canada) 21

Katz ruling (2008) 77, 87, 160
kidulthood, parallels between victimhood and 57
labelling of victims 28, 31–2, 33–4, 209, 212
LaGrand (Germany v United States of America) 160
Lawrence, Stephen 4, 35
local courts, informal 195
London bombings (2005) 35

makgotla 195
Mandatory Restitution Act (1996) (US) 182, 186
Maria Pupino case 76–7, 160
Marsy's Law 47–8, 112
Mason, Julia 112
material sources of international law 227
media 133
 and homicide survivors 35
 and moral panics 52–3
 and state compensation 171
mediation 195
 victim–offender 189, 191, 192, 198–9, 200, 205n
mental injuries, state compensation for 175, 178
Middle East 2
'moral custodians', victims as 209
morality, victimalization of 10, 207, 208–10, 212
'multi level governance' 88
murder victims, families of *see* homicide survivors

National Association of Victim Support Schemes (NAVSS) 18
National Center for Victims of Crime 102

Index

National Institute for Crime Prevention and the Reintegration of Services (NICRO) 19
national legislation 149–55
  creating new victim rights 153–4
  enforceability 150–3
  overlap with victims' charters 149–50
National Organization of Victim Assistance (NOVA) 18, 82, 100
National Victims Constitutional Amendment Passage (NVCAP) (2003) 20, 100, 108
Neighbourhood Justice Centre (NJC) 196–7
'neo-liberal' states 6
net widening 52
Netherlands
  child victims 117
  crime prevention 105
  defining victims 31
  discussion of policies 94
  domestic violence 111, 113, 123
  inclusion in research project 6, 7
  indirect victims 37
  people trafficking 118, 119
  restitution 183
  restorative justice 199–200
  state compensation 22, 169–70, 173, 177, 178, 179, 180, 181, 186, 211
  use of imprisonment 193, 200
  victim reform agenda 2
  victim rights 109, 145, 154, 155, 162
  victim surveys 16
  victims' charter 144, 146–7, 148, 149–50
  VSOs 18, 96, 97, 101
  vulnerable witnesses 46
new deal reform agenda 98
New Zealand
  child victims 115
  crime prevention 104
  criminal justice system
    efficiency savings 124, 125
  victim participation 157–8
  defining victims 32, 36
  discussion of policies 94
  ideal victims 49, 214
  people trafficking 119
  restitution 183–4
  restorative justice 2, 189–91, 200, 201
  sexual and familial violence 111, 114, 123
  state compensation 21, 169, 173, 174, 175, 177, 178, 179, 181
  victim notification schemes 145
  victim reform agenda, and the criminal justice system 44
  victim support 19, 43
  victims' charter 146, 149, 150
  victims' movement 23
  VSOs 19, 95–6, 101
  vulnerable witnesses 46
NICRO (National Institute for Crime Prevention and the Reintegration of Services) 19
NJC (Neighbourhood Justice Centre) 196–7
No Justice Beyond Criminal Justice 98
non-criminal acts 58–9
  victims 52–4, 222
North Africa 2
North America
  victim reform agenda 1–2
  see also Canada; US
Northern Ireland, restorative justice 141
NOVA (National Organization of Victim Assistance) 18, 82, 100
NVCAP (National Victims Constitutional Amendment Passage) (2003) 20, 100, 108

occupational cultures, effect on victim rights 159
offender rights *see* defendant rights
offender-based compensation
  distinction between state compensation and 185–6
  see also restitution

275

offenders
  distinction between victims and 16, 29–30, 48
  diversion from the formal criminal justice process 40, 58, 212
  and restorative justice 189, 201, 212
Office for Victims of Crime (US) 20
Organization for Security and Co-operation in Europe(2002) 86
'outsiders', fear of 225

Parole Act (2002) (New Zealand) 157, 190
participation in criminal justice, victim *see* victim participation in criminal justice
Payne v Tennessee 157
people trafficking 50–1, 84, 86, 117–21, 214, 218, 225, 229
  Council of Europe Convention 70
  definition 135n
  EU measures 78–9
  United Nations (UN) protocol 50, 66, 67
performance of criminal justice agencies
  measurement 130–1
  targets 125–6, 129
    for witness waiting times 129–30
'personal injury', state compensation for 175
PFI ('Private Finance Initiative') model of privatization 94
physical injury, state compensation for 175–6
plea bargaining, veto powers for victims 126
police
  attitudes to sexual and familial violence 111–12, 114, 214
  powers 83–4
  state compensation for injuries whilst assisting 175–6
'policy communities' 11, 93
  see also transnational policy communities
'policy environments' 93
policy making
  domestic 91–133
  and globalization 93, 224–6
  over-generalizations 93–5
  theories 92–5, 218–19
  to achieve punitive aims 221–3
policy networks 11–12, 93–5, 231
  influence of 216–23
  government 102
  law enforcement aspect 107
  as a model of policy making 221
  reflection in state compensation systems 181–2
  and restorative justice 195–6
  weaknesses in use 220–1
  see also transnational and international policy networks
politicization
  of crime 106, 107
  of victim issues 122
  of victim policies 12, 13
  of VSOs 99–102
'Poppy' projects 118
populist punitiveness 3, 10, 59, 103, 106–7, 127, 138, 216, 226
'positivist victimology' 16
Powers of Criminal Courts Sentencing Act (England and Wales) (2000) 184
pre-sentencing conferences 190
Presidential Task Force on Victims of Crime (US) 20
Prevention and Combating of Trafficking in Persons Bill (2009) (South Africa) 120
'principle of circularity' 219
Principles and Guidelines on the Rights to a Fair Trial and Legal Assistance in Africa (2001) 54
'Private Finance Initiative' (PFI) model of privatization 94
private prisons, adoption in South Africa 94

Index

Probation Services Act (1991) (South Africa) 19
Probation Services Amendment Act (2000) (South Africa) 194
'procedural protection' 67
procedural rights 24, 86–7, 139, 142
  distinction between service rights and 138
Prosecution Guidelines of New Zealand 147
Prosecutor's Pledge (England and Wales) 147, 148
protection of victims 58, 67, 159
  in victims' charters 146
Protocol to Prevent, Suppress and Punish Trafficking in Persons, Especially Women and Children (2005) 50, 66, 67
Provincial Offences Act (1990) (Canada) 185
psychological trauma 114
punitive aims
  and victim reform agendas 3, 221–3
  of victims 141
  and a zero sum game 142
'punitive populism' 3, 10, 59, 103, 106–7, 127, 138, 216, 226

The Queen v Zelensky 182

R v Billam 159
R v Davis (Iain) 167n
R v Gladue 191–2
R v Millberry 159
R v Mills 156
R v Perks 166n
R v R.E.M. 159
R v Secretary of State for the Home Department and another ex parte Bulger 157
'radical or anti-criminal justice' ideology 3
'radical victimology' 29
rape
  changes in the law 46–7, 113, 153–4
  definitions 33–4, 58
  see also 'secondary rape'
rape shield laws 153–4, 155, 156, 222
rape victims 105, 111–14, 214, 223
'rational' policy making 131
Re Torek and The Queen 182
Recommendation on the Position of the Victim in the Framework of Criminal Law and Procedure (1985) 71, 72
Recommendation R (06) 8 71–2, 82
Recommendation R (87) 21 71
referral orders 199
rehabilitation 179
'rehabilitation or resocialization' ideology 3
reparation 4, 21, 68
  restorative justice and 201
repeat victimization 105
Republic of Ireland *see* Ireland
research project 5–14
  data collection 8–9
  selection of countries 6–8
  theoretical framework, objectives and hypotheses 9–14
'resocialization or rehabilitation' ideology 3
respect for victims 144–5
Respecting Assistance for Victims of Crime (1988) (Canada) 31–2
restitution 68, 85, 141, 146–7, 168, 182–6, 211
  difficulties 186
restitution orders 146–7, 182
restorative conferencing 190, 191, 196, 198
'restorative detention' 200
restorative justice 2, 7, 17, 34, 107, 114, 139, 187–202
  benefits 199
  criminal justice and 40, 188, 202, 212
  definitions 187, 194
  effectiveness 196
  and efficiency concerns 128
  focus on less serious crimes 201, 212

277

forms 188
goals 187–8
as a lenient approach 192
offenders and 189, 201, 212
roots 189
and vengefulness 141
victim support 189, 194, 198, 201
victims suited for redress by 40, 58
'restorative warnings' 197
retribution 7, 52, 59
'retributive or criminal justice' model 3
revictimization, protection from 153–4
'rights' agenda *see* victim rights
Rome Statute (2002) 25, 32

Samuel Zamudio v California 157
satisfaction
   victim 5
   witness 222
Schadefonds Geweldsmisdrijven 169–70
Scotland
   ASBO framework 53
   defining victims 32, 38, 39, 55
   efficiency savings in the criminal justice system 124
   inclusion in research project 7
   people trafficking 135n
   restorative justice 187, 192, 197, 198, 200
   sexual and familial violence 111, 113
   victim notification schemes 145
   victim rights 153, 158
   victims' fund 185
   victims' movement 24
   victims as witnesses 42
   VSOs 18, 96, 97
Scottish National Standards for Victims of Crime 145, 147, 148
'second-order consensus' on law and order issues 223
'secondary rape' 112
secondary rules 227

secondary victimization 18, 30, 34, 40–7, 210
   definition 40–1
   effect of crime prevention 105–6
   protection from 46–7, 113, 153–4, 222
   United Nations (UN) measures 68
secularization 5, 10–11
Securing the Attendance of Witnesses in Court (2003) (England and Wales) 127
self-determination, denial 208
Sentencing Act (2002) (New Zealand) 183–4, 190
September 11th, state compensation 35–6, 171, 209
service charters *see* victims' charters
service rights 139, 161
   distinction between procedural rights and 138
   in victims' charters 144–7
Sex Offenders Act (2001) (Ireland) 113, 154
sex trafficking 118
sexual assault 120
   changes in the law 113
   definitions 33–4
   female victims 111–14
   special measures 153–4
   use of restorative justice 201
sexual history, questioning 46–7, 154, 156
Sexual Offences Act (2003) (England and Wales) 33
sexually transmitted diseases 83
Shipman, Dr Harold 35
Sn v Sweden 160
social workers, and ideal verses non-ideal victims 56–7
societal changes, and victim reform 207–16, 231
'soft law' 87, 230
South Africa
   breaches of human rights 54
   child victims 115

crime prevention 103, 106
efficiency savings in the criminal justice system 126–7
inclusion in research project 7
influence of *transnational* policy communities 94–5
people trafficking 120
restitution 183
restorative justice 193–6
rights discourse 109–10, 155, 163, 211
secondary victimization 40–1, 45
sexual and familial violence 45, 111, 214
state compensation 22, 171
surveys
  victim 27n
  witness 130
victim reform agenda 12, 23
VSOs 19, 98, 102
vulnerable victims 110
South African National Crime Prevention Strategy 115
South African victims' charter 2, 98, 144, 145, 147, 148, 149, 154–5, 163
compensation and restitution 146, 183
defining victims 31, 36
enforceability 24, 229
and restorative processes 146, 195
right to protection 146
state compensation 2, 21–2, 35–6, 43, 69, 168, 169–82, 202
distinction between offender-based and 185–6
justifying 169–75
singling out of crime victims 174
state compensation schemes 175–82, 211, 212
awards 179, 211
costs 173, 179, 181–2, 186
for 'deserving' victims 180, 213–14
eligibility 175–8
and victims' charters 146
state control
extending 121–2
facilitation 3
Statement of Basic Principles of Justice for Victims of Crime (2002) 82–3
status of victims *see* victim status
Stockholm Programme on justice and home affairs 81
suffering 10, 11, 33, 40, 57
defining victims by 210–13
of ideal victims 214–15
official recognition 211
types 5, 52, 212
see also 'emotional suffering'
support for victims *see* victim support
'survivors', use of term 34
Switzerland, VSOs 18
sympathy for victims 144–5

T and V v UK 160
Tampere Conclusions (1999) 73, 80
tape recorded evidence 45–6, 116
terminology 14
terrorism, Council of Europe Convention 70
Terwee Act (1995) (Netherlands) 183
Terwee Guidelines 144, 147, 148, 150, 162
'theoretical victimology' 18
Traditional Courts Bill (South Africa) 194
trafficking, people *see* people trafficking
Trafficking in Persons Report (TIP) 119–20
Trafficking Victims' Protection Act (2000) (US) 119
transnational crime 229
transnational and international policy networks 4, 12, 93, 132–3, 207f, 219–21, 226
aspects impacting on victim reform 95–132
crime prevention initiatives and populist punitiveness 102–7
customer-orientated criminal

279

    justice 128–32
    efficiency and monetary concerns 122–8
    people trafficking 119, 120
    the 'rights' agenda 107–10
    VSOs 95–102
    vulnerable victims *see* vulnerable victims
    dominance of 'balance' rhetoric 140
    and restorative justice 199, 200, 202
  transnational policy communities 93
    influence on South African policies and developments 94–5
trespass on railways, victims suffering personal injury from 176, 204n
Truth and Reconciliation Commission (TRC) 193–4

ubuntu 194
UK
  anonymizing witnesses 222–3
  customer-orientated criminal justice 131–2
  development of governance and policy networks 94
  people trafficking 51, 117, 118–19
  restitution 186
  restorative justice 141
  state compensation 21, 22, 168, 169, 175, 176, 177, 178, 179–80, 181, 211
  victim reform agenda 2, 23
    punitive impetus 106, 107
  victim rights 109, 156
  victim surveys 16
  VSOs 18
  see also England; Scotland; Wales
United Nations (UN) 22, 62–9
  and restorative justice 188
Universal Declaration of Human Rights (1948) 107

'unordinary' victims 213
  and the international policy scene 86, 218
US
  anonymizing witnesses 222–3
  child victims 115, 116
  courts users' surveys 130–1
  crime prevention 104
  defining victims 23, 31, 55–6
  development of governance and policy networks 94
  domestic violence 123
  efficiency savings in the criminal justice system 125, 126
  ideal victims 23–4, 49, 214
  inclusion in research project 7
  indirect victims 60n
  people trafficking 119–20
  questioning about sexual history 46
  rape 111, 112–13
    definitions 33–4
  restitution 182–3, 184, 186
    victims' funds 185
  restorative justice 198–9
  rights discourse 108, 145, 151–3, 156
  state compensation 21, 35–6, 169, 170–1, 173, 175, 176, 178, 180, 181, 209
  use of recorded video evidence 45–6
  victim impact statements 140, 141, 156–7
  victim reform agenda 1–2, 3
    punitive impetus 106, 107
  victim surveys 16
  and victimization from anti-social behaviour 54
  'victimless prosecutions' 106, 223
  victims' charter 143
  victims' movement 18, 19–20, 21, 23–4, 25
    comparison between Europe and 12, 20–1
  victims as witnesses 42
  VSOs 82, 100, 102

Index

Vaillant Guidelines 144
vengefulness 141
'victim advocates' 37
victim assistance initiatives 2
victim assistance organisations *see* VSOs
victim assistance professionals 60n
Victim Bills of Rights (US) 20
victim empowerment, tension between crime control and 106, 223
Victim Empowerment Programme (South Africa) 98, 110
victim impact statements 34, 56, 128, 148, 156–7, 213
 from indirect victims 37, 157
 influence 138, 140–1, 142, 223
 and legitimization of punitive stances 106
 therapeutic benefits 141
victim notification schemes 145
Victim Oral History Project 88–9n
victim participation in criminal justice 24, 138–9, 140, 142, 161, 222
 and domestic courts 157–8
 and the ICC 160
 and victims' charters 147–8
victim reform agendas 1–2, 57–8
 and achieving punitive aims 221–3
 and criminal justice systems 42–7, 58
 effect of crime control concerns 106
 influences 2–5, 10, 217–19
victim rights 1, 18, 25, 107–10, 137–63, 207
 balance and 139–40, 142, 158, 161
 conceptualization as unusual 162, 163
 distinction between human rights and 163, 229
 enforcing 142–3, 161–2
  through national legislation 150–3
 formal *see* formal rights of victims
 mechanisms for delivery and accountability 161
 normalization 161–3
 political use 122
 theorising 138–43
  appraisal of 142–3
 zero-sum game between defendant rights and 7, 142, 161, 209
victim satisfaction 5
victim status 28, 29
 advantages 209
 ideological convergence between left and right 210
 link between the harm principle and 28, 213
 recognition 182
victim support 1, 4
 globalization 12
 outside the criminal justice system 43–4
 as a principle of international law 226–30
 see also compensation
Victim Support Australasia 19, 82, 95, 100, 105, 162
Victim Support England and Wales 82, 96–7, 98–9, 101
 funding 20, 21
 manifesto 98
Victim Support Europe 2, 57, 80–1, 88, 95, 97, 220
 manifesto 82, 96, 99
Victim Support Ireland 97
Victim Support Netherlands 96, 97, 101
Victim Support New Zealand 95–6, 101
victim support organisations *see* VSOs
Victim Support and Rehabilitation Act (1996) (Australia) 184
Victim Support Scotland 96, 97
victim surveys 16, 130–1
victim–offender mediation 189, 191, 192, 198–9, 200, 205n

281

victim-orientated crime prevention 102–6
victimalization of morality 10, 207, 208–10, 212
victimhood
  expansion 5, 29–57, 58–9, 208, 210
    criteria 210–15
    in definitions 55–7, 215
    and the harm principle 1, 11, 28, 30–4, 57, 187, 210, 211, 213, 216
    ideal victims *see* ideal victims
    indirect victims *see* indirect victims
    secondary victimization *see* secondary victimization
    theoretical context 29–30
    victims of non-criminal acts 52–4, 222
  impact of cultural factors 208, 210
  parallels between kidulthood and 57
victimization 1, 29
  definition
    by reference to harm suffered 1, 11, 187
    expansion of 207–10
  see also criminal victimization; female victimization; 'hierarchy of victimization'; repeat victimization; revictimization; secondary victimization
victimless prosecutions 106, 223
'victimogogic ideologies' 3
victimology
  academic study 15–18
  disputes within the discipline 16–17
  effect on the state's role 121–2
  see also 'cultural victimology'; 'radical victimology'
victims
  as an emotive and politicized issue 132
  definitions *see* definitions of victims
  distinction between offenders and 16, 29–30, 48
  diversion from the formal criminal justice process 40, 58, 212
  labelling 28, 31–2, 33–4, 209, 212
  as 'moral custodians' 209
  prioritizing 59
  support for restorative justice 189, 194, 198, 201
  types 212
  as witnesses 29, 41–7, 58, 214, 222–3
  witnesses as 38–9, 211
    state compensation for 176
  as a yardstick for success in criminal justice 5, 10, 11, 58, 106, 108, 132–3, 174–5, 215–16
  see also child victims; 'derivative victims'; ideal victims; indirect victims; 'unordinary' victims; vulnerable victims
Victims' Advisory Panel (England and Wales) 149
Victims' Charter Act (2006) (Australia) 151
victims' charters 23, 24, 109, 112, 127, 128–9, 143–9, 162
  creating new victim rights 153–5
  enforcement 24, 144, 148–9, 151, 162
  overlap with national legislation 149–50
  and receipt of compensation 146
  service rights 144–7
Victims Compensation Program (California) 185
Victims of Crime Act (1984) (US) 20, 21, 23–4, 31, 49
Victims of Crime Act (1994) (Australia) 36, 39, 150–1
Victims of Crime Act (2001) (Australia) 151
Victims of Crime Act (2002) (New Zealand) 49, 214
Victims of Crime Assistance Act

Index

(2008) (Australia) 37
victims' funds 168, 182, 185–6
victims' movement 12, 85, 174
  and ideal victims 48
  impact of feminism and women's pressure groups 18, 21, 112, 114
  international development 15–25
    first and second waves 15–21
    third wave 21–5
  state compensation and 168
victims' needs 2, 10, 127–8, 223
victims of non-criminal acts 52–4, 222
Victims of Offences Act (1987) (New Zealand) 23, 36
Victims' Rights Act (2002) (New Zealand) 32, 44, 150, 190
Victims Support and Rehabilitation Act (1996) (Australia) 183
victims of trafficking *see* people trafficking
Victims and Witnesses Commissioner (England and Wales) 149
video-linked evidence 45–6, 71, 113, 116, 121
Vienna Declaration on Crime and Justice (2000) 66, 188
violent crime, state compensation for victims 175–6
'voice', giving a 93
VSOs 76, 81–2, 220
  development 18–21
  funding 20, 21, 44
  impact of transnational and international policy networks 95–102
  and indirect victims 36
  politicization 99–102
  unification 97
vulnerability, cult of 208–10
vulnerable defendants 122, 214, 222
vulnerable victims 110–22
  child victims *see* child victims
  female victims of rape, sexual assault and domestic violence 111–14
  as tools of the state 121–2
  victims of human trafficking 117–21
vulnerable witnesses 46, 110, 214, 222
Vulnerable Witnesses (Scotland) Act (2004) 46

waiting times for witnesses 129–30
Wales
  child victims 116
  crime prevention 103
  criminal justice system 17
    efficiency savings 125–6, 127
  defining victims 56
  domestic violence 123, 223
  inclusion in research project 7
  indirect victims 34, 37–8
  rape and sexual assault 111
    definitions 33
  restitution 184, 186
    victims' funds 185
  restorative justice 197–8, 199
  rights discourse 108, 109, 153, 157, 161
  use of recorded video evidence 45–6
  victim impact statements 156, 157
  victim notification schemes 145
  victim reform agenda 4, 104
  Victims Code of Practice 31, 38, 99, 129, 143, 145, 146, 148–9, 150
  victims' movement 19–20, 22, 23, 24
  victims of non-criminal acts 52–3, 222
  VSOs *see* Victim Support England and Wales
  vulnerable victims 110, 153
  witness waiting times 129, 130
WEISSER RING 19
'what works' 131
Wheeler v United States (1985) 116
witness intimidation 39, 58, 211

Witness Intimidation Act (2002) (Australia) 39
witness orders 127
witness satisfaction 222
witness surveys 130–1
Witness and Victim Experience Survey (WAVES) 130
witnesses
 anonymizing 222–3
 assistance when giving evidence *see* evidence
 difficulties 41
 as ideal 48
 targets for waiting times 129–30
 victims as 29, 41–7, 58, 214, 222–3
 as victims of crime 38–9, 211
  state compensation for 176
 see also child witnesses; vulnerable witnesses

women's movement, impact on the victims' movement 21, 112, 114
World Society of Victimology 1

Youth Courts 190
Youth Criminal Justice Act (2003) (Canada) 192–3
youth justice conferences 193
Youth Justice and Criminal Evidence Act (1999) (England and Wales) 46–7, 116, 153, 197, 199
youth justice systems 190, 192–3, 197
Youth Offending Panels 197–8, 199
Youth Offending Teams (YOTs) 146, 198

zemiology 25